Advanced Praise for

Women Peacemakers: What We Can Learn From Them

Women Peacemakers: What We Can Learn From Them *is a guide-book for all of us who strive to lead meaningful lives. Barbe Chambliss has committed to peacemaking in an unwavering and compelling way. By defining it and then sharing stories, honestly and compassionately, of women who have impacted others with peacemaking acts, Chambliss illuminates the transformational power of being a peacemaker. Finally, the invitation to us, as readers, to do our own act of peacemaking transforms this book from an outward panorama to an inward inquiry which leaves the reader with attainable and transformative steps. In a time when isolation and detachment are ever-present, Chambliss invites us to engage, collaborate, and act to improve ourselves and our world.*

~ C. Sheridan

The Peacemakers in your work have certainly inspired me to make positive change in my life moving forward. ~ Daniel B.

Today is Palm Sunday, April 6, 2020. The world is engulfed in managing the impact of the COVID-19 pandemic. At noon, as I participated in a worldwide pause for prayer, I felt the shared power of heartfelt concern for the well-being of all peoples as well as our planet. Reading Dr. Chambliss's book, Women Peacemakers *gives me that same sense of restorative empowerment. Here is a book that will guide you into a higher quality of life for yourself and your community. Don't miss this opportunity to be uplifted into a more peaceful world!* ~ Beverly B.

In Women Peacemakers, *Barbe Chambliss has written a moving and inspirational work that will touch the hearts of all readers, women and men alike.* ~ A___ A. MA

Women Peacemakers
WHAT WE CAN LEARN FROM THEM

BY BARBE CHAMBLISS, PhD

Illustrations by Dana Bishop

Credit to Brock Atiken for cover photo of Theo Colborn, bottom right image.

Though every effort has been made to obtain permission for quoted text, it has not been possible to do so in every case. Any corrections brought to the attention of the author will be rectified in future editions.

Published by Red Truck Enterprises, LLC
Paonia, Colorado

ISBN # 978-1-7348914-0-9

Library of Congress Control Number: 2020913235

Light of the Moon, Inc.
Partnering with self-published authors since 2009
Book Design/Production/Consulting
Carbondale, Colorado • www.lightofthemooninc.com

*I will write peace on your wings and
you will fly all over the world.*

Written on the gravestone of Sadako Sasaki
who died at age 12 from leukemia
caused by the bombing of Hiroshima

*There is peacemaking
and conscious peacemaking.*

This book is about the latter.

Foreword

This book comes to us at a time when chaos and discouragement are doing their best to distract us from the path of making peace in our world. Although there are many acts of peacemaking happening all the time, they are not always done consciously and they often go unnoticed, except, possibly, by the recipient. These hidden events rarely make the headlines and are sometimes not even recognized as peacemaking by the author of the act. As Dr. Chambliss says in the beginning of her book: There is peacemaking and there is conscious peacemaking. Her book is about the latter.

I've seen how just one sniper's bullet can condemn a family to three generations of suffering, never mind the human catastrophe of a missile attack. From what we have learned of the carnage of the past century, we humans now know enough about how to prevent war, that we can plan a viable world without war. And it is vital to stay conscious about making this happen.

We Peacemakers know we must be doing our work at both the macro- and the micro-level, at both the systems level and the individual level. With my current book, *The Business Plan For Peace,* I offer macro-level guidance and workshops for businesses, showing them how to recalibrate their corporate and social responsibility agendas toward building a world without war. Dr. Chambliss, on the micro-level, does the same for individuals with this book, giving them a pathway to consciously recalibrate their daily interactions with others by practicing behaviors of mutual respect and non-violence.

She does this with fifteen stories of individual women she interviewed throughout the world. These women started out as unknown, ordinary individuals and ended up doing extraordinary acts of peacemaking. In the beginning of each interview, most of these women called themselves doctors, nuns, clan mothers, activists, scientists, even ex-princesses. Dr. Chambliss helped the women transition into calling themselves "Peacemakers" by asking each of them their definition of peace, and then pointing out that their work fits their own definition of making peace. Hence the birth of fifteen conscious Peacemakers.

Dr. Chambliss also includes a chapter in this book that identifies more than twenty guiding practices she observed in the women she interviewed. This chapter reads like a recipe one can follow to practice peacemaking. It is written in language simple enough for a child to understand and wise enough for an elder to nod their head in agreement. It is short enough for an individual to glance at as he or she heads into a meeting full of unknown dynamics. It is compelling enough for a parent to think twice before they deal with a misbehaving child. It is grounded and realistic enough for a burgeoning leader to know what she or he has to do to succeed in bringing about a world based on non-violent mutual respect.

In her final chapter, Dr. Chambliss invites the reader to take on an act of peacemaking, however small or grand, and send the story of the results to her. Don't skip this invitation or underestimate the opportunity it offers you to make a vital difference in today's world.

Imagine a world with hundreds of businesses who come forth with their new corporate and social responsibility agendas! Imagine a world with millions, literally millions, of individuals doing one act of peacemaking each day for the rest of their lives!

Dr. Scilla Elworthy
author of *The Business Plan for Peace*
Founder of the Oxford Research Group and Peace Direct
www.thebusinessplanforpeace.org

It is time to put armed conflict on lockdown and focus together on the true fight of our lives. People caught in armed conflicts, which are raging around the world, are among the most vulnerable and are also at the highest risk of suffering devastating losses from COVID-19. It's time to silence guns, stop artillery, end airstrikes, and create corridors for life-saving aid. End the sickness of war and fight the disease that is ravaging our world.

U.N. Secretary-General Antonio Guterres

*Dedicated to all the women, men,
and children conscious Peacemakers
whose acts of peacemaking are
making this world a better place.*

TABLE OF CONTENTS

Introduction

When some people hear the word "peacemaker," they think of some-one who negotiates the end to a war. Not so the women in these pages. This book is about women Peacemakers who are purposefully leveling the field of opportunity for those who have been oppressed. By doing so, these women are proactively averting war, creating a world where war is unnecessary, possibly irrelevant, one person at a time.

When a war ends, there are always winners and losers. No one likes being in a "one-down" position of oppression. That's true whether it is a child getting bullied in school, a spouse in an abusive marriage, a prisoner behind bars, or a worker who doesn't have fair access to a healthy work-place. It is true with a group of people whose skin color, religion, or sex automatically puts them in danger or denies them access to life's oppor-tunities. In fact, any situation that has a domination/subordination dy-namic is another conflict just waiting to happen.

No woman who has carried a child in her womb for nine months, or even has the potential to do so, wants to see that child blown apart on a battleground of violence. She will, instead, choose every creative, non-violent, proactive way she can imagine to re-balance the scales of in-equity, long before the situation comes to blows. This is what these women Peacemakers are doing.

They pave the way for others to rise up by removing barriers and pro-viding opportunities. They know if you offer someone who is at a disad-vantage a fair chance at things like an education, a just outcome to a wrongdoing, a sustainable way to support themselves, they will embrace that opportunity and do something with it. Opportunities might look like a prosthesis to make one's body whole, or a workplace that is safe rather than deadly. It might be a chance for a newborn to thrive rather than die, or just a moment of hope and happiness after surviving a genocide. This work doesn't happen overnight; it is purposeful, organically evolving, and aims for sustainability. It is always non-violent. Sometimes the work lasts longer than the life of the Peacemaker.

Out of respect, these women Peacemakers don't do such things *for* those who are oppressed; they do it *with* them. They accompany those with whom they work, treating them with the same respect and dignity they want for themselves. They are catalysts that pave the way for others to fulfill their potential, just as they themselves are doing. This way of making peace is not exclusive to adult women; Nelson Mandala, the Dalai Lama, Desmond Tutu, and Pope Francis have used the same tactics. Greta Thunberg and Malala Yousafzai do the same.

When a path has been paved by a Peacemaker, two things happen. First, as the formerly oppressed individuals do the hard work to acquire what they were formerly denied, those who were angry quit trying to gain equality by violence. Those who were hopeless begin to have hope. They are grateful someone cared enough to clear a path for them. They gain confidence and begin to respect themselves. Their spirits begin to rise like corks that have been released from a net under water.

Then the second and incredibly exciting thing happens: These formerly oppressed, newly skilled individuals start giving back. They pay forward what they themselves were offered. They begin to mentor their siblings like someone mentored them. They upgrade the financial and health conditions of their families. They create a sustainable quality of life for their villages. They call for safe work places for co-workers. They use their stories of accomplishments as a beacon to encourage others. They become catalysts for upliftment, just as the women Peacemakers became for them.

The women in these chapters have looked around where they live and noticed a situation where there was a gap between domination and subordination. They have been awake when an opportunity floated by to recalibrate the dynamic toward a position of mutual respect, even a little bit, even for only one person.

They all started at the individual level. Some continued working with a few people at a time while others ended up providing opportunities for whole nations, whole cultures, whole classes of people to raise themselves up, one person at a time.

These are women that continued to wake up each morning and say "yes" to another day of assisting someone in a one-down position to climb the hill to a world that practices mutual respect with one another. Mutual respect is my definition of peace. This is why I call them Peacemakers.

A Peacemaker is anyone who narrows the gap between dominance and subordination, establishing a relationship of mutual respect. What makes an act of peacemaking conscious is being awake when the opportunity presents itself, and then saying yes every day to continuing the work.

In doing this, the women Peacemakers in these chapters are proactively eliminating war and infusing sustainable peace into the world today. Although they are often too humble to shout it, these women know down deep they have made a valuable contribution to the world, both for those with whom they work and as role models for others who might want to follow in their footsteps. And for these women Peacemakers, that is enough.

• • •

Chapters 1–15 contain the stories of fifteen women I have interviewed throughout the world who have done extraordinary acts of peacemaking. I asked each woman what advice she offers for others who want to do acts of peacemaking. Their answers are in Chapter 16.

By working with these women for thirty years, I noticed certain daily choices they made in going about their work. Twenty-four of these are listed in Chapter 17. They serve as guidelines for any man, woman, or child who wants to be a conscious Peacemaker.

Opportunity alert! In the last chapter, I offer the reader/listener an invitation and the guidance to do an act of conscious peacemaking in your own setting and then send me the story of how it plays out. Good luck!

*The planet does not need
more successful people.
The planet desperately needs
more peacemakers, healers, restorers,
storytellers, and lovers of all kind.*

—H.H. the Dalai Lama

CHAPTER ONE

Orphans Teaching Orphans

Chido Govera

• CHRISTON BANK, ZIMBABWE •

Peace Work:
Empowering African orphans and women
to care for themselves and contribute to society

Metaphor:
I am an eagle who rises above my troubles
to do my work from an inspired view.

Peace comes from being able to contribute
the best that we have, and all that we are,
toward creating a world that supports everyone.
But it is also securing the space for others
to contribute the best that they are.

—Hafsat Abiola

Chido's Book

One day in 2011, I was in my orchard pruning apple trees with my neighbor.

"How's your book coming?" Jon asked.

"It's coming," I said, "but slowly."

"Good," he said, "because I think I have another candidate for you. Do you have room for one more?"

"Always," I said. "There is always room to introduce another Peacemaker to the world."

He reached in his jacket pocket and pulled out a dog-eared paperback book with a picture of a young, scared, but smiling girl on the cover. The title was *The Future of Hope*. The author was Chido Govera.

"Read this," he said, "and let me know if you want help getting in touch with her."

"How do you know about her?" I asked.

"I'm affiliated with ZERI, the Zero Emissions Research and Initiatives group."

That night I Googled ZERI and found it was a global network of creative thinkers seeking solutions to the ever-increasing problems of the world. It was the brainchild of a Belgian man named Gunter Pauli. A statement on their website reads:

> *The members take on challenges others will consider impossible or too complex. Starting from ideas, based on science, the common vision shared by each and every member of the ZERI network is to seek sustainable solutions for society, from unreached communities to corporations inspired by nature's design principles. Innovative solutions are constantly designed by ZERI teams drawn from many walks of life and expertise.*

The idea was fascinating to me, but left me puzzled about what could possibly be the connection between this global initiative and the haunting eyes of the girl on the book cover. I started reading the book that evening.

Entranced, I finished the book around 2 a.m. I was host to a cacophony of emotions that would never let me sleep that night. As a trauma therapist, I had learned to keep my emotional balance while listening to stories of early childhood abuse, but that night I lost that balance as I read Chido's story. I knew I'd felt sadness because my pillow was wet with tears. The emotion that surprised me was a sense of pride. I had never met this young woman, and yet somehow I felt proud for her and what she had done with her life. Perhaps my strongest emotion was hope, not only for what one girl could do to change her own reality, but for the futures of so many like her. Her book title said it all: *The Future of Hope.*

The next day, I asked my neighbor how I could contact Chido to request an interview with her. She lived in a village in Zimbabwe. I was out of traveling funds, so I couldn't get to her village in person, but I was determined to somehow reach this young woman.

"Why don't you Skype with her?" my neighbor said.

"Skype? She can Skype from a rural village in Zimbabwe?" I replied, hiding my own concern that I was new to Skype myself.

"She'll figure it out," he said. "She's a pretty clever young woman."

And so she was.

Three months later, I dialed the number she emailed me on my Skype screen. I was sure I'd lose the intimacy of a face-to-face interview, but my worries dissolved when I saw her quiet presence on-screen, and heard a cheerful "Hellooo. How are you?" As she answered my questions, the tale of two decades of her life spilled out with dignity and truth. I heard not just her words but the certain grit and pluck, the hugeness of heart, and the focused determination of Chido Govera.

Chido's Childhood

Age seven is definitely too young to become the head of a household. And yet that was Chido's destiny. She never knew her father. When she was five years old, her mother began leaving home for long periods of time. During these times, Chido and her brother were taken to live with a cousin-sister's family. There, Chido experienced frightening and abusive events, which she was waiting to tell her mother when she came home. But when she looked at her mother upon her return, Chido realized her mother was ill and would not be able to take protective action with those who had hurt her, so the conversation with her mother never happened.

Her mother did, however, move herself and her two children to live with their grandmother in a hut behind her uncle's house in the small village in Marange. By this time, Chido, who had always been a frail child, was ill herself and staying in a tent nearby the round hut where her mother was convalescing. There was no opportunity for conversation or explanations for what was happening to their lives.

One day, Chido was told to walk with a cousin to see an aunt. The aunt put her arms around Chido and hugged her with unusual sadness. It was then and there that Chido realized her mother had died. It would be years before Chido would unravel the details of all the events that led up to her mother's death, including that her mother had died of AIDS.

However, what immediately became quite clear to Chido was that she felt bereft at not being able to say goodbye to the woman who had given her life. She felt angry that there would be no one to talk to about the abuse she had received at her cousin-sister's house. And, deep inside, Chido felt afraid, for she knew being an orphan girl in rural Zimbabwe meant she now had no one to protect her from future sexual and physical abuse that was commonly inflicted by men in the community.

Once her mother died, Chido was presented with two dilemmas. In Zimbabwe, as in much of rural Africa, the task of feeding her younger brother and grandmother immediately fell to young Chido as the girl child. She tried finding work in people's fields after she finished her school day. All too often she returned home empty-handed and had to face her five-year-old brother and granny going without food. There was no help to be had from her uncle, even though Chido was providing for his mother. Her uncle was also poor and struggling.

The second dilemma was that orphans, especially girls on the mother's side of the family, immediately dropped to the lowest level of societal status in the community. She had no rights or privileges, no voice or protection, and had to do whatever adults told her to do. In Chido's case, this meant enduring sexual advances from her uncles and their friends and other forms of abuse targeted to girls. And when Chido would come home with some money or food, her male cousins often stole it away. When her uncles had a bad day, they would beat her or explore their sexual fantasies with little Chido.

The Dream

When she was eight years old, Chido had a dream amidst this ongoing

11

nightmare. In it, she was teaching orphan children how to rise out of their circumstances and create new, productive lives. This dream planted seeds deep within her consciousness that would later bloom, manifesting as her life's work.

By the time she turned nine years old, it finally became intolerable to come home empty-handed after an unsuccessful day of foraging for food or looking for piece jobs after school. Chido dropped out of elementary school in order to spend the entire day working in other people's gardens, or seeking other ways to gather food. Whenever she was able, her grandmother contributed to the larder by taking Chido out in the woods to forage for local mushrooms. Though she was losing her eyesight, her granny knew where to find mushrooms in the wild and taught Chido how to identify the safe, edible varieties.

In the meantime, a girl cousin came to Chido with a plan to help escape her ongoing plight. There was a man, she told Chido, thirty years older who could not find a wife, and she would arrange for him to marry Chido. The most tempting part of the offer in Chido's estimation was that the man owned a car.

"Not just any car," Chido remembered as she told me this story, "but a blue car." Here was another dilemma for her. If she said yes, she would flee the abuse of her uncles but would not know the fate of her brother and grandmother. If she said no, she risked angering her cousin, and her life circumstances would remain the same. As Chido told me this story, I kept feeling the weight that must have been upon the shoulders of this slim child, less than a decade old. In the end, she declined the offer. To this day, Chido still takes notice of blue cars wherever she goes.

At this point, there really were no alternatives for this child beyond a life of abuse while trying to provide for her family against huge odds. Chido became an adult before she had even reached her teenage years.

The Miracle of Mushrooms

Miraculously, however, everything changed quite suddenly. When Chido was eleven, she was nominated by a Methodist church-going lady named Loveness Zengeni to receive a scholarship for one week of learning how to farm mushrooms at the Africa University in Mutare, Zimbabwe's third largest city.

A trio made up of the ZERI foundation, an African researcher named Margaret Tagwira, and a Chinese mushroom grower named Professor S.T.

Chan joined together in an urgent response to alleviate hunger and lack of resources in the marginalized rural populations of Africa. The team helped launch this Barefoot Mushroom Farming Training, funded by ZERI. Dr. Chan offered information from China's well established mushroom industry that utilized indigenous waste materials. Margaret brought extensive knowledge from her research project with water hyacinths, where she had been able to produce 450 kilos of mushrooms from 100 kilos of the plant's waste products. Together, they designed this training and taught orphan girls from African countries how to grow mushrooms from local waste materials.

Margaret identified fifteen female orphans to attend the training and arranged their transport, lodging, and food. Chido told me she was chosen because she was keen to learn how to feed her family without having to scavenge the fields. The idea was that in just one week's time, in a hands-on, show-and-tell training void of any scientific jargon, the girls would be able to return home equipped with the skills needed to grow mushrooms. These orphans at the bottom of the economic pyramid were to become budding entrepreneurs.

The course was a turning point in Chido's life in two ways. First, she now had a skill that would yield consistent food for her brother and her grandmother. Second, she could sell the mushrooms for money. She even began to gather enough money to send her little brother and other orphans to the village school.

But even more importantly, during that week away from home, Chido came to realize there was a world beyond the treatment of her uncles. Somehow, their hold on her was broken. She realized she could actually choose the people she wanted to include in her life.

Since ZERI's policy was "each one teach one," the fifteen scholarship recipients were expected to train other ZERI communities in their new mushrooming skills. What the sponsors had failed to foresee, however, was how valuable these newly skilled young girls appeared to the men in their villages. Shortly upon their return home, thirteen girls were married and no longer available to teach.

Chido and one other student held fast, remained unmarried, and were invited to return to the mushroom program for an additional three-year training. The other girl eventually married and dropped out, leaving Chido as the sole student in the effort. But first, Chido had to get permission from her uncle, who reluctantly agreed for her to participate in the program as long as she paid him a portion of her earnings. Her greatest worry was how her brother and grandmother would fare without her. She cried over this every day and night at the beginning of her new life. As often as she could, she made the ninety-minute trip from Mutare to Marange to pay her uncle and visit her family.

This advanced training focused on the extended skills of cultivating mushrooms on various kinds of substrates, primarily on materials that might otherwise be wasted. Margaret Tagwira became both a mentor and somewhat of a mother figure for Chido, inviting her into her home.

After completing her training in mushroom production at the university, Chido decided to complete the schooling that she had discontinued earlier in her life in order to feed her family. She became the oldest student in her school class, sometimes called "grandmother" by her younger classmates. Chido made up all her missed education in less than four years, and graduated from high school.

During this time, the founder of ZERI, Gunther Pauli, took a special interest in Chido and kept a fatherly eye on her from the age of eleven. Even though Gunter is a man of famed intellectual strength, Chido describes him as being very gentle with her. The relationship grew into a normal family connection, which brought to Chido not only a father figure with whom she remains very close, but five siblings and Gunter's wife, whom Chido respects as a mother figure. The added bonus was Gunter's sister in Belgium who became a beloved aunt: Tante Liesje. It was from this aunt's Belgian apartment that Chido was Skyping with me during our interview.

Overcoming History

When she was nineteen, Chido began to suffer multiple physical symptoms, including pain in various parts of her body. Intuitively, Gunter surmised that these symptoms might have something to do with her traumatic history. He introduced her to the Paracelsus Clinic in Switzerland where she was told that she had three options for treating her post-traumatic stress disorder (PTSD). She could speak to someone about her traumas, draw about her traumas, or write about her traumas. Still being rather shy, Chido opted to write about her history. As she wrote, she began to heal. In the process, she produced the very book, *The Future of Hope*, my neighbor had handed me in my orchard.

In her book, Chido not only wrote out her past traumas, but began to give voice to her eight-year-old dream of building a place in Zimbabwe where orphans could come to experience the same kind of rebirth she experienced herself. As she healed, Chido regained her focus, and began envisioning an actual place where she would teach orphans.

International Teaching Years

Chido fulfilled her teaching promise to ZERI by traveling throughout the world, teaching people how to grow mushrooms on their local waste products. By the time of my interview with her in 2011, Chido was twenty-five years old, and had taught mushroom cultivation skills in Colombia, India, Tanzania, the Congo, Ghana, Cameroon, The Netherlands, Germany, and the United States. In San Francisco, she taught young women entrepreneurs from the University of California at Berkeley how to start a business growing mushrooms on coffee grounds, winning her the Sustainability Award from the Specialty Coffee Association of America. Eventually, she would teach mushroom production skills to over 1,000 people in her travels throughout the world.

Everywhere she went, Chido used her skill of making complicated processes simple and understandable for all her students, regardless of their age or experience. She customized the lessons to make use of local waste products. She taught by doing and showing, so language barriers became inconsequential. Chido became known as one of the most knowledgeable Barefoot Scientists in mushroom farming.

Gathering Resources for the Future of Hope Foundation

In time, Chido continued accepting invitations to teach and talk about mushroom growing, but now it was with the new goal of making money for her own center, which she would call the Future of Hope Foundation. In 2012, on a speaking and teaching tour in the United States, Chido came to my organic farming community in Colorado. She told her story to two public audiences who were not only fascinated by her personal history, but were also willing to donate money toward her dream foundation. She conducted a training for several local farmers, teaching us how to grow mushrooms on our apple woodchips and spent hops waste from the local brewery. Each workshop participant came away with two bags of mushrooms ready to sprout in the coming weeks, while Chido came away with a $2,000 check for her new foundation.

The personal joy for me in Chido's time in my community was the time we got to spend together in my home, telling stories and laughing, sometimes like two mature women, other times like niece and auntie. She continued on to China where she spent several months studying the Chinese mushroom production process so she would have even more to teach her orphans.

As she traveled raising money for her foundation, Chido's vision became even clearer: she wanted to provide a place where children could learn skills that would sustain them, including mushroom growing and permaculture. She also planned to teach them nutrition, feminine hygiene, personal safety, and other basic human care skills they never were able to learn from their mothers, who died before they could teach them to their children.

Chido told me emphatically, "It's not just about mushrooms. It's about changing their philosophy, the way they think. I want these girls to believe they can stand on their own two feet." Equally important, Chido planned to help these children believe they could become happy, independent people who have something to give back to their communities. She planned to encourage the orphans to create a family and a community that would treat them with respect.

Her primary teaching tool for this would not be lecturing, but rather telling her own story. In her experience of describing her life to the girls in orphanages, they would say, "Your story is worse than mine, and look at where you are today. Maybe I can change, too." Chido envisioned for these children nothing less than what she had been able to create for herself.

She was aware that the abuse she endured as a child continued in many Zimbabwean homes and orphanages where children were routinely abused or neglected. This treatment left children believing they were of no value to anyone. Chido also understood that it is a lot to ask an orphan to return home to the same people who regarded her as worthless and to be able to sustain the sense of personal value she wanted them to gain in the training. She decided to invite women from each girl's community to attend the training. The job of these women would be to precede the child home to her village and pave the way for her community to respect this returning child as a worthy person with valuable skills.

I asked Chido if boys would be allowed to take the training. "Yes, eventually," she told me, "because both sexes have suffered from the abuse by irresponsible adults. And we need a place where boys and girls can learn to interact and respect each other as well as take care of each other." In the future, Chido also plans to open her training to other populations she calls "the unreached," who have been marginalized in society. When I asked how many children she might train at a time, she told me she planned to start with small numbers, maybe five, "to make sure that I thoroughly accomplish my mission." I will never forget one sentence Chido said during our interview, while looking directly at me on the Skype screen: "What I want is people taking ownership of their own empowerment."

Empowered, Not Power Over

Chido rankles at anything that feels like "power over." She told me a story about some people who had offered to buy land in Zimbabwe. They would permit her to live in a small house in the corner of the property and conduct her programs on a particular section of the land. When Chido asked how they might feel if the situation were reversed—if she owned the land and allowed them only a small portion, they replied, "Oh no. That would give you too much power over us."

"If you can't trust me to be equal partners with you," Chido queried, "how could you ever support me in empowering these orphans? Thank you for your offer, but I believe I'll earn the money for this foundation on my own, even if I have to wait several more months or years to see it happen." Perhaps it was this same distrust that made young Chido turn down the offer of an elderly husband with a blue car.

Forgiveness and Perseverance

When asked if she had forgiven those who had caused her harm or had not protected her, she answered, without hesitation: "I have to, because not to do so hurts me more than them. Otherwise, I couldn't be as happy as I am now." Similarly, when asked her thoughts about Robert Mugabe, the infamous leader of Zimbabwe who had not hesitated to exert "power over" people during his many years in office, Chido replied:

He is one person. The people need to take more responsibility. First we need to learn how to be at peace and trust ourselves. Then we won't sit back and do nothing. We will feel that we are respectable enough to change a bad situation. When you respect yourself and others, you become responsible.

17

Once when asked what wisdom she would share about her life journey, Chido answered: "I want to share the spirit of perseverance, forgiveness, self-belief, and hope. If I could go back to little Chido, I would say to her: 'Don't give up, forgive all the hurt, believe in yourself, and have hope for the future.' "

Creating the Future of Hope Foundation

During the time I interviewed Chido, she was doing more than simply raising money for her Future of Hope Foundation; she was searching for land and gathering a group of people that would support her dream. She was also putting the legal structure in place to keep her foundation safe in the face of a bully-prone political situation in her country. Most poignantly, she was carefully thinking through the philosophical intention for her foundation. Just like ZERI's "each one teach one" principle, she saw the underpinning philosophy of the Future of Hope Foundation as "orphans teaching orphans."

Chido sent me a working paper she had composed, entitled "Draft Introduction to the Future of Hope Foundation." Just as she had always acted older than her age as a child, this twenty-something young woman was now creating a mission statement for her foundation with a wisdom far beyond her years.

> *Orphans teaching orphans is a project aimed at breaking the normal thinking that someone else should, and will, come to the rescue of orphans or any other needy/disadvantaged groups of our communities. This project is aimed at encouraging pro-activity, encouraging all individuals to step up and take charge of their lives and change their predicaments. In the case of orphans, it has often been the case that they wait and hope for someone to save them from all their troubles. While there is nothing wrong with waiting and hoping in some situations, there obviously is everything wrong in letting the millions of orphans or any other disadvantaged groups believe that this is the only way.*

> *In Sub-Saharan Africa, it's estimated that about over 50 million children are orphans. It only makes sense to start encouraging these millions of children to start doing something for*

themselves. They understand their problems more than anyone else can understand them, and for this reason, if we are to deal with the problems of orphans effectively, we are better off giving them the tools and skills to do it for themselves, to stand up for each other. While emergency aid may be needed and welcomed, long-term solutions for the orphans by the orphans offer the best learning tools for vocational and interpersonal skills.

It is time we will all start seriously acknowledging the potential of these children, to believe and trust that the world needs them to step up. We have to give them a chance and mentor them. It is vital they are able to believe they can empower and inspire each other, not only be empowered, and that we support them in this. We have to stop pitying them and support them to break out of self-pity to understanding that they can change things; yes, they have gone through rough experiences but they must bounce back for their sake and that of the world at large. That is the future of hope, and it's not just for orphans but everyone that's considered "disadvantaged." When we can make everyone take responsibility and make things happen, when we can allow for that to happen without fear of losing control or feeling that our positions in power are threatened, then we stand a chance for a hopeful future.

The Many Dimensions of Chido

In order to know Chido fully, one must know her in at least three dimensions. The first is to meet her face-to-face. In this meeting, you will encounter a beautiful, lithe, soft-spoken woman, who will look into your eyes and answer your questions with clarity and humor, smiling often as she tells the story of her life, a life that might have broken any one of us completely. But as her story rolls out, you realize that Chido has something inside of her that won't break. It is as strong as a sword, but it isn't a sword. It is more like a force field of energy that simply will not be subdued.

The second way to know Chido is through learning what she has done in the three decades of her life. You can read about it, hear others' accounts of it, Google her website. Her accomplishments are impressive, amazingly productive, and clearly the manifestation of the dream she had when she was eight years old. Her accomplishments have taken place by

hard work and persistence, by luck and by pluck, with the helpful intentions of some people and in spite of the harmful intentions of others. I
have had the privilege of knowing Chido in these two ways.

The third way to know her is to quietly observe her in the midst of her
orphans: how she tells her story to them, how she answers their questions,
how she holds their hands as she walks beside them, how she makes them
feel safe, how she treats them with so much respect that they begin to respect themselves. Someday, I hope to travel to Zimbabwe to see her in
this third way.

Epilogue

Chido successfully secured the property and the network of people for
her Future of Hope Foundation. The place that became the site for her
Foundation was a former orphanage in Christon Bank, a suburb of Harare.
Rather than displace the seven girls that were residing at the former orphanage, Chido took them on as her children, became their mum, and
built the Future of Hope around them.

The Future of Hope Foundation was officially founded in 2013. Chido
held her first training for thirty-five girls and women late that year. Since
then, over 2,300 orphans and adults have directly benefitted from her
trainings in growing mushrooms and have been able to change their lives
and their communities. This is more than double the number of the one
thousand people she had taught internationally in her years prior to her
foundation.

At that time, the well-honed mission statement of The Future of Hope
Foundation read:

> The Future of Hope Foundation is an organization that works
> to capacitate and support women and girl orphans through
> food production with a specific focus on a Mushroom & Poul-
> try based Integrated Food Production System. The Foundation
> shares skills that promote and provide food security to vulner-
> able members of society and improve the conditions necessary
> for their self-development, with the ultimate goal to end

poverty, abuse, self-pity, and victimhood at grassroots level in Africa, by enabling them to step out of a victim role, turning their unhappy past experiences into a wisdom that equips them with strengthened energy to realize, find, and bring to life a purpose in life.

Chido also built a school on the Foundation property where orphans and women, like her, can complete an education that poverty delayed.

Chido and her students have built forty-five mushroom production units in the Zimbabwean communities where they live. Realizing this volume of produce needs a market, Chido established Hopefood, an entrepreneurial entity she created to support access to the market place for these production units.

Chido has grown from a vulnerable, overwhelmed orphan into an accomplished social entrepreneur, farmer, campaigner, educator, and charismatic speaker on edible and medicinal mushrooms. Simultaneously, she has founded The Future of Hope Foundation that is a life-changer for formerly disadvantaged individuals. Above all, she is an attentive, loving teacher and role model for the young women that come to the Future of Hope.

By thirty-two, Chido had won numerous awards for her work, her entrepreneurial innovations, and her philosophy of hope. She intends to pursue a master's degree. Not a bad intention for a woman who dropped out of elementary school.

When asked recently why she engages in this work, Chido answered:

When people take charge of their lives, they heal, they grow, and they can advance in life and bring change to their environment and the world at large. I also have a more selfish reason why I engage in this work. That reason is to heal myself and express my healing process in works that provide opportunities that I wished for when I was younger and weaker.

When I do public presentations about Chido, I am often asked, "Is she married?" After the blue car man, there have been some significant men in Chido's very busy life, but so far nothing has grown into marriage for her. During our interview, she told me she is looking for a man like her adopted father, Gunter Pauli. It's a tall order, but one befitting of her.

CHAPTER TWO

We Are the Ones the Prophecies Identified

Clan Mother Rachelle Figueroa

• STANDING ROCK, NORTH DAKOTA, USA •

Peace Work:
Interpreting the Original Laws of the Indigenous People to remind women it is their time to stand up in leadership

Metaphor:
I am like a rhinoceros when I have to be: I get thick-skinned and don't feel a thing when tough situations come at me.

Hear us:
You cannot make us go to war.
We are free, and many,
and as strong as water.
We will win,
because we will not fight.

—Adrianna Heideman

My Beloved, Ancient Orchard

It was my beloved, ancient orchard that inadvertently led me to this woman Peacemaker. These ninety-six-year-old trees were still producing apples, in spite of their history of several owners, some who nurtured them, and others who neglected them. It was 2016, an unusually productive year for all the fruit growers in our organic farming community. Our soil, our weather, and our hard work converged to yield apricots, cherries, plums, peaches, nectarines, and pears hanging off the trees in rare abundance over the summer months. And the apples, the last crop of the season, were not to be outdone. The 120 trees in my orchard alone bore twenty-six thousand pounds of red and yellow delicious apples, ready to be taken to the local juice company.

First News of Standing Rock

At the same time the apples were ripening, news began to trickle into our local and national media about Native Americans at the Standing Rock Camp near Cannon Ball, North Dakota. The Indigenous people in the camp were trying to protect their sacred lands and their water supply from the Dakota Access Pipeline (DAPL). This pipeline was to carry oil products that had been fracked and drilled out of the Bakken oil fields in North Dakota 1,170 miles to Illinois, where they would be shipped to international countries and corporations.

This news caught my attention because my own community had spent the last five years fighting several petroleum companies that had attempted to sink multiple oil and gas wells in our valley. The companies proposed to extract the gas using "fracking" methods, which were notorious for creating health problems for people, animals, and the earth. Their proposed sites for drilling their wells were near the water supplies for our organic farms, near the drinking water supplies of our towns, and near the schoolyards of our children. Twice our community galvanized itself and thwarted their efforts.

Native American youth had started the Standing Rock camp in early

2016 when they realized the construction route for the DAPL pipeline was slated to run through the sacred burial grounds of their ancestors. By one way of thinking, this was akin to burying a 30-inch pipeline through the Arlington National Cemetery where America's fallen war heroes and deceased presidents are buried. Moreover, this pipeline, owned by Energy Transfer Partners, carrying 570,000 barrels of oil a day, was slated to run underneath Lake Oahe, an important drinking water source for the Lakota Sioux near their sacred burial grounds.

The ranks of Standing Rock had grown substantially since its inception, with both Native and non-Native participants who, rather than calling themselves protesters, called themselves Water Protectors. There were now four camps instead of one. They needed to feed these volunteers that kept showing up. And here I was with an abundance of fresh, delicious apples.

Before the harvesting crew came to my orchard, I invited friends to come pick apples and squeeze them in our presses to take home as apple juice. I asked each of them to first pick some apples for Standing Rock, something they were happy to do. At the end of the day, I was left with thirty-five large, heavy boxes of apples and a question in my head about how to transport them the 880 miles to the North Dakota camp.

Forced Sterilizations

In continuing to track the media stories about Standing Rock, I saw a television interview with three Native American midwives at the camp. One, named Carolina Reyes, spoke about the forced sterilization by the Indian Health Services of 3,000 Native American women between 1973 and 1976, which decreased the birth rate for the Native population in the United States from 3.8 percent to 1.8 percent in the 1970s. I was skeptical.

I did some research to see what else I could find about this set of events. In fact, what Carolina reported was the tip of an iceberg. According to a research paper presented by Gregory W. Rutecki M.D. at the Center for Bioethics and Human Dignity in 2010, the U.S. Government Accountability Office reported results of its investigation of Native American sterilizations between 1973 and 1976 that happened in Aberdeen, Albuquerque, Oklahoma City, and Phoenix. In these four areas alone, there were 3,406 sterilizations of Native American women performed during this period, in most cases without consent. There was also coercion by threats to withdraw healthcare provisions or, more disturbing, to take over custody of Native American children already born. Dr. Rutecki pointed out that, percentage-wise, this would have been the equivalent of sterilizing 452,000 non-Native American women at that time. Further investigation of the Navajo reservation during a similar period revealed that sterilization procedures increased from 15.1 percent to 30.7 percent, while abortions increased by 130 percent.

I was shocked. I had received a bachelor's degree in American Studies, yet I had never heard of these practices. I suddenly realized as an American citizen, I knew more about the sterilizations that had taken place in Germany in World War II than I knew about such practices that had taken place within a few hours of where I grew up in the United States. I knew that the Native Americans in North America had been badly mistreated by the ancestors of my white, non-Native culture, but getting specific details such as these brought it home like a boulder. Not for the first time, I pondered what other details I didn't know about the dark side of my own cultural heritage. I planned to continue pursuing answers.

Apples For Standing Rock

I decided if I personally delivered my apples to Standing Rock, I might have a chance to interview Carolina Reyes about the work she was doing to overcome these practices and the subsequent loss of Native American population. It was tricky because Internet and phone communications at Standing Rock were significantly and purposefully interrupted, making it impossible to pre-arrange an interview. I rented a U-Haul trailer and loaded up the apples. A friend, Mike Straub, volunteered to join me. We filled the U-Haul with other supplies, like a wood stove with wood to fuel it, clothing, Milk of Magnesia to counteract the effects of pepper spray, hay for horses, and fresh produce donated by several of our organic farmers. Together we drove the 880 miles to Standing Rock, which allowed me to see a part of the United States I had never seen.

From watching the news coverage of the situation, I gleaned the conflict was between the Texas-based Energy Transfer Partners that was building the DAPL, and the Standing Rock Sioux Nation across whose traditional treaty land the pipeline was being constructed. The Native Americans, and their ally Water Protectors, felt the sacred ceremonial and burial sites were being physically and spiritually violated and the safety of their water supply jeopardized.

Indeed, it was not only Native resources that were in the path of DAPL. The Energy Transfer Partners had plans to pipe their oil under multiple streams and the Missouri River, potentially endangering the drinking and agricultural water for millions of American citizens. To make matters worse, this company had a reputation for oil spills.

The Energy Transfer Partners felt confident it had done everything the U.S. government required to grant permission for this section of pipeline. Legal and governmental complexities notwithstanding, this conflict was playing itself out on the backdrop of over five hundred years of broken promises and mistreatment of the Native Americans by the U.S. government. To top it off, there was a well-documented contemporary record of racial discrimination against Native Americans in North Dakota.

David and Goliath

By the time Mike and I approached Standing Rock, the ranks of both sides were swelling daily. What started out as one camp with two hundred Native American youth had grown to four camps containing six thousand people by the time I visited there. Phenomenally, and for the first time in history, over 320 Native American Nations gathered in one place in solidarity. Plus an equal number from Canadian First Nation tribes and members of Indigenous peoples throughout the world had come to contribute their support.

By Thanksgiving, two weeks after my visit, the numbers of Natives and non-Natives had increased to a reported fifteen thousand, including many young adults, medical personnel, movie stars, civil rights leaders, and over two thousand retired military veterans who pledged to protect the Protectors. A herd of over two hundred buffalo even made their presence known, no small contribution in the minds of the Natives.

The sheriff of Morton County, North Dakota became the public point person for enforcing the rights of the Energy Transfer Partners. His ranks also swelled, not so much by the numbers of people seen in the Standing Rock camps, but by an incredibly well-equipped law enforcement presence of local officers, state troopers, National Guard units from North Dakota and other nearby states, and allegedly even mercenary forces, known as Tiger Swan, hired by the Energy Transfer Partners. Their arsenal contained a full complement of modern riot equipment, including rubber bullets, tear gas, powerful water cannons, sound grenades, batons, police dogs, automatic weapons, helicopters and small planes, military ground vehicles, and a sophisticated communications transport unit the size of a semi truck. Moreover, they assumed, they had the might of the local judicial system and of the United States government on their side.

The tool chest of the Standing Rock Natives included prayer, a core of wise elders, a huge cadre of Native and non-Native men and women of all ages, a handful of horses, one drone, multiple Indigenous prophecies, and, not to be underestimated, lessons learned from decades of suppression by the U.S. government. They also had a level-headed chief who astutely took their cause public, including to the United Nations. And in the end, their requests were ultimately backed by the action of President Obama.

From the beginning, Standing Rock had a dedication to non-violence that was impressive; everyone that was involved in a direct action was required to go through a non-violence training. Neither weapons nor alcohol were allowed in the camps. If arrested, no one resisted, just like the days of Civil Rights protests.

It smacked of David and Goliath to me. Only this time, there was the media; mostly the alternative media with impressive on-site coverage of the interactions, often narrated by Native journalists. Watching the alternative news, one saw bareheaded Water Protectors in t-shirts, carrying banners that said "We are not armed," marching toward a line of law enforcement officers in full riot gear who appeared faceless as the sun bounced off their riot helmets and eye shields. As our U-Haul traveled closer to Standing Rock, I wondered what we were getting ourselves into.

The Peace of Standing Rock

We remained at Standing Rock for only two and a half days, but it felt like much longer to me. We arrived at night and settled in to our friends' tipi in the Rosebud camp. My first visual was at dawn the next morning. I saw a quiet, wide river flanked by camps dotted with combinations of tipis, tents, yurts, and sweat lodges, some nestled on the river banks and some spread out on a large, flat area. People were walking and talking quietly. I could hear a large group praying in a Native American language on the far bank of the river. Their drum beats felt comforting. The smell of wood smoke and sweet cooked apples was in the air.

My experience at the camp was one of feeling welcomed, appreciated, respected, and willingly assisted. And contrary to what one might think from the conventional media coverage, I felt utterly safe. There was a sense of order that was invisible yet palpable to me. I felt my contributions, whether unloading apples in kitchen larders, assisting with camp duties, or listening to people's experiences and wisdom, were all considered valuable and appreciated. I was thanked for everything I did.

One of the first things I saw at the camp's entrance was a full piece of upright plywood, with the following painted on it:

DIRECT ACTION PRINCIPLES
- *We are ~~protestors~~ protectors.*
- *We are peaceful and prayerful.*
- *'-------isms' have no place here.*
- *We are non-violent.*
- *Respect the locals.*
- *We are proud to stand, no masks.(?)*
- *No weapons. (Or what could be considered one.)*
- *Property damage does not get us closer to our goal.*
- *All campers must get an orientation.*
- *Direct action training required for all taking action.*
- *No children in potentially dangerous situations.*
- *We keep each other accountable for these principles.*
- *This is a ceremony. Act accordingly.*

The pace of life felt relatively calm, much like the pace of the Cannonball River that flowed between the camps. My feet were on dirt rather than asphalt as I walked among the well-maintained camps. People were talking to each other rather than focusing on their cell phones or computers. The lack of electricity in our camp sent folks to their dwellings soon after the sun set. The conversations that evolved in the magic of the fire in the center of our tipi during the night and early mornings helped forge those of us who started out as strangers into friends we may never forget. I felt a rare peace within myself.

There was something else going on as well, something I couldn't put my finger on at first. It felt a little like being in my orchard, which on the surface looks simply like 120 trees. But when I sit down under a tree and get quiet, I can feel the life force of the orchard. It took me some time to identify what this "something else" at Standing Rock was. I finally realized it was the life force of prayer.

From the minute I set foot on the ground there, I was included in someone's prayers. Somewhere in the camp, there was always someone praying, day and night. The prayers were for everyone, including the Water Protectors, the law enforcement officers, the owner of the Energy Transfer Partners, the ditch diggers, the bulldozer drivers, the President of the

United States, the animals, birds and plants, for Mother Earth and for me. Sometimes the prayers were audible, though often they were just silently part of the air in the camp. I missed them when we drove away.

A Serendipitous Connection

Although I waited all day near the midwives' center to invite Carolina Reyes for an interview, she was constantly occupied elsewhere in the large Oceti Sakowin camp. Serendipitously, as I walked back to our camp, I made the acquaintance of Danielle Gennety. When she heard about my book on women Peacemakers, she lit up, saying that a Clan Mother named Rachelle Figueroa was living in her tipi and would be a perfect Peacemaker to interview. Danielle and Rachelle had spent three days together in jail after being arrested during a Water Protectors' peaceful action.

Danielle made the introductions and Rachelle graciously accepted my invitation. As the interview unfolded, I realized this was really why my apples had led me to Standing Rock.

The UnPeace of Standing Rock

"I was praying," Rachelle told me when I asked her what got her thrown into jail for three days.

> We were lined up on the top of a ditch facing the burial grounds. We Elders, three or four of whom were in their eighties, were sitting down in chairs. Some had walkers. We were doing a chanupa ceremony and praying. (A chanupa is a sacred peace pipe carried by selected clan elders.)

> One young man was way up in the hills doing a vision quest about the pipeline situation. He was in a Hochika, a five-foot by five-foot space with a sacred altar he had erected, where he was to stay for four nights and five days. The officers went up and yanked him out of his sacred space and threw the buffalo skull and other items away off his altar.

> Suddenly, the sheriff's people came toward us. I just remember putting my chanupa with its prayer flags on my head and just praying. I heard the first line of officers say, "Go around the Elders." But suddenly, the concussion bombs and the pepper

spray and the rubber bullets got blasted into the group behind us. You could hear everybody yelling and screaming.

The second line of officers went directly for the group of Elders. All the Water Protectors, as they had been trained, formed a phalanx of bodies around their elders to protect them, Danielle being one of them.

One by one they plucked everybody away, and then they took us. When I came out I was curled around my chanupa. A cop took me over to the side of the road, and demanded that I put down my chanupa. I said, "No, this is a sacred item. It is not supposed to be separated from me." He twisted my arm and started pushing me down. I looked up and saw another officer. I looked at him, asking for help with my eyes. He came over and picked up my chanupa. The first cop yelled at him to just leave it. But the officer said, "No. I'll carry it for her."

That was one of the many miracles that happened. It was such a contrast, one irate crazy person with no consciousness of the sacred, and the other who knew it was something sacred and came right over. The world we live in is fifty percent dark and fifty percent light on all levels, spiritually, emotionally, physically. But you can't see the light unless you are in the dark. You have to understand the balance between what you can do and what is not for you to do.

Many Water Protectors, including the Elders, were arrested, put in handcuffs and made to sit in the sun for two to three hours. At that point, a bulldozer started up from the top of the hill, turned in front of the Water Protectors into the sacred burial ground and began bulldozing back and forth, back and forth.

We were just crying and praying. There was nothing we could do, just sitting on the side of the road handcuffed behind our backs. Everybody was just praying basically.

And then all of a sudden a young man yells, "Look! The buffalo are coming!" We turned around and out of nowhere this herd of buffalo start running toward us from a half mile away. And then another one comes from the other side and they meet, like Whoosh! I don't know if you have ever seen a large buffalo herd, but it is powerful! And the Elders said, "The ancestors…they are here backing us up!" It just lifted our spirits.

And then a helicopter chased them away, and we were depleted again. Some people said we had staged that. But some of our men from the Oceti Camp knew of a man that lived pretty far away who had a buffalo farm. They asked if he had anything to do with it. He said he only had a dozen or fifteen buffalo and they never moved off his property.

Things happened; eagles came, just different things. And we said, "Okay the ancestors are with us. Just keep going." And our medicine people were doing lodges and Spirit told them things that were happening and what we should do or not. They were telling us, "Just keep going. Keep standing up for Mother Earth."

The Water Protectors that were arrested that day spent three days in custody, being moved to three different incarceration centers. Rachelle and Danielle helped calm some of the younger women who were traumatized by the events. When they had quiet moments to share, these two women, both coming with substantial backgrounds in serving their people and Mother Earth, forged a friendship that had the potential to change the course of both their lives. They spent much of their time brainstorming how they could merge their work to serve the world, even more effectively together than they could individually. Rachelle would call this the second miracle that happened during her arrest.

A third miracle happened for Rachelle the moment of her release, at 11:30 at night on the third day. The Reverend Jesse Jackson just happened to show up at her detention center. This had special meaning for Rachelle. Being 65, she had grown up during the era of JFK, Bobby Kennedy, Martin Luther King, and Cesar Chavez. What Rev. Jackson told the Standing Rock folks that day was that not much has changed since those times. He said, "This is not the democracy we thought we had or were living in. We have to change it. If we don't change it, it is not going to get changed. If we don't speak up, no one is going to hear the injustices."

When I asked Rachelle to give me a metaphor for her work as a Peacemaker, she thought for a minute, then told me when she was in her corporate job in Hawaii, she heard a motivational speaker compare leadership skills to the skills of the rhinoceros. "They are thick-skinned and don't feel a thing when tough situations come at them. You just let them go by. If they run into you, you won't feel a thing. Just keep going, charging ahead. I think there are times when I pull up my rhinoceros-self," she said, "like when I was dealing with that first cop that tried to take my chanupa."

Growing Up As Rachelle

Rachelle was not always a Clan Mother. In fact, she was raised Catholic and had a former career as a national sales director for a large financial services firm in Hawaii. She was born to a mother who was Mexican, a Michoachon Indigenous native from Tarascan, south of Mexico City. She found her father's name on a census role the U.S. government made of Native Americans around World War II, as being from the Arapaho Nation around Wind River, Wyoming.

Rachelle was born in 1951, around the time the U.S. government was relocating many Native American people to three places in California: San Francisco, Riverside, and Los Angeles. Somehow in this shuffle, Rachelle ended up being put up for adoption in Los Angeles.

At age two, she was adopted and raised by a kind mother who was Czechoslovakian, and a generous father who was from Panama. Both her parents, who met when they were going to high school in Los Angeles, were very much involved in doing service in their community and were known for being generous hosts, helping many immigrant families. They taught Rachelle the values of service to community, and that everyone is welcome to the table.

When she was in college, Rachelle began the search for her birth parents, which proved quite difficult due to the minimal amount of information available. Mostly, she told me, she found them through Native ceremonies that she would learn later in her life. I asked if she had ever met her birth parents. Her answer was, "No, I never met my parents, but their parents, my grandparents have been with me since I was a little girl. Or maybe it was my great-grandparents. I just knew they were my ancestors. They came to me all the time."

As a youth, Rachelle had many questions about spiritual matters. The answers she got, especially from the Catholic church, fell short. In her mid-teens, she started reading Eastern philosophies, which gave her more satisfactory answers to her questions.

Rachelle was incredibly athletic. She played volleyball, softball, surfed and skied and could pretty much do anything she put her mind to. She was self-reliant and independent and loved to learn new things, from how to sew, how to do body work on her own car, and how to repair things around the house. She had a strong competitive streak, whether it was playing board games or catching the largest fish, even though she had a knack for making up the rules as she went along! She was incredibly stubborn and had her own way of doing things, but always with love. She was open-hearted and warm with a mischievous sense of humor and a well-developed sense for fun and adventure. She was an incredibly caring friend to all, human, plants, and animals alike.

When she was twenty, she and a boyfriend moved to Hawaii because they were avid surfers. This was in the 1970s when there was only one stoplight on the entire island of Kauai. On the north side of the island, she joined a community that was studying Hinduism and growing their own food. There she learned to meditate, chant, sing, and study the sutras. Because Hawaii was such a melting pot, she befriended Buddhists, Taoists, and others from many religions.

She described one of the people she met as "a wonderful Hawaiian man who was raised by his two fully-Hawaiian grandmothers." As Rachelle began to research her lineage in earnest, she sought out a shaman who told her she should start practicing things like holding sweat lodges, something she had never heard of. After locating some women who educated her about sweat lodges, she asked her Hawaiian friend to be her Fire Keeper and help her build a sweat lodge. He did his Ho'o-ponono practices (a Hawaiian forgiveness ceremony) and she did her Native American traditional practices. Together, they helped many children and families. Rachelle told me, "This was my first glimpse of the power of the Indigenous relationship with Mother Earth and all that is sacred."

As she continued to live in Hawaii, her life also took a more conventional path. She gave birth to and raised her two daughters, and she became a corporate national sales director in a financial firm, where she supervised five regional vice presidents.

Clan Mother Rachelle and the Grandmothers

In 2000, Rachelle returned to Los Angeles to care for her mother who had fallen and broken her hip. In doing so, she realized she had been gone for thirty years and that both her parents were aging and going to need her help. During the next six years while she was caring for her aging parents, she began meeting with Native people in Los Angeles and becoming more involved in their community activities and gatherings.

After many years of traditional Native ceremonies, and organizing and supporting Indigenous communities all over the world, Rachelle was given the name Oyate Wi Ca Yu Wita Winyan, which means She Who Gathers The People On This Turtle Island. (Turtle Island is the Native phrase for North America.) She was also a Traditional Practitioner, a Sundancer, and a Sweat Lodge facilitator of the Lakota Tradition, and she was honored and invested with the responsibility of carrying a chanupa—a sacred peace pipe. Through her work in the community, she become very close with and eventually spiritually adopted the young Chief of the Choctaw-Muskogee-Yamassee Nation, and he in turn, honored her with the role of Grand Matriarch for their tribe. In addition, she was given the honor and responsibility of caretaking the Sacred Staff of Peace and Unity of the Maya Council of El Salvador. She travelled all over Turtle Island and all the way to Sri Lanka to spread its important message.

She told me that Los Angeles had the largest urban population of Native American youth in the United States. The Native children raised in this environment are often missing the vital link of learning their Native culture from their family and ceremonies. Most poignant, Rachelle feels, they get disconnected from their grandmothers.

> *There's something about traditional grandmothers that I can't really put into words; it's just a feeling of home, and trust, great trust and respect. And most of the nations on Turtle Island, that's part of what they always had ... Elders they could go to. The parents, they have their role; but the grandparents, they have a different role. Often the aunts and uncles do the discipline. The grandparents bring in all the love.*

Later in the interview, when I asked Rachelle what advice she would give a young Peacemaker, she told me, "Tell them to go find an Elder."

As she worked with the Native American population, Rachelle realized the need to help these urban Natives who had spent decades in the cities, isolated from their places of birth and their traditional ways of interacting with each other and with Mother Earth. They needed to reconnect with their heritage, their traditions, their ceremonies, and to do this they needed to connect with each other in the old ways.

Rachelle founded the Morning Star Foundation along with her friend Leon Siff, from Friends of the Universe. She had seen a vision of this foundation in her mind's eye during a Sundance ceremony on Black Mesa in Arizona. The mission of this nonprofit organization is multi-faceted: to support the needs of Native/Indigenous traditional Elders, women and youth; to educate and create public awareness for the protection and preservation of Native/Indigenous Nations; to protect the Sacred Traditions, Ceremony, Songs/Language, Sacred Sites, Burial Grounds, and Environment. No small mission. Where to begin?

Rachelle decided to begin by working with the grandmothers.

> *It seemed there was a great need, especially for women, to reconnect with the Grandmothers. Inherently, there is something in being around the Grandmothers that brings back some memory from their childhood. It was someplace they could come and really feel reconnected with the sacred ceremonies again that a lot of them had left behind, left at home on the reservations.*

Predictions of the Mayan Calendar

"There are natural and spiritual laws that were given to us eons ago," she explained. One example is the Mayan calendar, which actually is a medicine wheel. Because Rachelle is a Carrier of the Sacred Staff of Peace and Unity from the Maya Council of El Salvador, she has intimate knowledge of this calendar. It explains that the natural evolution of life is unfolding in a series of successive medicine wheels. The year 2012 marked the beginning of a new medicine wheel. Not only is this revealed in the Mayan prophecies, but in many different Indigenous cultures, like the Hopi Tribe, the Iroquois Confederacy, and the Six Nations in Canada.

> *The Mayan call it the time of the Glistening Trees, the change from the fifth to the sixth world. Looking at the last five hundred years of what has happened to Turtle Island, there's been*

such a patriarchal control of the planet. Because of so many wars and so much disharmony and non-peace, it has come to a point to where the prophecies say that this is the time now that the leadership is of a female face. The male dominant time is over with now.

Mother Earth is not just a synonym or a metaphor. The Earth is a female spirit. And the women are the ones that are most connected because we are life-givers. We have now come to this point where unless the women stand up together, unless the women understand the power that they hold within them to make this shift, this new shift that is happening now, then there is a good chance that the planet will fall apart.

I told Rachelle I felt something like that happening at Standing Rock. When it came to who would be on the front line of the direct actions, there were just as many or more women as men who were taking the non-violence training and joining the front line. She told me the women were doing both kinds of jobs.

There are just as many women not on the front line in the camps taking care of the kids, taking care of the Elders, cooking, bringing that energy of love and food so those warriors are strong when they get out there.

Right now many of our prayers are for the men because the men are having a really hard time. They don't understand what is going on energetically. The shift has already happened. We have already moved out of the masculine. But consciously, nobody knows what is going on. On a spiritual level, and energetic level, it is already taking place. But the men are having a hard time. I talk to men all day long. I see them struggling so much because they don't understand where they are supposed to be now. They understand in their mind what they have been told a warrior is. But then they ask why are the women so much stronger than us?

After the Water Protectors returned from their three-day incarceration ordeal, Rachelle decided to do a sweat lodge for the women who had just gotten out of jail. She asked one of the Elder men if there was any message he wanted to give them.

He just closed his eyes and said,

> *You know, over the past five hundred years the invaders have come, they have constantly been pulling us apart, our nations, putting us here and putting us there, separating us. They did-n't want us to be together. They wanted to separate us purposefully. And they put us on the reservations and they tried to destroy us in the boarding schools … but here at Standing Rock, we have made history because we have all come back together again, all the nations have come back again to stand up for the Sacred Water and Mother Earth. But we have new warriors. Tell the women they are the new warriors.*

When the women in the sweat lodge heard his message, they cried. They were just beginning to understand how powerful they were. And it wasn't just about being a warrior on the front lines. Rachelle reminded them:

> *The other part is about holding that loving space with compassion and forgiveness and gentleness and nurturing. As life givers, that's the life we've been given. And we were not taught that growing up. That's why Morning Star is helping them learn this. We are at a crossroads now. Because not only Native people, but all women, especially in the Western cultures have had this idea that they had to act like the men in order to become successful and go up that ladder. So instead of the natural flow of women being in cooperation, women have been in competitiveness.*

Rachelle also shared with me a quote from Chief Phil Lane Jr. of the Ihanktonwan-Dakota Nation. "In order for the Eagle of Humanity to soar to its highest potential it must use **both** wings: one is Woman and one is Man."

Do Not Let the President Get in the Way of Doing Your Service

I reminded Rachelle that four days prior to our interview, a very "male

male," Donald Trump, had become the president-elect of the United States, even though the popular vote had been won by Hillary Clinton, who had made her way up through the competitive ranks of different positions in the U.S. government. I asked Rachelle if she had any advice for us. Her answer was refreshing and full of common sense.

> *Do what the Elders say. Prepare. Don't be blind. Do what you need to do to prepare for all these changes. My service is to bring the Elders together, to bring all the youth together, to teach them and hold that space in prayer. I don't care if this president is a Martian. I just do what I can do. Just think if everybody did what they knew was right, if everybody stood up and spoke for the voiceless, spoke for Mother Earth, spoke for the water, spoke for the animal relations, if all the Indigenous, all the people that are conscious, would stand up and just do what they know is right, no one can stop that.*

"Standing side by side with men of good heart and clear mind"

At this moment in the interview, I found myself looking inward. I thought, "I am willing to stand up as tall as I can to be part of correcting the compass of our world. And I am also getting clearer and clearer that I don't want to be alone in doing so. The responsibility of leading our world out of its current dilemma is incredibly daunting; we need both wings of that bird working together."

Just when I was convinced by listening to Rachelle that everything in the future was up to women alone, Rachelle showed me a speech she had given at the International Day of Peace. The title was "The Native Circle of Peace." The sentences that stood out strongly for me read:

> *It is time for the Women Nation to come together in Unity and accept the leadership role with Love and Compassion.* **Standing side by side with Men of good heart and clear mind,** *we can balance out the negative forces of hatred, greed, war, and planetary destruction.*

We need each other. We need partners, collaborators, whether it is a good man as the prophecies suggest, or two women as Rachelle and Danielle might have found in each other. Or a whole slew of men and

40

women on the front line at Standing Rock who were willing to brave concussion bombs and tear gas to look into the eyes of the law enforcement officers hiding behind their riot helmets. What Rachelle gives us is the selection criteria for knowing such a partner when we come upon them. She told me to "look for the *person* with a good heart and clear mind." With these words, I found myself able to fully breathe for the first time in taking in her message.

We Are the Ones the Prophecies Identified

Clan Mother Rachelle had answered my interview questions with her personal opinions, which is what I had requested. Yet her answers came from someplace deeper, further back in time. She was sharing wisdom from eons of Indigenous teachings. In our interview, she often referred to the Natural Laws that had been given by Great Spirit. I felt as if I was having an interview with the ancestors of all mankind, and perhaps something even beyond that.

Before our interview closed, Rachelle had one more message to give me, one hard to ignore:

> *We should all acknowledge that each one of us was put on this planet, at this important time in history, for a reason. It is our duty and responsibility to speak up for the voiceless. To pray humbly for strength and courage to speak up against injustice, greed and the destruction of our Sacred Water, Air, and Earth Mother. Let us join together in the Sacred Hoop of Life, the Sacred Circle of Peace, and live in goodness for the benefit of our present and future Relations.*

> *These prophecies are always talking about what will happen in the future, but they are actually talking about us. This **is** the future they were referring to. And what they have prophesized, we are now living. We are it. So now whoever is on the planet at this time will determine what is to happen to our planet. We can't wait. It is us and it is now.*

Epilogue

Two weeks after I left Standing Rock, over two thousand U.S. military veterans, Natives and non-Natives, arrived there to "protect the protectors." They helped build winter dwellings, chopped wood, and they created a nonviolent human shield around the Water Protectors during direct actions with the law enforcement.

They also apologized. In a historic gathering of Natives and non-Native civilians and military veterans, Wesley Clark Jr., a soldier in the U.S. Cavalry and son of the four-star general and Vietnam veteran, addressed the Native elders. Dressed in his cavalry uniform, reminiscent of the uniforms of General Custer's army, Clark spoke the following message:

> *Many of us, me particularly, are from the units that have hurt you over the many years. We came. We fought you. We took your land. We signed treaties that we broke. We stole minerals from your sacred hills. We blasted the faces of our presidents onto your sacred mountain. Then we took still more land and then we took your children and then we tried to take your language and we tried to eliminate your language that God gave you, and the Creator gave you. We didn't respect you, we polluted your Earth, we've hurt you in so many ways but we've come to say that we are sorry. We are at your service and we beg for your forgiveness.*

Three Native men and women, Chief Leonard Crow Dog, Faith Spotted Eagle, and Ivan Looking Horse, accepted the apology with dignity. They offered forgiveness, and spoke a plea for world peace. They also reminded us that "We do not own the land; the land owns us."

Presidential Turn Abouts

On December 4, 2016, in his last days of his presidency, President Obama ordered the Army Corps of Engineers to halt the progress of the DAPL pipeline until a thorough Environmental Impact Statement had been completed. Less than two months later in 2017, the new President, Donald

Trump, reversed this order and authorized the completion of the DAPL pipeline by Energy Transfer Partners, in which he had personally invested a substantial amount of money.

Recalibration

A brutal and long winter storm began settling into the Standing Rock area. Although many were willing and prepared to brave the dangers of the coming winter months, a decision was made to dismantle the camp for many reasons, not the least of which was the desire for no human life to be lost to the elements. For many whom Standing Rock had provided a place to find purpose in their life, to forge lasting friendships, perhaps even to let go of addictions to alcohol, busyness, or anger, leaving Standing Rock was a difficult and a sad transition.

However, the energy behind the movement was not lost. Many of the Natives and non-Natives simply dispersed into other arenas throughout the United States to help correct the imbalance of domination and subordination, to protect the water, and protect Mother Earth.

DAPL

Oil first flowed through the DAPL pipeline in June of 2017. In January 2018, an article in *The Intercept* stated:

> *The Dakota Access Pipeline leaked at least five times in 2017. The biggest was a 168-gallon leak near DAPL's endpoint in Patoka, Illinois, on April 23. According to federal regulators, no wildlife was impacted, although soil was contaminated, requiring remediation. DAPL went into operation on June 1, along with its under-the-radar sister project, the Energy Transfer Crude Oil pipeline [ETCO], a natural gas pipeline converted to carry crude oil. Together, the two make up the Bakken pipeline system, transporting crude oil from North Dakota to the Gulf of Mexico. ETCO leaked at least three times in 2017. The most significant of these spills was a 4,998-gallon leak on the ETCO pipeline in Dyersburg, Tennessee, on June 19 ... The series of spills in the pipelines' first months of operation underlines a fact that regulators and industry insiders know well: Pipelines leak.*

Rachelle

In December of 2016, Rachelle left Standing Rock as the camps were shutting down, and returned to Los Angeles to visit with her family for the holidays. Shortly thereafter, she fell ill and was unable to recover. In early February, she was diagnosed with stage IV colon cancer and underwent emergency surgery. Although her surgery was a success, her cancer had already advanced to such a severe state that her doctor prescribed intense chemotherapy treatments in an effort to prolong her life. But Rachelle refused this treatment. She felt strongly that she wanted to live what remained of her life in the best way possible and did not want to subject her already weakened body to what she considered to be poison. Instead, she used traditional and holistic medicines to improve her condition and lived out the remainder of her days at home, in a loving environment, surrounded by friends, family, prayer, and sacred songs.

On July 25, 2017, her daughters sang to her as she crossed over, to return to her Creator and reunite with her ancestors.

CHAPTER THREE

No More Generational Violence

Judith Jenya

• FORMER YUGOSLAVIA •

Peace Work:
Providing safe places for war-torn children

Metaphor:
I am a Chinese dragon that is idealistic
and charismatic and who champions causes,
takes risks, and courts peril.

When the next generation asks us,
why didn't you do something,
why didn't you speak up,
what will you say?

—Jeff Flake

Volunteering at a Summer Camp for War-Torn Children

The Bosnian War nearly did me in … twice; once when I couldn't do anything about it, and once when I did do something about it.

As an American in 1996, I knew very little about the war that was brewing and then erupting in the former Yugoslavia. I later learned one reason for my ignorance was due to a concerted political effort by the U.S. government to keep much of the news about that conflagration out of the American media. I didn't even know that I didn't know. As information began to leak into our news, I went from feeling ignorant, to frustrated, to deeply disturbed. I simply felt that I had to DO something about the horrific war going on in the Balkans. I was on my way to "helpless" when I found a letter in my mailbox from a friend who knew my feelings.

Inside the envelope was a request for donations to an organization called Global Children's Organization. A note was attached from my friend Marcia:

"Check this out. It might help."

It described an organization that provided a two-week summer camp for children that had been caught in the Bosnian war. I found myself calling the number on the brochure. A woman named Judith Jenya answered the phone. I told her that I couldn't make a donation, but I wondered if she took volunteers.

"Yes!" she said energetically. "That's what this is all about. Doing something about this situation!"

I'm not sure what I meant when I suggested volunteering, but I had vague thoughts of helping out in the kitchen of a kids' camp in California. Judith, however, was very clear about what it meant to volunteer in her camp. I would be a counselor in a camp in the former Yugoslavia, along with other American volunteers. There would be Bosnian teenagers to help out as interpreters and mentors for the children. I would pay $480 for my own food and lodging at the camp, and another $480 for a camper to attend. I would pay for my own air passage to and from the camp, which, by the way, was in Croatia, not California. Additionally, the American volunteers were responsible for providing everything that happened at the camp, including music for singing, swimming suits for swimming, art materials for art activities, basketballs, soccer balls, toys, soap, costumes, dance music, you name it. It would clearly have been easier and cheaper to write her a check for $100, but something inside me, perhaps the lurking fear of once again feeling helpless, simply signed me up to be a volunteer.

As I boarded the plane a few weeks later, I wondered if I was crazy, or just plain irresponsible. I had farmed my own children out to members of my family, gone into my savings to pay for this venture, and was now paying the overweight fee for the two 60-pound duffel bags I was checking. I asked myself who this woman, Judith Jenya, was and why I felt so compelled to join her in this endeavor?

Growing up Judith

Judith is the daughter of refugee parents. Her mother was separated from her family after the 1917–1918 Russian Revolution. Her father, a Zionist, was a political prisoner for seven years. He emigrated from Germany, first to Palestine and then to Southern California, where he worked his way up from being a migrant worker to getting a degree in agricultural engineering from the University of California at Berkeley. Her mother and father met there. Judith grew up in several small blue-collar, working class towns, mainly in southern California. Judith's mother role modeled a cross-cultural mentality for her family by being the first person to establish a bilingual system in the Los Angeles school libraries.

As she moved from place to place, Judith kept realizing "there were no other people like us." Her family lived for five years in the first federal housing project in California, near the shipyards in San Pedro where her father worked at the time. Many of the other residents were people from the Dust Bowl in Oklahoma, who had been displaced during the Depression. They were all white, largely fundamentalist Christian and anti-Semitic. During this period, Judith's family celebrated Christmas and Easter but no Jewish holidays.

Always an Outsider

Judith experienced first-hand what it was to be an outsider because her family members were always the only Jews and her parents were the only foreigners wherever they went. She described it as such:

I was always an outsider. But the thing about it was that they were very anti-Semitic there and at that time we weren't practicing Jews. I didn't even know we were Jewish because my mother was raised as a Russianized person and my father had become a Zionist where they didn't believe in religion. So there wasn't anything that was Jewish about what we did. We celebrated Christmas. I did not even know we were Jewish, but everybody else knew. So they painted swastikas on our house and stuff like that. But I didn't know really what was going on, only that we were different.

And when I was in elementary school in Altadena, California, they had this thing called Religious Release Time. People could go out during the week to their church. Everybody would leave and I would be there in my class because I didn't have any place to go. I wanted desperately to be Mormon or Catholic or something. I really wanted something because I didn't like not having anything. And then when my father decided we were Jewish, it was a very watered-down Jewish and it didn't come from the soul and it didn't have anything to do with anything. So there was always a sense of estrangement.

To complicate things even more, Judith, unlike her sister, was born with dark skin and dark hair. Growing up in Southern California, she was always taken for being Mexican. Her first grade teacher even said, "Get out of this class, you dirty little Mexican." As such, she experienced what prejudice on the basis of skin color felt like.

Judith's family also sponsored other immigrants, some of whom lived in their home long enough to feel like siblings to her. The ethos in her family was the Jewish principle of "tikkun olam: you share and you take care and you help people." Her parents were also Socialists who disapproved of any accumulation of wealth or material goods. Combining these two philosophies, she learned that "money was bad, but sharing was good." Judith has had a hard time with money all her life because money was something one wasn't supposed to have. She, like so many of the other Peacemakers I interviewed, is not wealthy. And like the other Peacemakers, rather than this fact hindering her peace work, she simply finds a way to creatively "source" the funds needed for each of her camps.

The Path of Peacemaking

When I asked Judith what led her down the path of peacemaking as opposed to some other path, she told me it was the time she contracted a life-threatening disease that didn't take her life but left her with powerful insights into what to do with the life that was saved. As a twenty-four-year-old, Judith had a life-altering experience. She contracted encephalitis, which catapulted her into a coma where she had to fight for her life for days on end. She was one of several victims of a small encephalitis epidemic in San Francisco. Although she was the only victim to recover, she was left with a legacy of reduced coordination and memory difficulties. And it shifted her perspective on life:

> As a result, I first became aware of the fragility of life and the unpredictability of everything. I was aware of the necessity of taking action NOW… that things cannot be put off for a better, more convenient time, since it may not arrive. Secondly, I gained great empathy for people whose lives have been adversely affected by an outside force and have lost physical capabilities such as I lost. I felt when I recovered that I had a purpose to have survived, so it became an obligation for me to do something of purpose with my life. I became very tolerant of ambiguity and impermanence and not very concerned about risks. That led me to peacemaking, which is my purpose. It involves great uncertainty of outcome and the willingness to take risks. The fragility of life I now know means that the ephemeral is more important than the concrete and that my peacemaking work was real.

Because Judith was willing to call herself a Peacemaker early in her career, one cannot tell if her definition of peace is born out of her work, or perhaps vice versa. She sees peace as an evolving process rather than a specific outcome to be achieved. Regarding her view of what peace is, as well as what it is not, she told me the following:

> Peace is acceptance of others and it is also the absence of hatred and fighting and intolerance. Peace is an energy and a spirit of and a willingness to admit that there is diversity, and then to cooperate. It is also a quest. It is not a thing. It is a

process, as opposed to a thing you achieve. It's a spiral that goes up and down. Peace is something that you seek to attain, an ideal that you work toward.

The constant theme underpinning Judith's peacemaking work is to curb the cycle of hatred that travels from one generation to another as a result of oppression. She had honed her thoughts on this from both her personal experiences and what she had seen in her worldly travels:

The concept of hatred growing in the hearts and minds of yet another generation of children is abhorrent to me. I think one of my motivating desires is to do something to break the cycle of hatred, so that children have something other than the stereotypes and animosities and legends that make each generation hate the next. And one way to do that, in my view, is to interrupt it with goodness, the power of goodness.

These kids, whether they're from Northern Ireland or Bosnia, or the Middle East or wherever, have suffered from violence themselves. And they have been trained and taught to hate other people, because they are "other" people, and to only trust their own kind of group. The definition of who is in your group is narrowed down; it's got to be someone similar or identical in some way—color, ethnicity, religion, family name, something. And then that makes everybody else 'the other' and you don't have to treat "the other" as human. You don't have to treat them with respect. You can just kill them. You can do whatever you want because they are not 'us' and they're not people.

But through giving opportunities to volunteers, Judith took the concept of "other" and made it positive. We American volunteers were clearly "others" in the camp. We came from different religions, cultures, ethnicities. We had no axe to grind, nothing to gain. We weren't righting any wrongs from our personal pasts, nor were we settling a score. The Bosnian War had much to do with settling scores of incidents that had smoldered in Yugoslavia from both the World Wars. It challenged the children's thinking to believe that we were volunteering simply because we cared what had happened to them. They kept asking Judith, "Why are you here? Why do you care? Are you doing this for God … Mary … Allah?"

Judith feels this thinking is entrenched in whole societies. She tells the story of going to Northern Ireland where she was asked if she was Protestant or Catholic. When she replied that she was Jewish, she was asked if she was Jewish-Protestant or Jewish-Catholic. In their minds, there were only two options for her religious affiliation.

The Role of Forgiveness in Peacemaking

When I asked Judith if she felt forgiveness played a role in peacemaking, she told me this was a complicated question for her. After some thought, she answered:

> *By forgiveness I mean that act of letting go of the energy that ties you up and leaves you unable to move ahead because some of you is still in the past with the unforgiven. I do not mean the act of condoning or forgetting. I think forgiveness is about getting free of hatred and anger inside yourself. It can mean also reaching an awareness of the humanness of the other, but some things are so horrible they cannot be forgiven. They can be 'defanged' so that a person can move into peacemaking. But peacemaking does not require forgiving the other party, just letting go of the hurt and anger inside oneself.*

Rainbows, not Black and White Boxes

This concept of only two boxes, of black and white, violates everything in Judith's nature. She believes it is simply a matter of different categories, a rainbow of colors, in fact shades of these colors. Her whole being manifests this preference. Her apartment is covered with her vividly colored paintings. Judith says she cannot paint in black and white, doesn't photograph in black and white, and literally can't see that way. Even her closet is carefully arranged by hues. One of her favorite places to spend time is in Hawaii, with its symbol of the rainbow. Judith divides her time between the land of the boxes and the land of the rainbows.

The Birth of the Summer Camps

When the brutal news of the Bosnian War began to leak into the American press, Judith also found herself unable to stand by and do nothing.

As a divorcee with grown children out of the nest, she was free to travel so she could see for herself what was only being alluded to in the news.

One day, while visiting a Croatian orphanage, the administrator got in her face and hissed, "I hate all you humanitarian aid-types. You come here and take photos and feel sad and no one does anything." Unruffled, Judith asked him what it was he thought the children needed most. He said they needed a safe place to play and to get away from the war. Judith thought, "Well, that's doable. How hard can that be?"

This was the birth of the summer camps for war-torn children that Judith and her volunteers were to put on for several years to come. Even as both the bullets and the snow were flying, Judith would spend part of her winter months in the former Yugoslavia finding a place that was close enough for the children to attend but safe enough to be out of harm's way. For the location of our camp, she picked an island off the Dalmatian Coast of Croatia, where the war had left somewhat fewer scars and visual reminders of the war.

Gathering the Children

Finding the children and getting permission for them to travel to the camps were no easy tasks. Food, lodging, and transportation had to be negotiated at black-market prices. Once a united country, the former Yugoslavia was now split into several countries, each with different currencies, each requiring different visas at the border crossings. Sometimes at the borders, people would be called off the bus and never get back on. Visas called for birth certificates, but birth certificates weren't always available for a family who had fled for their lives in the middle of the night. Parental permission was needed, but often one or both of the parents were missing, killed, or on the Front Line. Now Judith was offering parents a difficult decision: to allow their only remaining child or children to leave their side and travel for hours by bus to an unknown place with an unknown American woman for a chance at what they wanted most for their child … a temporary safe respite from one of the most brutal and ugly wars of the century.

The year I was a volunteer, Judith's efforts resulted in 80 children being transported by bus and and then boat to our camp. Around half of them were from Sarajevo and other urban centers, while the other half came from Srebrenica, a more rural part of Bosnia. Only months prior, these children from Srebrenica had watched as Serb soldiers invaded their village and either outright killed their fathers and any brothers over the age of ten, or marched them away with their hands tied behind their backs, never to be seen again. Some watched as Serb soldiers raped their mothers and sisters. All of them fled with their mothers and remaining family members sixty miles away to Tuzla, a city that had doubled its population with the influx of displaced survivors.

Gathering the Volunteers

Judith persisted because this agenda of providing an opportunity of safe play for these war-torn children meshed perfectly with another agenda that had always been close to her heart: providing opportunities for volunteerism.

> *One of my missions is to create opportunities for service and volunteerism, the experience of giving and sharing which is, in my belief, the most enriching experience there is: to create these opportunities and let people experience genuine people-to-people connection, giving and sharing with another person and to realize that they, of course, get more than they give.*

Besides gathering the American volunteers, Judith also offered volunteer opportunities to a second group: a handful of Bosnian adults who had, themselves, barely survived the war. They had horrendous stories that over time, as trust was built, they shared with us. Many had spent four years with their entire family sleeping, cooking, and living in the hallways of their Sarajevo apartments. The other rooms with windows were too visible in the scope of sniper rifles. Most were left penniless by the war, even though their four-year-old clothing hinted of times more grand. One doctor was the only pediatrician left at her hospital in Sarajevo, a city where thousands of children were wounded and died for lack of medical supplies. A man's sister had been shot through the heart in front of her children by Serb soldiers who were displeased with the way she registered herself when they entered her village. A young woman was getting divorced, a rare thing for a Muslim, because upon return from his military service her husband had turned to alcohol and domestic violence. Another young woman's boyfriend had spent ten months in a Serb concentration camp, and had witnessed horrors of which he would not, could not speak.

The third and most remarkable group of volunteers were Bosnian teenagers who had aged before their time during the four years of the war. They were bilingual, creative and generous, and endlessly energetic as interpreters. Some were beleaguered by the depression of post-traumatic stress disorder. All were mature beyond their age as they tenderly made themselves available to the younger children.

Judith had chosen well. These teens were from the cities of Sarejevo and Mostar. They had known prosperous times: times when they listened to Michael Jackson CDs, when Adidas and Guess jeans were important, and when their families had gone to their second homes in nearby ski villages for vacations.

But the last four years for them had been spent hiding in cellars, going to funerals of their friends who were killed on soccer fields, and wondering when their time to die might come. Schools were shut down. Computers and bicycles were destroyed. Pets died from lack of food. Families first burned every tree in their yard, and then every stick of furniture in their homes to keep warm during the freezing winters after the snipers shot out the windows of their homes. Parents left their teens in charge while they risked their lives, darting from cover to cover several times a week when the water rations were made available. Things like flirting and falling in love had become irrelevant in settings like the army, concentration camps, and rape crisis centers. Kids lost weight for lack of food. Parents' teeth turned brown as they gave anything with calcium in it to their children. Most communication was cut off, including mail, television, radio, and newspapers, and what news remained was cruelly distorted to justify the ethnic cleansing. These teens thought no one in the world knew what was happening to them, because if anyone knew, surely this war wouldn't have gone on for four years. They begged us to tell their story to the world when we returned home from the camp.

In all its horror, the war had quelled neither the spirit nor the gentleness of these teenage volunteers. It had destroyed their physical world, but, miraculously, not their spirits. I never heard one word of retaliation from their mouths. One beloved young man who worked with me said he felt that the best Peacemakers would be women, because women carry the children in their wombs and therefore know peacemaking from their hearts, not their heads. He hoped to do humanitarian work for children when he grows up.

Camp Guidelines and Conversions

Judith had done her homework. She researched the causes of the war, how to deal with the children's fears, and what to do and not do to create this period of safety for everyone. And she passed all this information on to the volunteers. Above all, she told us we must never make a promise that we could not keep to the children, for the byword of this war had been "betrayal." She warned that everyone would want to take a teenager home with them to the United States, but it was precisely these youth that would build back this country after the war. I needed that advice. Without it I might well have taken a set of twins home with me on my flight back to the United States.

We divided into groups of ten children, with two adults and two interpreters. In our group we played trust games, told stories, held talking circles, did art projects, sang songs, took turns telling what we would do if we had a million kuna (Croat dollars), and went on short excursions. One day we came across an empty wine bottle. We each wrote out our wish for the world and threw it out to sea.

These children were good at fine motor skills, like playing with Match Box Cars, things one can do while hiding in a cellar, but many of them were just learning gross motor games such as basketball and soccer. The favorite activity was swimming in the ocean, which we did twice daily. Many of the children had never seen the ocean. They worked hard at learning how to swim, sometimes practicing their strokes in bed at night before the lights were turned out. Although we provided all the children with a swimming suit, many chose to swim in their underwear because the swimming suit was the best piece of clothing they now owned. Judith made her way from one group to another, robed in her beautiful colors, sometimes putting out fires, sometimes just smiling at what was unfolding.

After dinner there was always a ripsnorting disco dance outside under the stars, each night having a different theme. The dress-up preparations became more elaborate with each theme. At first the children's bodies were stiff, as habitual fear told them it could be unsafe to partake of such outdoor activities, but within a few nights, they limbered up. Breakdancing skills emerged. Serbs and Bosnians, deadly enemies on the battlefield, were joyful partners on the dance floor. Americans and young campers did the Twist with each other. Teenagers were flirting with each other in spite of their different ethnic origins and religions. Nearby villagers couldn't help but join in. Judith was often the first one on and the last one off of the dance floor.

Bedtime took a long time. We went from room to room helping kids wind down. The nighttime was when the war would revisit some of them. Some children could only sleep completely engulfed in blankets, even though the nights were hot and humid. One wet his bed. Another twirled her hair until it came out.

I Miss Their Feet

I was assigned bedtime duty for a roomful of ten-year-old boys, many of whom had become the "head of the family," when all other males in their families were killed, often in front of their eyes. Each night I made a ritual of rubbing their feet. I don't know why I started doing this, but it gave me a way to make safe physical contact with them. At first they thought I was crazy. So did I. Their feet were filthy and stiff as boards. By the end of camp, however, they would hurry to wash their feet and have them sticking out of the covers when I came in to say good night. Sometimes we would swap phrases. I would say "laku noc" and they would return "good night." Sometimes when I sang softly, their minds would float a million miles away, and their feet became softer and softer. I miss their feet.

In the safety of the trust that we provided, and in the healing waters of the Adriatic, the children changed. Skin sores healed. Beds were wet less frequently. Nightmares diminished. The hair-pulling ceased temporarily. Rigid bodies turned into lithe disco dancers and breakdancers. Individual talents began to re-emerge. Older children assigned during the war as protectors to young children began to have some time off. Children who had spent years prohibited from playing outdoor sports became skilled ball players. Teenagers fell in love with each other, regardless of origins. Some kids even indulged in the brief luxury of getting mad at each other.

Visions of War's Toll

At the end of the camp, the campers begged the Americans to come back to their homes and refugee centers so we could see for ourselves and tell the stories of how war devastates. As the travel homeward unfolded, we Americans watched the children put back on their defense mechanisms. And rightly so, for when the bus rolled into Sarajevo I could not imagine how anyone lived through the incessant dangers and senseless destruction of this beautiful Olympic city. And after visiting the temporary housing where some of the displaced families resided in Tuzla, a city bulging with refugees, I understood what it meant for a nine-year-old boy, who won all the breakdance contests last week, to now have utterly nothing to do all day long.

The Sarajevo teens invited us into their homes so we could see from the inside what conditions their families had endured for the past four years. To their credit, it was important to them to make sure we saw what had happened to their national library. The regal building had been devastated by grenades lobbed by the Serbian soldiers from the hills surrounding the city, leaving it in tatters of hanging concrete shards. But even more devastating, once the structure was compromised, incendiary grenades had been launched to burn every book and document that once recorded the many centuries of Balkan history.

Returning Home Changed

I returned home to Colorado, having given away everything I had brought in those duffel bags, including the duffels themselves. During the plane ride home, I slowly realized that Judith had given me an opportunity to combat helplessness by doing something of service. Among other things, she gave me the closest opportunity I ever hope to have to really see what war does to places, to people, to hopes without jeopardizing my own safety.

It took a week before I felt like going outside or beginning to work again. I missed the bond and camaraderie I had built with my fellow volunteers. Mostly I just wanted to be with my children. This experience affected me on so many levels. It could have been my undoing. Instead of breaking my heart, it broke my heart open. It became the beginning of being conscious of my potential, my responsibility to be a Peacemaker.

And Judith? She was already working on next year's camps, not only in the Balkans, but in Northern Ireland.

Advice to a Young Peacemaker

When I asked Judith what advice she would give to a burgeoning Peacemaker, her answer was extensive:

> *To be a Peacemaker requires a sense of mission, purpose, and commitment to the principle and the goal. It requires a belief that is not always based on what seems possible at the moment but which one knows is possible through focused effort and adherence to the purpose. More than anything it requires*

a belief in the value of each life and the value of making a small difference that can be multiplied. The pitfalls occur when your efforts are derailed by events and when hatred seems to have the upper hand.

Have a great vision, but not expectations; learn to not take things personally. Develop great flexibility; study aikido or other techniques of getting to your goal indirectly but surely. Have clarity about your desired outcome but not attachment to the outcomes that happen. Be open and willing to change tactics, schedules, actions, but not stray from your basic values, principles, and goals. Regard each small gain or victory as validation and encouragement, but don't dwell on the losses or discouragements as a statement about the purpose. Be willing to walk a lonely, often solitary road and not be attached to recognition when it does or doesn't come. Treat others with respect and compassion and be willing to meet people where they are. Get angry at injustice, deceit, betrayal, and then move on. Take time for yourself and have recreation and beauty in your life.

Epilogue

More camps were conducted in the ensuing years, some in the Balkans and Kosovo, some in Northern Ireland, and some in Los Angeles. Some were conducted by Judith, and after new endeavors took her in other directions, some of them were conducted by former volunteers that remained dedicated to the value of providing what these camps offered.

Rape Determined to Be a War Crime

During the Bosnian War, somewhere between twenty and fifty thousand women were victims of rape, sometimes in rape camps. In 1996, the International Tribunal for War Crimes in Former Yugoslavia indicted eight Serb men for sexual assault. It was the first time in history that an international tribunal charged someone solely for crimes of sexual violence.

The verdict was based on the testimonies collected by Nusreta Sivac and Jadranka Cigelj. These two women, both victims of Serb rape camps during the Bosnian War, had helped many other women who were war rape victims find the courage to come forth and provide testimonies of what had happened to them during the war.

A *Christian Science Monitor* article dated March 9, 2013 reported that "to date, thirty people have been convicted at the international war crimes tribunal in The Hague and another thirty cases are ongoing."

Latest Findings about the Srebrenica Massacre

July 11, 2015 was the twenty year anniversary of the Srebrenica massacre. At that time, the International Commission on Missing Persons, using DNA human identification methods, verified the finding of approximately seven to eight thousand bodies buried in multiple mass gravesites near Srebrenica. As a result, these crimes against humanity committed at this time constituted the worst massacre in Europe since World War II.

Judith Today

Many years after my interview with Judith, I came across a speech she had given at an International Women's Day Event in Mexico in March 2012. An interviewer asked her if she felt one person could really make a difference in the kinds of wars and conflicts we are experiencing today. Judith gave the following answer:

> *The situation on the ground does not change militarily or politically by my actions. But, for individual children, one person's caring action and love does make a difference. And the recipient person can multiply the effect. One person caring, taking the time, putting themselves at risk when they don't have to, makes a difference.*

Judith moved to San Miguel de Allende, Mexico where she is a full-time artist and writer. She is now finding personal peace in her retirement and her relationship with her new husband.

CHAPTER FOUR

I Was in Prison and You Visited Me

Sister Sarah Clarke

• LONDON, ENGLAND •

Peace Work:
Tending to the needs of Irish
political prisoners and their families

Metaphor:
I often felt like Daniel in the lion's den.

The smallest act of kindness
is worth more than the greatest intention.

—Kahlil Gibran

How I Found Sister Sarah

One snowy evening in rural Colorado, I attended a community concert put on by the Cassidy family of five Irish brothers. After the performance, I went backstage and struck up a conversation with the musicians. I told them of my search for a woman Peacemaker in Ireland.

"We wouldn't know about such things," they said, "but our sister, Fenula, is a disc jockey in Dublin. She has a talk show where she interviews lots of women. She'll have somebody for you. Here's her phone number."

In fact, when I rang up Fenula, she had two "somebodies" for me. One was Sister Sarah Clarke.

When embarking on this project of interviewing women Peacemakers, I had made a decision to include my children in the process as much as time and finances allowed. I have always felt our future rests in the hands of our youth. The stories these women told of their work contained a rich harvest of experience from which my children and I could learn. I wanted to offer them the opportunity to meet these women, to see and hear them speak of their experiences, and to learn how practical and passionate these women were.

As my nine-year-old son and I flew across the Atlantic Ocean, I wondered if I could really accomplish walking out my front door in Carbondale, Colorado and showing up at Sr. Sarah's doorstep on Bartholomew Street in London at the appointed day and time. I wondered many other things, too. Fenula told me that Sr. Sarah's work involved visiting Irish political prisoners in the London jails. I wondered how visiting prisoners constituted peacemaking. How dangerous is that kind of work, I wondered. Probably not very dangerous, I surmised. Oh, how naïve I was. Little did I know how many times Sr. Sarah would use the word "terrified" in describing her work.

Nearly Missed Appointment

I nearly missed the appointment. After my son and I got settled in our lodging, we had three hours to do a bit of sightseeing before our interview with Sr. Sarah. About halfway through our tour of London's highlights on a double-decker bus, the jet lag caught up with my son and he fell soundly asleep on my lap. I had to carry him over my shoulder like a sack of flour back to our lodging. I was sure that he would wake up in time to take the Tube to our interview, but I was wrong. No attempts to wake him succeeded. I hired the lodging owner, who said she would check on him regularly and entertain him until I returned. Giving her Sr. Sarah's number if she should need me, I hailed a cab and reached Sr. Sarah's door with two minutes to spare.

Irish Tea

She met me at the door, dressed in a traditional black and white habit, and warmly invited me into her flat. It was neat, clean, and flooded with light. There were large paintings on every wall, some bright and colorful, and others somber black and white, often of the crucifix. She had prepared tea for us. She had made triangular sandwiches with trimmed crusts, a wonderful cucumber sauce, sweet biscuits and since it was near Easter, she had a chocolate bunny that I took back to my sleeping son. She served the best cup of tea I have ever tasted, with ample sugar and milk to be had. Sr. Sarah pointedly told me this was Irish, not English, tea. All of this detail was made even more special by the fact that Sr. Sarah had lost her eyesight in recent years and was now, by her own description, "stone blind." Moreover, in the not-too-distant past, she had been in an auto accident serious enough for a priest to administer the last rites to her.

When I asked for her definition of peace, she answered:

> *Well, I find it hard to give a definition of peace. Peace is at the graveyard, and you can have peace at the church pew. But if you haven't justice, if you haven't truth, you're not going to have peace. I dedicated my life to justice and truth, and let's hope peace will come of it. I'm only in a very small corner doing this. There are so many ways to learn how to go about making war, but I don't think we even understand what making peace means.*

Growing Up Sister Sarah

Sr. Sarah wanted to be a nun ever since she could remember. When she played dress-up, she dressed as a nun. She knew it would mean sacrifice to give up her comfortable life with boyfriends, dances, being a bit wild, and her favorite thing, lavender perfume. But she wanted to "serve God and other human beings."

She grew up in Southern Ireland, knowing nothing of the plight and political conflicts of those in Northern Ireland. The Clarke family was known to have a "Midas touch," so things that she did always succeeded, even when they shouldn't have. And she admitted, "It wasn't good to be successful. I think people got jealous, and I think it wasn't a good thing in a religious life anyway."

Looking back, she can see how the starkness of her training and life as a nun completely paralleled the lives of the prisoners with whom she would later work. As a novice, she had to break off all ties with her family, never returning to her childhood home until the death of her mother. She laments her mother's terrible grief at having "lost" her daughter to the religious life.

Novices were not allowed to speak and had to do whatever the Reverend Mother assigned them to do. Incoming and outgoing letters were read and censured. Permission had to be asked for every move, including going to the bathroom. No newspapers or television were allowed. Sr. Sarah describes this process as "becoming thoroughly institutionalized." When the Vatican II proclamation finally relaxed regulations for Catholic clergy and nuns, she was unprepared for the world into which she was now allowed to venture.

This process of reentering the world left Sr. Sarah in a state of depression and depleted health. However, she speaks of this period as "a useful and illuminating phase of my life; it gave me some intimation of what it was to be down and out, to be marginalized, to exist on the edges of society where life is lonely."

Subsequently, she was given permission to attend Chelsea Art School in London, where vitality returned to her as the artist in her awoke. Not only did she develop her painting career at the school, but she was surrounded by many young London artists whom she found delightful. "Chelsea opened my eyes and mind to the very different thoughts and lifestyles of the students around me."

In retrospect, Sr. Sarah told me it was easier to see behind their punk hairstyles and occasional marijuana smoking than it was to tolerate the unjust and deceitful behavior of the British Home Office she would encounter later in her life. After her schooling was complete, the church gave her an assignment of teaching art at Chelsea. She spoke of how much she enjoyed those halcyon days.

During this time, the Second Vatican Council published its landmark decisions. The words of the Council that were most encouraging to Sr. Sarah were addressed to those in the religious life. They were to combine the "burning zeal of an apostle with wise judgments toward coming to the aid of others in need." As she later wrote, "Chelsea had given me back my sense of worth as a person. The Second Vatican Council gave me the license to begin the work I eventually would choose to do."

Out on a Limb

It was at the age of fifty-three when Sr. Sarah "slipped" into her peace-making work. A priest named Father Faul suggested she might want to take on the volunteer position of secretary of the Civil Rights Association. He warned her, "Sister, there'll be no honors, no promotion for us in this. You don't set out for honors." She volunteered for the position because it seemed to be exactly the kind of aiding others in need that Vatican II encouraged. And so, Sr. Sarah set out upon a path that would lead her places about which she never dreamed.

In the beginning, Sr. Sarah continued to also work at the assignment the church had given her teaching art at Chelsea. The civil rights work was an avocation. The church didn't assign her to that work, but they didn't stop her either. Sr. Sarah spoke several times in our interview of "getting permission to do the work that became her life's passion but not getting any support from the church in doing it."

This concept of Sr. Sarah of being given permission but not receiving support for an assignment was, at first, hard for me to understand. What did that mean exactly? When she was a novice, permission and support seemed synonymous. Being given permission to go to the bathroom also meant that you would be supported by relieving you of whatever duties you relinquished while completing the task. But this civil rights work was something different. This made me think of being given permission to climb a tree, but if you got yourself stuck out on a limb, no one was going to bring you a ladder.

That tree-climbing metaphor was not so far off the mark. As Sr. Sarah's life turned to full-time work with the plights of the Irish prisoners and their families caught in the onerous web of lethal conflict and wicked doings of the British Home Office, the church never forbade her, giving what might be assumed as tacit support. Yet often the church ignored her or gave her words of discouragement. "The church family kind of ignores me and hopes I go away. Sometimes I think that they are right behind me. And then sometimes, I feel that there's nobody behind me and that I'm out there alone, dangling on the edge."

When I asked Sr. Sarah why this was the case, she answered, "Because, you see, the church in the Western world always took the side, right or wrong, of the Establishment."

There were some exceptions. Because her work involved so much travel to prisons, airports and docks, solicitors' offices and courtrooms, she was allowed the use of a car, although it broke down more often than not while she was driving it. Many prisoners often told of meeting Sr. Sarah for the first time and noticing that her hands were smeared with grease from attending to something under the bonnet of her car. Toward the end of her career, the church allowed her to live in a flat of her own at her request. As her eyesight failed her, she was provided a special computer that spoke what she typed, so that she could correct her typographical errors as she continued sending messages to prisoners and their families and submitting articles to the press.

There were a handful of exceptional people she could count on to help her. The first was Father Faul, who had asked her to be the secretary of the Civil Rights Association and stuck with her throughout her work. And there were a few solicitors and Members of Parliament that would answer her calls to assist the Irish families. Occasionally she found a colleague in another nun or priest who would either assist her or at least have sympathy for the work she was doing. Sometimes it took an outsider to realize the true value of Sr. Sarah's work. One of her highlights was when a bishop from Texas accompanied her to visit some of the prisoners in the local prisons. After he saw the rude and threatening way she was treated by the guards and the Home Office personnel, he sympathetically compared her life to Daniel in the lion's den.

Why Stick with Fearful Work?

If the Mother Church was not responsible for her dedication to this difficult and dangerous job, one might ask why she consistently chose this path for herself in her later life. It was Sr. Sarah's heart that called her to the work, and Vatican II that gave her the license to do it. The Bible passages that spoke of Jesus's work with prisoners and the disadvantaged became both the justification and the guidance for her work. But in the end, it was the gratitude of the prisoners and their family members that kept her choosing to get up each day and continue doing the work in the face of an imminent possibility that she might be arrested as a terrorist for her work.

Before she knew it, Sr. Sarah's was immersed in the work.

> *I was getting all these phone calls. Families, people were missing. People had disappeared. They were traveling, and they hadn't arrived, this kind of thing. And it was my job to go and find them. And it was a rather terrifying job because of the way I was treated by the prison guards and the Establishment. Everyone was afraid. Everyone was afraid to speak about Irish people at the time because there were a lot of bombs going off, and they were called "persona non grata." And by sticking out your neck and helping people who were arrested, you were accused of being a member of the IRA and detained and tortured for any number of days under the Prevention of Terrorism Act.*
>
> *I was in danger myself. I didn't know the day or the hour that the Big Hand would come on me. And I often wished that the phone wouldn't ring. But I had to answer the phone. I couldn't say no, but I was frightened to say yes. And I would go out in the car, drive out of the convent grounds, and wonder if I would ever come back. And wonder would anyone help me if it were to happen to me? Or would I end up being strip searched?*

The Link Between Prisoners and the Families

Sr. Sarah became the link between the prisoners and their families. While the arrested people were being detained, she informed their families of what was going on. She called solicitors for the prisoners, took them parcels, visited them, gave them hope, encouraged them to fight "not with their fists, but with their pens." She lobbied to have them sent to prisons in Ireland closer to their relatives, and encouraged journalists to write newspaper articles about the injustice and misuse of the arrests under the Prevention of Terrorism Act. She visited them when they were on hunger strikes; she held their hands on their deathbeds; she rejoiced with them on the rare occasions when justice was served and they were declared innocent and sent home.

Beginning in 1974, and for the first twenty years of the Prevention of Terrorism Act, 7,397 people were held and questioned, and many thousands more were routinely stopped for short periods of time at ports of entry. Many of the prisoners were eventually found not guilty even though they had served many years in prison by that time.

She became a link to reality for the "Birmingham Six," the "Guilford Four," and the "Maguire Seven," alleged underground groups held in London prisons, sometimes for years before their trials took place. Some were eventually released after being found innocent of any wrongdoing. She called their families in Ireland and gave status reports. When family members were able to make the arduous and expensive trip across the channel, she met them at the docks and airports and found free housing for them. She helped them fill out the necessary papers to obtain visitation rights, stood in the long prison queues with them, prepared them for the possibility of being strip searched, and tended to their broken hearts as they left.

And because she knew from her own experience how difficult it was to come out of institutionalization, she tried to prepare both the prisoner and their families for the difficulties they might face upon release. Many of them had terrible problems adjusting to their newfound freedom and especially to the demands of family life with wives and children.

All this even though Sr. Sarah did not have a penny to her name. She made a pragmatic and symbolic choice to continue wearing the traditional black and white habit when Vatican II allowed nuns to have a clothing allowance to wear regular clothes. Pragmatic, because she then took the habits discarded by the other nuns, raised the hems to fit her, and used her clothing allowance to buy the parcels of cigarettes, pens and writing paper, and underwear for the prisoners. It was symbolic because it gave the prisoners and families a sense of security to see the traditional black and white habit. Sr. Sarah wouldn't let on that she, herself, never felt safe at all.

While she was working with them, Sr. Sarah's intuition told her if the prisoners she tended were guilty or innocent. In either case, she did not discriminate. "Oh well," she pointed out to me, "Christ was innocent. And Christ also identified himself with everybody, even the greatest thug. You never know until their trial if they are innocent or guilty. And once you've taken them on, you don't ever drop them." In fact, Sr. Sarah found many of these prisoners to be lovely youngsters, from lovely families. Some of them had three or four academic degrees.

Sr. Sarah's job became substantially more complex when Britain passed The Extradition Act. This allowed the Home Office to arrest and hold for five days anyone they even slightly suspected might be related to or have information about Irish criminals. Irish people who had lived in England for decades and established successful businesses were suddenly extradited back to Ireland because they were suspected of aiding a long-lost cousin who was suspected of making trouble in Ireland. Mothers and wives were picked up and taken and detained. Their clothes were stripped from them. They were endlessly interrogated while their young children, who were left at home alone, were questioned about the whereabouts of family members until the wee hours of the morning. As I listened to Sr. Sarah's descriptions, I tried to imagine what it might be like to have something like that happen to me and my family. It felt chilling.

Compiling Information

Sr. Sarah saved every news clipping, every letter from prisoners and families, and every piece of red tape from the prison processes. She also kept a detailed daily journal. In 1995, she was asked to write a book revealing all the events and the miscarriages of justice by the British Home Office. She sent me home with an autographed copy of her book entitled *No Faith in the System*.

Indeed, she had lost her faith in both the political system and in the church system. Because of her work, Sr. Sarah was shunned and in many ways persecuted on every front. She explained, "I'm a persona non grata. Nobody wants to talk to me. The Embassy gives a party and I'm left sitting on the lawn alone."

The British police tapped her phone, followed her car, kept surveillance on her home, and often denied her requests to see prisoners. There was some speculation that her car accident might not have been an accident at all. By the time of our interview, Sr. Sarah told me the Home Office had banned her from entering the prisons. The agency characterized her as a security risk though she was, even in their words, "a blind, old-fashioned nun, who had never knowingly broken a law or a rule in her life."

Sr. Sarah described her life during these times as a nightmare: "These years were marked by increasingly draconian British attitudes toward the

Irish and by a mounting death toll. I was officially barred from visiting Irish prisoners in English jails but continued to offer whatever help I could to the many beleaguered families who were often neglected."

When I asked Sr. Sarah what she would tell a young person who wanted to become a Peacemaker, she replied, "You should try not to offend anybody, but you will always end up offending the Establishment, and it's not a pleasant position to be in."

Paint Like Mad

It was her faith in Jesus and the wisdom of the Bible that carried Sr. Sarah through the rough times. When she would come home stressed after something awful, she would take out her paints and paint like mad.

> *That's why you see all these crucifixions on the walls, and the paintings of the gospels. Because these were the only things I had. I used to say to myself, "How am I wrong ... no, how am I right and everybody else wrong?" Because everyone made me feel dreadful for doing this kind of work. And then I'd take up the gospel and find that this is what I was meant to be doing. Like the stripping of Christ, I never knew what that meant before; but after meeting women that had been strip searched, I understood enough.*

To do this work, Sr. Sarah had sacrificed her safety, her pension, her salary, and a beloved career teaching art to children. Yet she knew that her decision to do so, difficult as it was, was a choice she had on a daily basis. In contrast to the prisoners with whom she worked that were stuck in prisons, she could "pack it up any day." Her compensation for it all was the gratitude, the "lasting gratitude," from the families and from the prisoners, who continued to visit and write to her.

The Irish prisoners Sr. Sarah worked with were fighting back against the power differential between their country and the colonial attitude of England. Once in prison, they were confronted with an even greater power differential between themselves and the British Home Office, with no way to speak out except with their fists and their hunger strikes. Sr. Sarah became the advocate for their powerlessness. She encouraged them to fight not with their fists, but with the pens she provided for them. She role modeled nonviolent confrontation by using the tools of the telephone, by choosing carefully selected solicitors, by facilitating communication between the prisoners and their families, and by her incessant pursuit of truth for the oppressed prisoners. She used her pen to write an entire book about the miscarriages of justice. Most of all she modeled the powerful tool of never giving up.

The last words in her book read as follows:

> *My diaries vibrate with hundreds of lives related to the struggle for justice and my quarter-century commitment to Irish prisoners and their families. People who have known me might express my work in the single line from Matthew's Gospel, 'I was in prison and you visited me.' That would be the greatest highlight on the canvas of my life.*

Epilogue

During our interview I told Sr. Sarah that my older son who was studying art in Canada was coming to London to be an exchange student. She said she would love to meet him and give him some tips about the art student population.

A few months later on the appointed day, I couldn't help thinking about the meeting that my son was having with Sr. Sarah. He called me soon after he left her flat.

"How did it go?" I asked.

"It was good," he said. "But after I left and was about two blocks away from her flat, I had an attack."

"An attack?" I said a bit alarmed. "What kind of an attack?"

"A best-day-of-my-life attack."

"Oh," I said with a relieved grin. "I had one of those in just about the same spot."

Sean

Sister Sarah was eighty-one at the time of our interview. Several years later, I was at a retreat for Dances of Universal Peace in Mexico. The dances took place on the beach and anyone passing by was welcome to join us. For three days, a somewhat crippled fellow watched the dances. On the fourth day he joined us, introducing himself as Sean.

After the dances, Sean and I struck up a conversation. I could tell from his lilt he was from Ireland. I mentioned I was writing a book on women Peacemakers. He asked if I had interviewed any women in Ireland. When I mentioned Sr. Sarah's name, Sean became very quiet. To my surprise, tears began to roll down his cheeks. When I asked if he knew her, he told me that he had become crippled from being beaten by the guards in the London jail. "But," he said, "once Sister Sarah started helping me and my family, I quit fighting 'em."

I asked if she was still alive.

"No," he said. "She died at the age of eighty-two." When I asked if she was alone when she died, he replied, "Not at all. She was surrounded by the families and friends that she had helped. She was known to us as the Joan of Arc of the British jails."

When peace is made, it is a synonym for respect.
The main point is that when people respect each other,
they are willing to share power.
Sharing power is the opposite of using military power,
of occupation and oppression.
Live and let live.
Don't try to know what is better for others.

—Ruchama Marton

CHAPTER FIVE

Do Not Lie To Me

Ruchama Marton

• TEL AVIV, ISRAEL •

Peace Work:
Founder of Physicians for Human Rights – Israel, an organization
working to end the occupation and create the right to health for
all people living in Israel and the Occupied Palestinian Territories

Metaphor:
I am a donkey. I am overworked,
underpaid, and very, very stubborn.

Wherever there is injustice, there is anger,
and anger is like gasoline –
if you spray it around
and somebody lights a matchstick,
you have an inferno.
But anger inside an engine is powerful:
it can drive us forward
and can get us through dreadful moments
and give us power.

—Scilla Elworthy

Growing Up in Peaceful Palestine

"It was so peaceful growing up in Palestine, before Israel," Ruchama said in a voice that beckoned me into the memory of her childhood. It was a leap for me to get there, because getting to her house in Tel Aviv for this interview was anything but peaceful. Getting through security after landing at the airport took over an hour because they dismantled my son's Gameboy to make sure there were no explosives inside it. Convincing the Israeli authorities that we were there on an academic mission took another half hour and lots of documentation. Driving to the interview from a nearby town reminded me that Israel is a small country with not enough miles of highway for the number of cars, resulting in inevitable traffic jams and consistent late arrivals for appointments. Everyone had a lock on their steering wheel, as a guard against theft. Peaceful wasn't the first word that came to my mind.

But once I passed through her gate and walked down the garden path to her home, my whole system began to settle down. I heard her talking on the phone, something that would happen several times during our interview, often in different languages. In this interview, I would learn that her telephone was one of Ruchama's primary peacemaking tools.

Childhood

As she began to tell the story of her childhood, I felt privileged to join her in this very peaceful image of a bygone Israel. Ruchama was born in 1937 in Jerusalem, to Bilha and Aharon Smuelevitch who had arrived from Poland ten years earlier. Her parents were poor, their family of four sharing a dwelling with two other families. Her grandmother was an important part of their family. All of these newcomers to Israel were very hard workers.

"I was born and brought up in Jerusalem," she began. "It was, of course, before 1948. It was a village at that time, a big village, maybe a small town, Jerusalem was. Not even a city. Extremely nice, which disappeared totally. Oh, never mind."

During World War II, her grandmother had made a vow to God to visit the Wailing Wall once a week. Every Wednesday she took Ruchama along on her walk to the Wall. Her immediate neighborhood was full of hard working pioneers, like her parents. Most of them were European Jews who were not born in Israel.

> *But part of this neighborhood was Jews who were born in Jerusalem, from Sephardic origins, so different from my parents and the European-descent people. Next to them were the most religious Jews. There is no one in the world more religious people than they. All these neighborhoods were so close—three, four, five minutes walking. On the north side, there was a whole neighborhood of people who came from eastern Europe and in another corner, people who came from Kurdistan. Jews, all of them. So different. Different origins, different songs, different language, different clothing, and different food. Even their religions were different even though it was all Judaic. And then in less than twenty minutes, there were the Palestinians. At least six or seven very different communities living in the same small town. There was no love; there was no hatred; we were just all together like this, being our own different selves.*

"So this is your point of reference?" I asked.

"Yes," she said. "This is what life should be like. And I experienced it. This is not an idea in Heaven. It is not such a naïve way of looking at things. I was there. For nine years I was there … so it is possible."

At a time when it was not common for girls to attend school, Ruchama had the luck to attend the Lemel School, a non-religious school for girls established by a European baron. Ruchama described herself as a "good little girl." When she was nine years old, her parents moved to Tel Aviv where she went to high school. Because they were poor, her parents chose to live far outside the town in the middle of three different Palestinian villages that no longer exist today.

> *We all lived really nearby each other. The Palestinian children were my friends; we played together. They didn't go to school like I did, even the boys did not go. Every day they tended*

their sheep. Our language was a mixture of words and sentences in Hebrew and Arabic. And the communication went perfectly. The parents were more distant because they didn't know each other's languages. But they were happy for us to play five or six hours a day together as children. The Palestinian family owned a big beautiful garden, full of figs and other trees.

The War of '48

"Then came '48 and then '49. One morning, when I was about ten years old, I saw our neighbors putting everything they had on their two donkeys, including their grandmother. As they headed east, our soldiers were pushing them, yelling, 'Hurry up! Go away!' My really good friends were gone. When the Army is present, life is … different."

As the new Jews began to fill in the voids left by the Palestinians, they were called the "Second Israel," which meant Jews that came from North Africa, Iraq, or Yemen. As a teenager, Ruchama began to notice that they were not treated in a very just way. They were deprived of many things that her family was provided. It was because they were "different."

Two Strong Dislikes

This was the beginning of Ruchama's awareness of one of her two clear dislikes about the world in which she was growing up. They began as strong concerns and they grew into driving forces for the rest of her life. The first was unjust, unequal treatment. She didn't like it at the individual level, and she especially hated it at the system level. Her second abhorrence was being lied to.

This second lesson came to her like a storm when she was fulfilling her military duty at age eighteen. Military duty was obligatory for both young men and women. "It was unthinkable not to go," Ruchama told me. "That was the atmosphere. So I went in the military like everyone else."

It was 1956, and she was assigned to a fighting unit, which had some of the esteemed national heroes that had fought in 1948. These were people that Ruchama's generation adored. What an honor to serve under one of these revered men. It was a very short war called the Sinai War, or the Kadesh War as it was known in Israel.

"I was cheated," Ruchama said abruptly at this point in the interview.

"How were you cheated?" I asked.

"The myth in Israel was once again that the Israelis were attacked and therefore it was a war that was enforced on us. And it was a pure, sheer lie. It was a confabulation between the U.S., the French government, and the British government. We were the ones that attacked Egypt.

> *And there was another myth I found out about at the same time. One should never come very close to a myth, because then it breaks. I was with these men day and night as my leaders. Most of them were ... (big pause searching for the right words) ... far from being good, or adult, or whatever. They were cold, not good friends, fighting all the time among themselves, and grabby. And they looted from different Egyptian places that we passed. They took a lot of things and broke other things. Having been raised to be a good, honest girl, this was horrible to me, shocking. Not only that, from then to the end of the war (which was a very short time), they shot the Egyptian prisoners of war. Some of this happened in front of my eyes. There were Egyptian soldiers coming down the desert dunes who were hungry, thirsty to death, without arms, and without shoes. And our soldiers went to them, humiliated them, and then shot them.*

> *I broke down. I couldn't eat. I couldn't sleep. I couldn't do anything. After a few days, they sent me back to Israel. That was the breaking of my innocence and my believing in Zionism. I can't tell you how terrible it was. We were always told how pure, clean, and just we Israelis were. When I saw the lie in this, I turned to look at other things. That was when I discovered the whole war was a lie.*

Her commanders did not like her questioning the treatment of the prisoners of war. She was given an early release from her duty, and she hitchhiked back to Israel. One thing led to another, and Ruchama started to ask questions at a time when asking questions was an unspeakable misconduct in Israel. In her words, "One of the most characteristic things about the whole society in Israel at that time was not to see, not to ask, and not to question things, especially not things political."

Incredible Loneliness

I asked, "Were you asking these questions of yourself or of your elders or someone else?"

"No!" Ruchama exclaimed. "The most upsetting thing for me was that I had no one to talk with. It was an incredible loneliness in this respect. Otherwise I was my normal social self, but this part of me had no one to talk to. Not to mention that no one would have had the answers to these big questions. I had to find the answers by myself, very painfully. This is how I gradually became an outsider and gradually a fighter for more justice and less discrimination."

This search for answers, Ruchama feels, formed much of her adult personality. As a child, she had learned to look for and find the good side of people's behavior. Now, as a young woman she was looking for justice, where it existed and where it did not. And she didn't just ask questions, she set about correcting some of the injustices she discovered.

Over time she managed to find people who were more or less thinking the same way. But even that had its challenges.

> I realized that it wasn't only about individuals; the whole system was involved. I became very sensitive to what the whole Israeli systems were doing. For instance in my twenties, most of my core thinkers were men. Only gradually I discovered that in a way they were also cheating. The socialist, extremist, leftist wonderful men around me were cheating because of the way they were treating women—their girlfriends and wives."

Medical School

After she recovered from her military duty, Ruchama went to medical school at Hebrew University in Jerusalem. During her time there she also gave birth to her daughter, Orna, and her son, Yuval. She began studying to be a pediatrician, but after a year she changed her focus. She went into psychiatry so she could study how and why people behave the way they do and how, if possible, to change it. She wanted to study the mind, the soul. Those were the real focus of her questions.

She discovered that the medical school had a rule that only ten percent of the student body could be women. Moreover, the women were not allowed to wear pants. Her discrimination radar went off and she went about changing both injustices. Neither situation changed overnight; however, over time and working with a colleague, both policies were changed.

During her twelve years working as a senior psychiatrist at Shalvata Mental Health Center, she strove, sometimes with colleagues, to bring services to communities. She initiated the first survey in Israel of private psychiatric hospitals to determine whether hospitalization was justified, whether the medication patients received was appropriate, and whether patients could be released if there was improvement in their mental state.

She went to extensive effort to make sure the medical school equally weighed the humanity grades and the math and science grades for those pre-med students applying for entrance. She felt this would improve the relationship between doctors and their patients. For two years, she worked with a group of medical students to process their experiences with patients in hospitals. This became a model that was then incorporated into the medical school training.

The War of Independence for the Palestinians

Then came another war that launched Ruchama on her next step in pursuing justice, and a big step it was. Most Israelis called it the Intefada; Ruchama called it a War of Independence for the Palestinians.

It began in December of 1987. There were lots of rumors of what was happening in the Occupied Territories in Gaza and the West Bank. "The media didn't provide us with any answers. I really know when the truth is not being told. I didn't know what the truth was, but I knew they were telling us lies."

Unable to sit in peace and quiet, she decided to go there and see for herself what was really happening in the Occupied Palestinian Territories, a mission that was quite dangerous. Believing in group work, Ruchama picked up her telephone and started calling anyone she knew in Gaza, as well as many of her friends. Two weeks later she had organized a small group of medical friends to go together to Gaza the following Saturday.

Foray To See For Themselves

One month after the Intefada began, this group of eleven medical volunteers spent one day in the Shiffa hospital in Gaza. Ruchama vividly described what they had found:

> *We talked to people. We realized what was really going on. Almost nothing the media had said was true. It was awful.*

We saw people beaten practically to death. We saw lots of people with broken arms and legs. A group of Israeli soldiers would break into a house; one would grab a person by the shoulder and the other one would grab him by the hand, and a third one would bring his rifle down on the arm and break it. Some were beaten unconscious on their heads with fractures to their skull. Others were shot at from a very short distance. It was really horrible.

I asked Ruchama if the victims were soldiers or civilians. "Civilians," she answered. "Because the Palestinians had no army at that time." The Palestinian leaders had decided that their people would not use guns in the beginning of this war. Instead they used non-violent means of resistance, such as not going to work or not paying taxes. The medical care they received as victims of Israeli's brutal "Iron Fist" policy was sorely inadequate as the Gaza hospital was so poorly equipped.

One week later the group visited the Mukassed Hospital in the West Bank in east Jerusalem and found the same thing. It became evident to these volunteers that this was a situation of systematic war on the Palestinians, although this was not the way it was presented to the public. From these two visits came the birth of the organization that is currently known as Physicians For Human Rights–Israel, or PHR-I.

The volunteer observers started to write letters and do whatever they could to make the truth known. But they found that no one would listen. They kept getting more creative about how to get the truth out to the public. They took media teams with them on their trips. Ruchama decided to spread the word outside the country. She had no money for travel, so she got herself invited to give lectures in Europe and the United States, with her passage paid by the conferences where she spoke. She told them what she had witnessed happening in Israel. It worked like a boomerang and got back to the Israeli government officials, much to their anger. For example, Yitzhak Rabin, then Minister of Defense, punished the Gaza Strip by cutting the health budget. This left those living in Gaza without any health services. People were dying from illness and injuries.

I wrote a letter to the Minister about it but didn't get any response. I traveled to London and talked to the BBC, telling them what was going on in Gaza. They didn't believe my story so I told them "Go to Gaza and see for yourself." A BBC team came to Gaza and issued a short story. It worked like magic. In no time Mr. Rabin returned sixty percent of the health budget back. That was a most important lesson for me: pressure from abroad works!

The First Woman Leader of the First NGO

In less than two months after their first visit to Gaza, the volunteer membership of Physicians For Human Rights grew from the original eleven members to 100 members. In less than a year, it would have two hundred members. Ruchama's tiny two-room apartment became a very crowded headquarters for this intense activity. At this point in the interview, Ruchama told me something that I heard from several of the women Peacemakers:

Then I found myself leading this group. It was not intentional. I didn't sit down and say, "What group am I going to invent?" People referred to me, in a way, as the leader by asking me what we should do. I didn't have the answers, but it happens often in motherhood when your children are asking us what to do. And then you find yourself giving answers, only because you were asked. And so I gave answers. We did a lot of thinking together, but more and more I found myself in this grownup position with children, although all of them were adults, some even elder than myself. They would ask what we should do, and I would figure out the answer.

So without intending to do so, Ruchama became the first woman leader of an Israeli non-governmental organization. And PHR-I was the first NGO to introduce the concept of human rights to the Israeli public. They used the "right to health for every person" as their criteria for determining if human rights were being violated. They interpreted the word "health" in the broadest possible way, as *physical, psychological, and social well-being including access to water, sanitation, education, electricity, sewage, work, and free mobility.*

More Acts of Peacemaking

Although PHR-I was her most famous undertaking, Ruchama would go on to found or co-found many organizations that addressed injustice in the Israeli society. She was quite clear that her intent was to correct injustices by any sector, whether it be Israeli, Palestinian, or otherwise.

I asked Ruchama to give me her definition of peace.

"When peace is made, it is a synonym for respect. The main point is that when people respect each other, they are willing to share power. Sharing power is the opposite of using military power, of occupation and oppression. Live and let live. Don't try to know what is better for others."

When I asked for an example, she told me a story of one of the earlier trips she and her volunteers made to the West Bank. They had received $1,500 from an American organization to do whatever her organization thought would be useful. They purchased baby food, powdered milk, some medications, and other staples for a Palestinian refugee camp. Ruchama had made a list of specific things that each family needed.

When they arrived, the people were extremely happy to see them even though they were Jewish Israelis. Everyone came to help unload, even the children lifted heavy boxes. They organized themselves spontaneously. Ruchama wished a video had been taken of the teamwork between the refugees and the volunteers. No one was less than or better than; everyone was working side by side.

The process went slowly because Ruchama, "like a policewoman," made sure that the right boxes went to the right people. Both the givers and the receivers respected this because everyone knew that otherwise the load of goods would have been confiscated by "the big chief."

She spoke of another example of equal respect. The doctors took their clinic to a different village every week (because taking it to the same village wouldn't have been fair). After a massacre in Hebron, PHR-I brought their mobile clinic to tend to the medical needs of a village next to Hebron. They were warned not to go to this village, as they would be hated and harmed because of the recent massacre.

Normally the villagers gave them lunch, but the volunteers knew that it was Ramadan, the time of fasting for Muslims, so they expected no lunch that day. To their surprise, besides having lived through a massacre and not having eaten all day, these villagers had prepared a meal for the volunteers. To not eat the meal would have been disrespectful. The Jewish volunteers sat at the table and ate while the Palestinians stood behind them, observing their Ramadan tradition of not eating. "This," Ruchama said, "is one of my best examples of mutual respect."

Working at Both the Individual and the Community Level

She also told me she was working with a woman who had been beaten and raped by her husband, who had also beaten and raped their children. Ruchama had found shelter and medical care for the wife and children. She was unable to bring charges against the husband because he was a Palestinian from the Occupied Territories where, at that time, no court had been established. However, she made his behavior known to her friends where he lived so that his conduct would not be shielded by secrecy.

"So you work at both the individual level and the community level?" I asked. Her reply was clear, making me think I was not the first to ask this question:

> I work at both levels. This is very important in my mind, not to give up the individual work. Many people, mostly men and one very 'man-ish' woman, kept telling me I was wasting my time and energy working with individuals. They thought I wouldn't have time and energy to solve the real problems, like resisting the occupation and religious hatred. But I tell them this is not true. Both are equally important. I make sure I balance my time between both. I really believe this is a feminist way of thinking.

And then in a way I had come to know as characteristic of Ruchama, she added, "But I'm not going to give anyone the possibility to make me choose."

Complicated Attitude toward Forgiveness

When we broached the subject of forgiveness, Ruchama became pensive.

> I really don't know. I personally have a big complicated attitude towards forgiveness. Matter of fact, I don't know if deep, deep, deeply I do understand exactly what forgiveness is. Is forgiveness to forget? For me that is impossible; I have such a good memory for details even if I don't want to remember them. So do I forgive or do I not? I can understand not to be angry anymore, and I can behave like this, but is this forgiveness? Maybe?

"Let's take the example," I said, "of someone in Gaza whose arm had been intentionally broken by the Israeli soldiers."

"There were lots of them," Ruchama said.

"OK," I said, "let's say hundreds of those folks. Do you feel like forgiveness is something that is possible or is necessary in order to make peace between those people and their oppressors?"

"I believe they should be compensated," she said.

"By their oppressors?"

Yes, and it should be mutual. One should know that he or she should receive compensation and the other side should know that it is his or her obligation to give all kinds of compensation … by word, by money, by deeds, by any measure that one can find. One of my hardest jobs is to convince the Palestinians to accept the reparations. I push them, both sides, to ask for and to give compensation. One deserves to get it and one is obliged to give it. If this is forgiveness, I fully agree.

An Interviewer's Near Mistake

At this point, I almost made the biggest mistake I could have made in my interviewing career. In order to respect Ruchama's time frame for our interview, I said, "That was a beautiful inquiry into forgiveness. We are done," and I began packing up my recording equipment.

Ruchama quietly added, "I am suing the state of Israel."

"What!? You are bringing a suit against the whole state of Israel?" I asked, quickly turning back on my recorder.

"For compensation," she said. "And I hope that they will compensate willingly. But they are not. But even by doing it not willingly, it is so much better than not doing it at all."

"Can you give me an example?" I asked.

There are many examples, but I will give you one. A Palestinian man who was tortured for thirty-two days. He was really broken, totally broken. And I am suing the State of Israel to compensate him for what happened to him. In the family there are eight brothers and a father and a wife of this person. I had to persuade them that it is their right, and it is their right for dignity to get compensation. It was not easy.

"Who is actually bringing the suit against the Israeli government?" I asked.

"My organization. It is not me, Ruchama. It is being done in an organized way."

"And you have hundreds of these cases?"

"Tens of these cases," she replied.

"So you are saying that forced compensation is better than no compensation at all?"

"Yes, yes, for both sides. Even for the giving one," she said convincingly.

One Last Question

Having bought a few more minutes of time, I asked Ruchama one last question. "If you could paint me a picture of what the world would look like if your concept of peace were in place, what would that picture look like?"

"I already told you," she smiled. "It would look like walking to the Wailing Wall with my grandmother."

Epilogue

I viewed a YouTube coverage of the courtroom procedure in which Ruchama is suing the State of Israel for mistreatment of the prisoner she mentioned in our interview. Sitting next to the brother of the tortured victim, Ruchama is being cross-examined by a very aggressive male lawyer. This is a public trial in which the State of Israel is being accused of doing something wrong, embarrassingly wrong.

Occasionally the camera pans to the torture victim, who has trouble holding his head up and appears mentally unable to follow what is going on. Ruchama speaks in a calm but assertive voice throughout the proceedings. When she is frequently interrupted, she calmly finishes her sentence anyway. When there are incorrect allegations, she corrects every one of them in the same calm voice.

In our interview, I had asked Ruchama to give me a metaphor for herself as a Peacemaker. She told me she was a donkey because she was overworked, underpaid and very, very stubborn. Watching her in the courtroom scene brought to mind the very, very stubborn aspect of her metaphor. But there was something very feminist and enduring about her stubbornness, transforming it into quiet, unstoppable determination. I had seen the same thing in so many of the women Peacemakers I interviewed.

After our interview, Ruchama went on to pursue the elimination of torture and mistreatment of prisoners within Israel as another focus of her human rights corrections. She co-founded the Public Committee Against Torture in Israel. In 2005, she co-founded the Committee For Political Prisoners, and a year later, the Committee for the Rights of Residency. She also co-founded the organization of mental health workers for peace known as Verification. Again, as a co-founder, she helped start the organization Palestinians and Israelis For Peace, which organized seminars and discussion groups to help advance the peace process. She even co-founded One in Nine: Women for Women with Breast Cancer, an advocacy group for women who had breast cancer. And, never losing her commitment to work at the individual level, she continued to volunteer her work with female victims of sexual assault in Tel Aviv.

Eightieth Birthday

In September 2017, on the occasion of her eightieth birthday, Ruchama spoke with Alon Mizrahi for 972+ Magazine. In her interview, she is clear she feels that Israel has been practicing colonialism:

> *And the first thing a good colonialist does is dispossess. Dispossess of what? Of anything he can. Of what is important, of what serves him. Of land. Of natural resources. And, of course, of humanity. After all, it is obvious that in order to control someone else you have to take away their humanity. Dispossession is an unending task. Those occupied people, those dispossessed people, whether they are inside the Green Line or outside of it, they do not agree. They do not give up. They don't agree to be dispossessed of their land, of the water, of their humanity.*

The root problem, as Ruchama sees it, is segregation:

> *Segregation exists within our society as a central political principal. After all, we are divided here into first-class and*

second-class Jews, and beneath them are Palestinian citizens of Israel, and the Palestinians in the West Bank are even lower. At the very bottom of the ladder are the asylum seekers and the refugees.

The Right to have Rights

Ruchama went on to say she deeply shares the views of the philosopher Hanna Arendt who wrote about the "right to have rights."

Ruchama told Mizrahi:

Without political rights, there is no human being. Political rights come before everything else—before the right to property, movement, assembly. Those are all very nice but they are secondary. Without political rights, everything you do is charity. Without political rights, there is nothing.

When Mizrahi asked her what were today's chances in Israel of treating the Arabs humanely, Ruchama replied:

I don't want humane treatment of the Arabs. I want political rights. After that you can be humane or whatever you want. Without political rights you continue to be a colonist, an occupier, an apartheidist. A human rights organization that is not willing to fight for that is howling at the moon. It is meaningless.

Ruchama feels the biggest achievement of Physicians For Human Rights–Israel has been the trips to Gaza and the handing out of medicine to all humans in need out of solidarity, because this has shattered the segregation.

PHR-I

Currently, Physicians For Human Rights–Israel has grown to over 1,500 Jewish and Palestinian volunteers. They continue to operate their mobile clinic in rural villages in the West Bank with both Israeli and Palestinian doctors, pharmacists, and other medical and non-medical volunteers. They maintain their reputation as a consistent place of trust and solidarity where people in need can receive medical assistance.

In addition, they operate the Open Clinic in their permanent headquarters in Jaffa, where the volunteer staff treats over six thousand patients a year on a free or minimal fee basis. In its inception years, most of the patients were migrant workers, but in recent times there is a growing population of refugees and asylum seekers receiving services.

Over half of the volunteers of PHR-I are non-medical members. Their efforts are divided into four arenas. The first is the Occupied Palestinian Territories Department. These folks investigate and publicize testimonies of human rights violations in the Gazan population, the West Bank and East Jerusalem. This includes limitations on the right to move and reside freely in the West Bank for Gazans, and interrogation by the GSS of patients at Erez Crossing. They advocate getting passes for Gazan Palestinians to get necessary medical care in Israel. In the West Bank, the staff deals with water shortage, medical problems, mobility issues, arrests of Palestinian children, and the violence of the Jewish settlers against Palestinians.

The second area is the Prisoners Department, which sees to the health care of all prisoners in Israel, including criminals, those being detained for questioning, administrative detentions, and for asylum seekers. This department investigates and publishes their findings on mistreatment of prisoners, torture, and denial of treatment. They identify physicians who collaborate with the mistreatment. They also lobby against the privatization of the prison system.

The third arena is the Residents of Israel Department, which keeps its focus on equalization of health care for all residents of Israel, whether Jews or Arabs, urban or rural. For the many populations that are not recognized by the Israeli government but live in Israel, such as the unrecognized Bedouin villages in the Negev, they attend to individual cases of inequity of health care services.

The fourth arena, known as the Migrants Department, attends to the health care of all persons residing in Israel who do not have civil status. This includes Palestinians, refugees, asylum seekers, migrant workers, children who are not recognized as residents, victims of human trafficking, returning residents, and persons deprived of citizenship through the Law of Citizenship and Entrance to Israel.

After decades of fighting the occupation from within, Ruchama feels outside help is needed. She would like to see the current international support for Israel's practices of Palestinian oppression replaced by International boycott, divestment, and sanctions, which she calls BDS, to pressure Israel to comply with international law.

About her own life of speaking truth to power, and fighting for what she believes is just, Ruchama, at eighty, says her fighting days are behind her. "After thirty to forty years, I've had enough. Maybe I didn't succeed in everything, but I did in some things. I'm very proud of it."

There are many who feel that Ruchama has done far more than "some things," and that her accomplishments have been extraordinary. She has received many awards for her widespread influence, both internationally as well as in Israel. She was nominated as one of the 1,000 Peace Women Across the Globe. Most poignant, She received the Right Livelihood Award in the name of Physicians For Human Rights–Israel for her role as a Peacemaker. At her acceptance speech in Stockholm in 2010, Ruchama spoke the following words:

> *We are part of the community; we are citizens just as we are physicians, thus our obligation to social justice and human rights. We raise our voice with the voiceless; the tortured victims, prisoners, and all the disempowered people and groups in our society.*
>
> *For all of us, this award gives a moment of pride and recognition to lives of continuous struggle that is often rebuked, lonely and rejected. It is not an easy decision for a physician or nurse to joining PHR-Israel. They are criticized by their peers for being "political," as if medicine can be a neutral profession. Because health is used by the regime as a means of controlling its citizens, of undocumented people and Palestinians under occupation, it is through the right to health that we can best struggle against such control and oppression.*
>
> *I humbly accept this award in the name of Physicians for Human Rights wonderful and relentless staff, board, volunteers, and membership; in the name of our dear Palestinian partners from the occupied Palestinian territory; and in the name of all who support us. From Israel and from the Occupied Palestinian Territory, I bring you back their gratitude, and the commitment to building societies that we will not be ashamed of, but rather proud of, for their conduct towards human rights. Let us join voices and be heard loud and clear. For silence is the language of complicity, but speaking out is the language of change.*

CHAPTER SIX

The Match and the Fire

Connie Ning

• VIETNAM & GUATEMALA •

Peace Work:
Microcredit Plus/Educating Girls

Metaphor:
I am the match. They are the fire.

*May the Spirit bless you with discomfort at
easy answers, half-truths and superficial relationships
so that you will live deep in your heart.
And may the Spirit bless you
with the foolishness to think
you can make the difference in the world,
so that you will do the things
which others say cannot be done.*

— Interfaith Council for Peace and Justice
Ann Arbor, Michigan

Insight Tour

It was a hot, cloudless day. I was wandering up one of the steep cobbled streets of Santiago, a village on the edge of Lake Atitlán, a large and beautiful body of water in Guatemala. There were two girls about elementary school age, shyly watching me and giggling. With sign language and my very broken Spanish, I asked if I could take their picture. Little did I know they did not understand Spanish, broken or not. Their heads nodded yes, but their body postures became even more shy.

I was traveling with a regular camera and a small Polaroid camera. I took the Polaroid picture first. By the time I had snapped the other camera, the Polaroid picture was rolling out. I showed it to the girls, and their eyes grew wide as it came into focus. All shyness forgotten, they started chattering questions in their native language, Tz'utujil . They handed it back to me, but I assured them it was for them to keep. They raced up the hill to show their mothers.

Finding myself at the entrance of a small *tienda*, or outdoor shop, I looked around at the goods for sale. I was delighted to find clothing items decorated with colorful, intricate embroidery. I looked closely to see if it was machine work or handwork. Clearly someone's hands had created each stitch in the story told on the blouse. I was impressed.

The woman in the shop spoke the only two broken English words that she knew, "Friendship Bridge?"

"Yes," I nodded. "I am here with Friendship Bridge," the name of the nonprofit organization that had arranged an "Insight Tour" for a few Americans to see this Mayan life up-close and personal.

Before I knew what was happening, the woman took both my hands and somehow made it very clear that I was to stay in her shop while she ran somewhere. She took off at a lope up the steep street. There was no worry about me stealing anything from her *tienda*, because apparently, the words "Friendship Bridge" had acted like a magnet, and I suddenly found myself surrounded by several shy, smiling Mayan women.

When the *tienda* owner returned, out of breath, she thrust something into my hands. I wasn't sure what it was but I knew it was important. She flipped through several pages showing me her handwritten figures. Slowly it dawned on me that this was her loan payment booklet for the microloan she had borrowed from Friendship Bridge. Microloans are small loans typically for financing entpreneural projects by impoverished individuals and groups in poor or developing regions.

She had not missed a payment. Then I made the connection that this *tienda* was the result of her microloan. When I put it all together, I looked up and saw the other women, eyebrows raised, nodding and smiling and inviting me to see the products of their loan dreams. Before I left, embroidered blouse under my arm, the shop owner and I hugged each other as only two women who no longer feel like strangers can do.

It took me all afternoon to walk that steep street. I saw milk for sale, as well as baskets and towels, belts and shoes, and small household tools, but mostly I saw short women standing tall, happy with their successes, humbly proud of their accomplishments. I thought to myself, "What a gift it is for me to witness this microloan epiphany. Who in the world made this possible, both for the Mayan women as the borrowers and for me as an American visitor?"

I knew that my travels to Guatemala were offered by an organization called Friendship Bridge. I promised myself I would learn more about this organization when I returned to the U.S. To my delight, I found that one of the co-founders was Connie Ning, a woman who lived in my home state of Colorado. Soon after I returned from Guatemala, I called to ask her for an interview. She agreed heartily.

Genesis as a Peacemaker

A few weeks later, I found myself interviewing Connie Ning in the Friendship Bridge office in Evergreen, Colorado. She had blond hair and striking blue eyes. She was one year shy of her sixtieth birthday, but she appeared to have the energy of someone decades younger. It didn't take me long to realize that to fully grasp everything Connie told me during our interview, I had to both listen to her words and watch her eyes, which were full of expression. She introduced herself as the co-founder of Friendship Bridge, a nonprofit that has assisted poverty-stricken people in both Vietnam and Guatemala.

When I asked how she got started on her path as a Peacemaker, Connie told me how originally she had been a very busy psychotherapist. Plus she and her husband, Ted Ning, a well-respected doctor in Denver, Colorado, had six children—three birth children, one adopted from Vietnam, and two from Korea. Her life was full; she had no plans to do anything else. She said if anyone had told her then she would turn out to be a banker, it would have been impossible for her to imagine.

Shortly after they were married, Ted was drafted into the American Army Medical Corps during the Vietnam War, where he did health work in orphanages and villages in Vietnam. He returned home safely to the United States. Not long after the end of the War, Ted wanted to go back to see what had happened in the interim to the orphanages, hospitals, and families he had known during his service. Connie wanted to accompany him so she could learn more about the birth country of their adopted daughter. This was not an easy thing to do, as there were no post-war diplomatic channels between the two countries.

After several years, Ted and Connie were able to go to Vietnam. Connie describes the conditions as:

> *Abysmal. It was like visiting a medieval hospital. In the nursery, there were rats around the milk, and there were women dying postpartum because the doctors didn't have soap to wash their hands. They didn't have any pain meds either. No antibiotics, no pain meds. That's what political sanctions do. And the diplomat that was showing us around didn't know how bad things were.*

> *There was a woman in the hall. She was dying of cervical cancer, which is totally preventable, and her husband was holding her hand next to her. She was young. And I looked into her eyes and just lost it. So I had to leave. I just cried and cried uncontrollably. She spoke to me in a way that I just can't verbalize. All that suffering was so unnecessary. It was ridiculous. It was inhuman; that women should not be suffering like that. Nor should anyone be suffering like that. Much less die!*

> *So I went back to my hotel room and then I became very mad, because I was in a choiceless situation. I truly mean it was choiceless. I just knew I had to return to Vietnam with some antibiotics and some pain meds. There WAS no other choice.*

I'm no heroine. It was just the way it was. So I went home, and I talked to friends.

And so began Friendship Bridge, a nonprofit organization that she co-founded.

"And who was the other co-founder?" I asked.

"The Vietnamese woman in the hallway," she replied, unpretentiously. "If she hadn't looked in my eyes, there would have been no Friendship Bridge. She died two weeks later."

Ah, I thought to myself. It's true that there would be no Friendship Bridge without the woman who looked into Connie's eyes. But there also would have been no Friendship Bridge if the window to Connie's soul had not been open at that moment on that day.

Friendship Bridge-Vietnam

Connie went back to the United States and began exploring ways she could correct the situation she had just left. Two friends accompanied her on her next trip to Vietnam where they delivered antibiotics and pain meds she had purchased with donated monies. She discovered that there was enormous waste of barely-used medical equipment in many hospitals in the U.S. If, for example, a surgery kit was opened and then not needed, it was discarded. Her husband Ted was instrumental in contacting medical facilities to donate medical equipment. Many were happy to give the unused or barely-used equipment to their cause. One hundred forty tons of it, in fact.

By this time, Connie had recruited a cadre of friends to help her in gathering these supplies. Among them was a woman named Mimi Schlumberger. Mimi would remain Connie's sidekick in her humanitarian work for many years to come. For the time being, one of the much-appreciated jobs that Mimi took on was cutting through the complicated red tape of getting visas to a country that had no embassy in America.

Then there was the cost of transporting one hundred forty tons of goods. Connie gave more talks about her mission, something that petrified her, as she was quite timid about speaking publicly at the time. The Catholic Church gave her the $3,000 to cover the transport costs. Catholic Relief Services in Thailand also donated money to buy burn cream for the numerous Vietnamese children who had suffered burns from hot oil spilled out of woks overturned on the floors of the Vietnam homes.

One thing led to another. Friendship Bridge did several medical personnel exchanges, taking American doctors, nurses, and therapists to Vietnam and bringing the Vietnamese medical workers to the United States.

And somewhere along the way, Connie told me, she got bored. When I asked why, her answer revealed that it wasn't the boredom of someone who had too little to do. It was the boredom of someone who is only scratching the surface of a bigger situation.

For one thing, you could see it was just a black hole of endless needs. Endless. What is causing all this cholera, polio, malaria? Well, it's poverty. So what causes poverty? Economic disadvantages. I think people who are poor see themselves as beasts of burden. Their lives are just barely putting one foot in front of the other. Almost unable to think because they are so tired and so hungry. I couldn't stay in their shoes for a couple of hours. Half a day and I would be flat on my nose in the middle of a road somewhere.

Early Microloans

Now Connie and Mimi started looking into how to help the Vietnamese overcome the economic poverty of the post-war era. They decided to make loans of money, which they would raise in the United States. They started a small loan project in the Mekong Delta area of Vietnam.

"We had fifty borrowers," Connie told me candidly. "We did everything wrong. The borrowers were all men. We had no savings component. We had no meetings for the borrowers. We didn't charge interest. At least we didn't hurt anybody, I don't think." It was refreshing to hear her chuckle about her early mistakes.

It was around this time that Muhammad Yunus began speaking about his Grameen Bank microcredit program in Bangladesh. Connie and Mimi went to study with him. Connie remembers Yunus saying that credit is a human right. Connie often challenges people in the U.S. to think about how their life would be if they never had access to credit by asking: "Could you buy a house? Could you buy a car? Could you send your kids to college? Access to credit makes all the difference in the world."

On their second round of loans using Yunus's teachings, Connie and Mimi did things differently. They only lent to women. They charged interest and required their borrowers to set aside savings. They found the

Vietnamese people to be literate and entrepreneurial, both of which contributed to the success of their program.

When I asked Connie why they changed to having only women as borrowers, she was bursting to give me her answer:

> *OK! Globally women pay back at a better rate, probably ninety-seven or ninety-eight percent, and men come in at about eighty-five percent. But more importantly, loaning to women levels the gender field a bit. And when you give women economic power, they then have more decision-making power in their families, which globally leads to more nutrition for kids, more kids in schools (especially girls), a decrease in spousal abuse, a decrease in the number of children born. It's birth control.*

Connie also told me that many of the women that took out loans ended up working in collaborative partnerships with their husbands on the new projects they spawned.

A Family Vacation to Guatemala

During this time when the microcredit program in Vietnam was highly successful, issuing five thousand loans a year, Connie and her family decided to take a Christmas vacation in Guatemala. And once again, she was awake at the most unlikely, yet perfect, moment.

They were drawn to visit the area around Lake Atitlán, especially the town of Santiago, where I had my *tienda* experience years later. On a whim, Connie made an appointment with a local priest. Connie and Ted explained a bit about what they had been doing in Vietnam and asked if there might be anyone in this area that might need help. At which point, the priest jumped up and said, "Oh my gosh, I've got to go do mass! It's Epiphany!" He immediately appointed Ted and their son to join the procession as two of the three Kings journeying to visit the baby Jesus. The rest of the Ning family was recruited to offer gifts at the manger. Everyone loved the spontaneity of the process.

During the homily, the priest told them to come up to the front and tell the congregation what they had shared with him. Connie described it as "looking out at this sea of about six hundred Mayan people." The Nings told their story in English, which the priest translated into Spanish. Then one of the Mayan parishioners translated the Spanish into Tz'utujil, the local language of the Mayans. At the end of the service, the president of the radio station that broadcast to the Mayans on Lake Atitlán came up to them and said, "I've been meeting with a group of about thirty women. They would be very interested in your loans."

And thus, Friendship Bridge-Guatemala was launched.

Around this time, for a variety of reasons, the government of Vietnam took over the work that Friendship Bridge had been doing in their country. This allowed Connie and Mimi the time and energy to focus their attention on the Mayan women in the Lake Atitlán area.

Guatemala was in the process of a slow, fragile recovery from a brutal thirty-six-year period of oppression, violence, and genocide, known as *La Violencia*, instigated under the dictator General Rios Mott with alleged undercover assistance by the United States. Over 200,000 people, mostly Mayan men, women, and children were killed. Many were murdered and dumped into mass graves. Boys were forced to join the armed forces that were slaughtering their own people. Exploitation, rape, and murder of the Mayan women were widespread products of this "war that was waged by men on the bodies of women." When the Nings were launching Friendship Bridge Guatemala, many of the women in the Lake Atitlán area were trying to scrape out a basic subsistence for their remaining children while sorely grieving the loss of their husbands and sons who had "been disappeared" during *La Violencia*.

Friendship Bridge-Guatemala

Connie and Mimi honed their already successful model of microloans by adding three new components: monthly meetings for the women, sending the children of a borrower to school, and the Insight Tours where people like me could become educated about the needs and beauty of these unique humans.

First, Connie explained that adding the monthly meetings for the women added several benefits that the loans alone could not accomplish. The meetings became forums for teaching skills that included how to incorporate hygiene into family life and how to start a small business. They also provided rare moments to forge connected friendships between these women whose hard work as soles family providers usually kept them isolated from each other. And the women discovered things about themselves. Connie told me it was not uncommon for women to tell her: "I

101

never knew I had a voice; I never knew anyone would listen to me," or the most common phrase she heard, "I never knew I was smart."

Second, Friendship Bridge added an educational component to their loans. If a woman was successful in repaying her first loan and elected to take out a second loan, Friendship Bridge would pay all the costs for her children's educations. This they called Microcredit Plus.

Insight Tours

Third, by starting the Insight Tours, Connie offered up-close and personal opportunities to introduce the "Haves" in the world, like me and those people on my tour, to see the realities of the "Have-Nots" lives that these impoverished women lead. In the process, the tours also raised money for the microbank. With the funds, they were able to make small loans to the Mayan women to finance small entrepreneurial projects. During the tours, we gringos were invited into the women's monthly meetings. I went to a group where the women were acting out the story of Jonathan Livingston Seagull, which had me fighting tears. Things were changing for them, their families, and their newly-spawned dreams.

Most touching of all, some women invited us into their homes. These were usually one room structures with dirt floors swept to shininess. As the women continued to borrow subsequent loans, a second room was sometimes added to improve the hygiene and safety of the home. In the home I visited, Maria told us she got up early to make 120 tortillas for her family of five to take with them to school and to work. When they were on their way, she started milking the cow that she had purchased with her microloan. Then she would make the rounds to sell the milk in the village.

One of the comments I remember most about my interview with Connie was when she said, "The poor have so much to teach us! I'm on my knees with humility for what they have taught me with their courage and their spirit and the joy they have in the face of unbelievable odds."

Overcoming the Fear of Public Speaking

They also taught Connie the courage to overcome her fear of speaking to groups of people and organizations when she was raising money. She told me, "When I think about all the faceless people I represent … all the women who will never have a voice, who will never be able to stand in front of anyone and tell their story, then it's a pretty big obligation on my part to do my best."

The interest paid by the women on their loans made enough money to continue providing more loans for the Mayan women. However, the finances needed to cover the costs of administering the loan program was something altogether different. Among other things, there were prodigious licensing and legal fees to operate in the country. This required fundraising by Connie and the Friendship Bridge Board of Directors in the United States throughout the year. Not only did these funds go to pay for uniforms, pencils, and school fees, but also new components were added to the monthly meetings to help the mothers learn how to support their children's school experience. Connie describes going into the home of one mother who implored her: "Please give my children another chance next year to go to school because they all flunked this year, and it's all my fault. I didn't know they had to go to school every day. I didn't know they had to show up for tests. I sent them down the coast to work with their dad. And then they came back, and they had missed out."

"How would she know?" said Connie. "She had never been in school herself."

What Role Forgiveness Plays

I asked Connie what role she felt forgiveness plays in peacemaking work. Her immediate answer revealed to me that her concept of forgiveness was all about self-forgiveness. She said, "We have to forgive ourselves for what we have done unknowingly." This prompted me to remember what I had learned about the role the USA had played in promulgating both the war in Vietnam and *La Violencia* in Guatemala. She said:

> *I continue to forgive our whole country for what we are doing, again unconsciously. But I think almost all cruelty is unconscious. Part of the whole idea would be, as best you can, to help people to become more conscious, to give them opportunities to become more conscious. That is what the Insight Tours are about.*

"It certainly worked for me that way," I told her. I asked what she had learned about forgiveness from the people she worked with.

> *In Vietnam, they have little animosity towards Americans, in spite of what we did there. And the Mayan women, they are*

shy with tourists, but they are very hospitable. I don't know if they have time to hold a grudge. I mean, one thing about the desperately poor is that they live in the present.

When I asked Connie to paint a picture for me with her words of what the world would look like if her concept of peace were to successfully happen, she didn't hesitate for a moment:

OK, if peace were to successfully happen on this planet, then the first thing is that people would realize we are all interconnected. That for whom the bell tolls, the bell tolls for all. So that if we are all interconnected, if we are all brothers and sisters, then everybody has to have a place at the table. So we have to make a way bigger table. And we, the Haves, wouldn't have to give up that much for a whole lot of people to have a good life, a decent life.

She went on to describe an ever-expanding table where the food kept multiplying and the chairs kept coming for all Haves and Have-Nots that kept showing up.

"But I think part of the problem," she continued, "is that we up here in North America participate in enormous cruelties, without knowing it."

"And how would you help someone get out of that ignorance?" I asked.

Anger Doesn't Work

That's a really good question, because it's tempting to get mad and to get angry, and that is the very thing that won't work. I'm not talking about the Haves getting angry. I'm talking about me getting angry at the Haves. But it doesn't work because people don't respond to anger by writing a check. The bridge goes both ways. I think that helping the Haves understand the joy that they could experience by giving is as good for them as for the person borrowing their money.

"Especially if they don't know why you are angry with them," I said, "That's why the experiential part of the Insight Tours has made such a difference for me."

This made Connie smile. "We at Friendship Bridge agree with you."

Match and Fire

I asked Connie to give a metaphor for her peacemaking work. Her answer was that she was a match and the borrowers of the Friendship Bridge loans were the fire. The women have their dreams and do the hard work of building the material for the fire, but they need the microloan, the funds raised by Connie and her Board of Directors, to be the match that lights the fire allowing their dreams to catch hold.

Advice for Peacemakers

In response to my question of what she would tell a young Peacemaker, her answers just kept rolling out:

> *Stay under the radar of the government, who could care less about the poor as long as they are not arming themselves or getting too vocal. You have to be willing to be pretty counter-culture and be willing to get in trouble. A friend told me, 'If you are in the work of doing charity, you will probably get awards or get your picture in the paper. If you are in the work of doing justice, you will probably go to jail.'*

> *Stay small enough that you can make ninety-degree turns. Have a team culture with your Board and staff. Every organization, nonprofit or for-profit, needs a culture. It's critical.*

> *Admitting your mistakes is a fast track to success. And if your Board can do that, you've got a great Board. I couldn't do this all by myself. I would never want to run an organization by myself.*

> *There is a spiritual component. Among other things, it carries you through the rough times, like when an employee steals from the organization. It's like having a bigger perspective. This also helps keep you from burning out. It is that spiritual component that is the grace of knowing it is not me that is making it happen.*

> *Mostly, I'd tell a young Peacemaker to go for it! You can do far more than you ever dreamed you could do.*

At the end of the interview, I asked Connie if she had anything else she wanted to add. She was silent for a minute and then spoke of another metaphor for herself that touched me deeply. It seemed to describe all the women Peacemakers that I have been interviewing. She said, "Actually, I'm a sort of a conduit. I'm a pass-through. I feel like it's not me that's making it happen. Because things just could not work out this well on my own."

When I asked her what was passing through her, she tilted her head and said simply, "Grace."

Connie is a woman who initially wanted to focus her energy on raising her family, a worthy goal indeed. She has done that and so much more. By creating opportunities for Vietnamese and Mayan women to live out their dreams, Connie is living out hers. She is also giving Mayan mothers the gift of watching their daughters attain places of dignity and opportunities that La Violencia stole from them. By being awake at auspicious moments in her life, Connie is making the world a place where the ripples of equal respect and equal opportunities are actively creating a more stable and peaceful world.

Epilogue

Rethinking Causes of Poverty

After our interview, Connie kept updating her focus on the causes of the poverty cycle in the Mayan population around Lake Atitlán. The statistics revealed that Mayan girls are at the bottom of every measurement of human development, including education and gender equality. The average Mayan woman only completes four years of education at the elementary level. One in ten thousand Mayan girls attended college; and even if a student qualified, there were no scholarships that would enable a Mayan girl to attend a college or university. These Mayan girls are largely outside of the education system, illiterate, and stuck in a cycle that positions them as overlooked citizens in their own country.

The Starfish Program

Connie, Ted, and Mimi decided to rethink, reimagine, and redesign innovative ways to beat poverty and uplift an entire cross section of the population. They asked the question: "What if we backed up and focused on a Mayan girl before she was married and had several children, before she had the opportunity to even believe she could take a different path, and set her on a different trajectory?" In answer to this question in 2008, the three of them formed a new organization named Starfish. The premise was simple:

> *Look for girls in poverty with high aptitudes and see what would happen if each were able to realize her full potential. How far could she go? What kind of transformational changes would she bring?*

> *We find her just after sixth grade, when she is about to abandon school for economic reasons. She joins Starfish, and her new trajectory launches. A local, professional mentor guides her and her family along an unprecedented journey through middle school, then high school, and well into the beyond. Along the way, she acquires knowledge and know-how that have eluded Mayan women for generations.*

> *In Starfish, we are betting the farm that five hundred Girl Pioneers, each with her talent fully developed and empowered, will be infinitely more effective than we can be as an organization. Our task is to innovate effective responses that embolden these women to continue to blaze a new trail and become powerful women outliers where before there were none.*

> *Forget the incremental change stuff! These women are leaping over four to five generations. Can the daughter of an illiterate, single mother become a physician? We think so, and we are going to find out what happens when she does.*

Girl Pioneers

The idea is to identify the young women who are bright, resilient, determined, and positive, who are willing to find their voice, and who want to help their people. Each girl who is selected and her family are assigned a personal mentor for the next six years, someone who is from their village.

This mentor is a university graduate, almost always the most educated member of their own family, and someone who has personally overcome many of the hurdles these girls will be facing. Throughout the next six years, the mentor provides both academic support for their school work, as well as a curriculum of life skills such as reproductive education, women's rights, personal finance management, nutrition and health, leadership, critical thinking, and environmental stewardship.

Rather than trying to simply elevate a young woman above her traditional family patterns in an isolated way, Starfish works to educate her family in how to support their daughter in being a pioneer for the entire family. Monthly home visits with the family mentor, with mandatory attendance by the whole family, encourage buy-in and education of the entire family, which, in turn, supports the Girl Pioneer. Every other month, sessions for the families of all participants at the school are held, creating community, and allowing parents to network and discuss the challenges and successes they are experiencing.

Middle and High School

In middle school, the young women participate in the *Poder* (Power) program, where they learn study skills and resilience. They learn how to find their voice in their classes by raising their hand, speaking up with confidence, and asking questions. In their weekly mentorship session, the Girl Pioneers are introduced to subjects outside academics such as life skills, health and personal hygiene, and financial literacy.

In high school, the Girl Pioneers transition into the *Puente* (Bridge) program, which covers more advanced age-appropriate subjects such as sexual rights, financial literacy, and reproductive health. The girls have a bank account, an email account, and do regular community service in their village. Through weekly tutoring, Starfish's mentorship program provides ongoing academic support to keep each young woman on track to finish high school and achieve her goals. The family support groups and home visits continue throughout this period.

Three Options Upon Graduating

Once the Girl Pioneers graduate from high school, Starfish supports them to go onto one of three tracks: find employment, launch her own businesses, or go to university. Graduates can choose to pursue one, two, or all three of these tracks.

If a girl chooses the track of starting her own business, Starfish has a Small Business Program where they can learn skills such as how to navigate the regulatory process, how to write a business plan, and how to make proposals to organizations that provide seed monies to start a business. They are exposed to local, national, and global markets. They are encouraged to think outside the box and develop a business that capitalizes on their talents while also boosting the economy of their village.

Steep Challenges for University Seekers

If a girl chooses to go to university, there are steep challenges to be met. Due to the substandard education offered in public schools throughout rural Guatemala, it becomes almost impossible for a Mayan girl from this rural school system to pass the entrance exams required by the universities. A four-hour school day, teachers unfamiliar with the curriculum subject matter, and a system with low expectations take a toll on the chances of a Starfish Girl Pioneer from even entering the university system, much less finding the financial resources to pay for such a higher level of education. And the universities are located hours away from their villages.

With the Starfish program in good hands, Ted and Connie decided to focus their personal attention on this population of Starfish girls who were seeking to go to university. These girls had begun to believe in themselves as learners. They had learned the value of asking questions and seeking information on the Internet. Their families were understanding and supportive of their daughters reaching for more education. Some of them wanted occupations to bring back to their communities that required a university education.

And yet, none of them passed the entrance exam to get into university.

The Quetzal University Fund

Connie and Ted started the Quetzal University Fund, named after the national bird of Guatemala. They created a new Board of Advisors of six women, including Connie, and set about raising funds ... lots of them. It costs the equivalent of $2,500 per year for each girl to attend the weekly classes at one of Guatemala's universities. Room and board expenses have to be provided. For girls choosing to work in their villages during the week and travel to university classes on weekends, the annual cost is $1,500 per student. Connie figures the budget for this program to be one million dollars.

But the young women have an equal challenge. They need the raw determination to make a go of it. Two women have been hired as staff, whom Connie calls the backbone of the academic and emotional support needed by the girls to navigate the program.

When none of the girls passed the university entrance exam, they took classes and worked with the staff until they did pass. A personalized pathway of educational pursuit through the university system was then designed for each girl.

Each year Connie asks the Starfish mentors to recommend twelve to fifteen girls from the high school graduating class that they feel have enough desire, motivation, and skills to complete a six-year course of studies at the university level. Connie interviews each girl personally. She is looking for perseverance, resilience, a grade point average of over 80, and that very critical trait they learned from their mothers, hard work. If they have these traits, they are welcomed into the Quetzal University Program.

Connie cites Juana as an example. As a weekend student in business administration, Juana had trouble navigating the requirements for both her math and logic classes. She asked the staff for help, and they found her a tutor. Because she had learned computer skills in the Starfish program, she continued to learn more from YouTube videos on the Internet. By the end of the term, Juana had the highest grade-point average in her class.

Another example is Concepcion, who comes from a very poor family. Her brother died from a disease that was neither diagnosed nor treated. Concepcion's life goal is to become a nurse to help impoverished people so they will not suffer as her family has. She travels two and a half hours by bus to the university on the weekends. She also works for a U.S. non-profit organization that provides care for disadvantaged mothers during the week. In three years, Concepcion will become a nurse. In three more, she will earn her bachelor's degree in nursing.

As of 2018, there were forty-one Starfish girls on the university track. By the time they have completed their six-year university programs, they will have earned degrees to become engineers, nurses, lawyers, business administrators, teachers, and psychologists. These girls are truly on their way to becoming the change agents for themselves and for their Mayan communities. In the process, Connie and Ted have discovered a blueprint for helping Mayan girls succeed in the Guatemalan university system.

CHAPTER SEVEN

Paralyzed Into Action

Muffy Davis

• IDAHO, USA •

Peace Work:
Changing mindsets to support
disabled people accomplishing anything they want

Metaphor:
I am a mountain climber.

*The well-being of our grandchildren
is directly related to the well-being
of our enemy's grandchildren.*

—Jon Paul Lederach

Olympic Dreams

When I asked Muffy Davis how she came to do her peacemaking work, rather than follow some other path, she said the best answer to that question was a line out of a song by Mary Chapin Carpenter: "Accidents and inspiration lead us to our destination." I assumed she meant she had been lucky in the opportunities that had accidentally been gifted to her in her life. I had no idea she was speaking literally.

Muffy grew up an independent young woman. She knew a lot of things about her future even when she was a little girl. She knew she wanted to help people when she grew up, and she was sure the way to do that was to be a doctor like her dad. She was also a spunky, competitive kid who grew up in Sun Valley, Idaho, one of the premier ski areas in the United States. Sun Valley was the nurturing ground for several women Olympic skiers. Two ski runs on the mountain, Gretchen's Gold and Christin's Silver, were named after two of the local Olympian daughters of the town, Gretchen Fraser and Christin Cooper. Muffy wanted to join their championship ranks before she went to medical school, In fact, more than anything, she planned to win an Olympic medal and have the slope nestled between Gretchen's and Christin's runs to bear her name.

Everything in her life was on track to complete these dreams. She clearly had family and community support to accomplish her Olympic aspirations. She clearly had the will. All she had to do was hone her skills and keep winning qualifying races.

Accident

One day when she was sixteen and skiing fifty miles per hour on a training run, she met with an accident, literally. She flew off the track into a tree, and careened off that tree into another with such force that it split her fiberglass helmet in half. She was rushed to the local hospital where X-rays were taken.

A wail was heard in the hospital lab as the radiologist on call that day, who happened to be Muffy's father, read her future in the black and white films. She had broken her back and become paralyzed in both legs. Being confined to a wheelchair had never been part of Muffy's plans, but in an instant it was her only plan.

When the reality of her situation settled in, her very first muddled thought was that she would never have another boyfriend. Her second more devastating thought was that she would never ski again. The loss of her mobility was shattering. It was a tragedy not only for her, but for her whole family and the close knit community of Sun Valley. Everything that she wanted to do now seemed impossible. As far as she could see, she could not imagine a life for herself. Her memory of the accident shrouded her in anger. Her sense of her own future infused her with doubt and fear. Mostly she wanted to die.

Inspiration

And that is when inspiration stepped in. And it came in many forms. While she was in the rehab hospital, she had a dream. She recalled it in crystal clarity during our interview years after it happened. Something, perhaps her Higher Power, perhaps an angel, she wasn't sure which, woke her out of her sleep and told her that all this had happened for a reason. It told her that once she had learned all that she could learn and helped others by passing on her knowledge, then she would walk again, perhaps in this lifetime, perhaps in another. It left her with a palpable sense of peace. When her mother came into her room the next morning, Muffy told her that things were going to be alright and it was time that she started learning the things that she was supposed to learn.

Inspiration also came in the form of her mentors and her parents. Olympian Gretchen Fraser gave her a gold four-leaf clover with sapphires in the middle that had been gifted to her by a very important Olympian dignitary.

Her family was her rock. They would not let her feel sorry for herself. They stood behind her, pushed her, encouraged her, and, in her words, were just there for her. Her father played devil's advocate when she told him she wanted to help other people. He would push her to say how, exactly, she would help people. It would drive her crazy but it made her learn to think, and articulate, and fight for what she believed in. She began to gain clarity on how she wanted to help others.

Muffy was admitted to Stanford University. When she found out she had an Asian roommate, she felt nervous because she had never been around people from different cultures. Her mother said, "Muffy, you're disabled and that may feel like a different culture for her. Deal with it." In the end, she and her roommate were a perfect match, and their friendship became another source of inspiration. She learned that exposure could dissolve fear-based thinking.

By the time she graduated from Stanford with a degree in human biology with an emphasis in disability studies, Muffy had begun to get back on the ski slopes. It didn't come easily, however. The early adaptive ski equipment did not provide enough trunk support to keep Muffy upright on the snow. Over and over again she fell sideways. The ski patrol loaded her into toboggans so often they finally quit strapping her in. And then eventually, through an improvement in the adaptive equipment and two handicapped ski programs, she learned to master the mono ski. The new equipment made all the difference and by the end of her first week of using it, she had entered a race and her competitive juices began to flow once more.

When she was twenty-six, she joined a rafting trip down the Grand Canyon. A gregarious, entertaining, and creative fellow named Jeff Burley, who had graduated with a degree as an Adaptive Recreation Specialist from the National Ability Center, had volunteered to assist on the trip. Little did he realize what a pivotal decision that would be in his life. Jeff was taken with the beauty and aliveness of this woman who seemed to hardly notice that she could not move her legs. Lucky for both of them the attraction was mutual.

Four years later, Muffy and Jeff were married in a ceremony on the rim of the Grand Canyon. By this time, Muffy had brought home a bronze medal for skiing in the 1998 Paralympics in Nagano, Japan.

I asked Muffy if Paralympics referred to paralyzed people.

"Not at all," she told me. "It was so named because it is the Olympic competition contest that is held *parallel* to and always two weeks after every Olympic game. It is open to elite athlete contenders with physical disabilities."

Peace Trees—Vietnam

I first met Muffy and Jeff in Vietnam while on my trip to interview women Peacemakers in Southeast Asia. The two of them were on a nine-month trip, which they dubbed *Access the World*, traveling around the world and working with a variety of nonprofit organizations that served people with disabilities.

We met in Quang Tri Province of Vietnam, the area that had been the boundary between the North and South armed forces during the Vietnamese War. It was the area where the greatest quantity of unexploded ordinances, grenades, and land mines had been buried. It was also the location where an American helicopter pilot, Lt. Dan Cheney was shot down and killed during the Vietnamese war.

Muffy, Jeff, and I were with a handful of other Americans on a visit arranged by a nonprofit organization known as Peace Trees Vietnam. This is a humanitarian organization started by the sister of Lt. Dan Cheney, Jerilyn Brusseau, and Dan's mother, Rai Cheney, in memory of their brother and son. Their idea was simple: Clear the land of the land mines and other remnants of war and plant trees and fresh hope in their place. Over time, their mission has broadened to include returning the land to productive use, building schools and libraries to educate future generations, and advancing economic development to ensure a prosperous tomorrow.

They hire professional de-miners who have removed hundreds of buried ordinances and planted innumerable trees. One of the many impressive accomplishments of Peace Trees Vietnam is the construction of a learning center, the Mine Risk Education Center, where school children and other local citizens come to learn what these buried ordinances actually look like and how to avoid them. They also are the first responders to ordinance accidents, and they provide services for victims of exploded ordinances and their families with medical care. They provide financial assistance for the family to find new ways of making a living so that someone can stay home to provide care for their disabled family member.

Our group spent time in this Mine Risk Education Center. I was awash in the thought of what it must be like to feel that your home, your child's playground, or your rice field were not only a source of sustenance and activity, but also a potential source of harm or death.

Lai

We then traveled into the countryside of Quang Tri Province where we stopped outside a modest home. As we walked around the house to the backyard, I saw the pink snouts of three pigs and heard their eager grunts as they waited to be fed. On a long table, a substantial number of rice noodles hung on wooden racks to dry.

At another table under an eave, a young man sat alone, his family gathered quietly, almost shyly, some distance away. His body posture, head curled downward, shoulders slumped, spoke more of dejection than curiosity at his foreign visitors. Lai was fourteen years old. Three years earlier, an undetonated ordinance had exploded in his hand, leaving him blind in one eye and missing three of his limbs.

While our group waited with the family, Muffy and Jeff respectfully approached the table and joined Lai, Muffy rolling her chair and Jeff sitting on the bench across from him. With the help of an interpreter, they heard the story of Lai's accident. Peace Trees Vietnam had given his family the pigs and the rice noddle machine so they could make a living from their home and provide the care Lai needed. He was discouraged about his future; he could not play soccer any more. Walking to his school 2.5 kilometers away each day was a very painful experience because of the awkward fit of the leather and wooden prosthesis he had been given. He wasn't sure what he was fit to do any more.

Jeff talked to him about new soccer balls that were available that had bells in them so they could be "heard" as they rolled toward a blind soccer player. Muffy told Lai her story of being so discouraged after her skiing accident and how her love for skiing helped her find a way to regain her mobility again. She asked Lai if there was something that he loved that much. He told her he loved learning and school and that was why he endured the painful walk to and from his school every day.

Muffy showed Lai her wheelchair, how it worked, and how much mobility it gave her. She knew of an organization in the United States that was dedicated to providing wheelchairs like hers for people like Lai. When she asked if he would like to have such a wheelchair, he quietly said yes, he would be most grateful.

That night when we returned to our lodging, Muffy contacted the University of Utah Rehab Center who said they would immediately ship a wheelchair to Lai. She was also formulating a plan to bring doctors and technicians from Utah to Quang Tri Province to provide better prostheses for the disabled population there. While I had been struck by Lai's sense of hopelessness, Muffy told me that she had been struck by Lai's potential and the spirit inside of him. She felt as soon as he realized what was possible for him, he would pass that on to other people.

The Muffy-Jeff Team

Talking to people with disabilities and matching them up with the right equipment are two ways that Muffy and Jeff motivate them. Another way

117

is to live a life of mobility in a public way, setting a very visible example of what one can do.

A powerful example of this was provided the next day when our group visited a Buddhist temple and sanctuary in Quang Tri Province. The statue of Buddha was at the top of a set of over one hundred steep, uneven stone steps. I found myself wondering if one hundred high steps in this country of diminutive people might not be some sort of test of their Buddhist faith. Before I could put on my backpack and start climbing, Muffy and Jeff were nearly a third of the way up the staircase, Muffy facing outward and Jeff backing up the stairs, hauling her chair backwards up each step.

My first thought was one of pity for Jeff's back. However, the closer I watched them, the word "hauling" didn't seem the right verb. After every step, Muffy moved her hands forward on her wheels, which stabilized her chair from falling forward while Jeff was free to step backwards up to the next level. When Jeff began to pull her chair up the new step, I watched Muffy do half the work with her hands on the wheels. They had this step thing down to a fine art. Muffy told me later during our interview that at night she and Jeff massage each other's muscles that have done extra work that day.

I was not the only person watching them that day. The temple was flooded with tourists. I could only imagine how many people they would encounter on their nine-month trip around the world that would recalibrate their beliefs about traveling with "disabilities." Muffy's way of putting it is that she and Jeff are a great team; together they can break down any stereotype people might have about people with disabilities.

Debunking Stereotypes

Muffy doesn't like having someone else's beliefs serve as a limitation to her or to others. She speaks at TED talks and motivational speaker gigs to large groups to educate audiences about the abilities of persons with disabilities. She shows them the multiple medals she has won skiing in the Paralympics. She shows them pictures of herself water skiing, paragliding, horseback riding, scuba diving, and weight training. She also shows them pictures of her being the first woman with a disability to climb Mt. Shasta, a 14,000-foot mountain. How, you might wonder? In a SnowPod, an arm-powered device that crawls up a mountainside. Taking a journey through Muffy's website makes for fascinating viewing. It is no surprise that Muffy's metaphor for herself as a Peacemaker is a mountain climber.

Muffy also loves visiting with groups of children because they aren't afraid to ask basic questions like, "How do you go to the bathroom?" and "Can you have babies?" She feels that getting questions answered at young ages helps these children grow up without the stereotypes that many adults harbor. One of her most beloved audiences are the children with terminal illnesses in the *Make a Wish Foundation*.

She also works one-on-one with people with disabilities to help them quit setting limits on themselves. She volunteers in the local hospitals to visit those who are newly disabled, to share her story, and to give them some hope for their own futures. She encourages them to transition their intentions from surviving to thriving, and reminds them being different doesn't mean "less than." She tells them and their families how her family and friends supported her through the tough times. She also helps them learn the importance of asking for help, and the skills of how to do it. She brings her medals from the Paralympics and lets people try them on.

As strong a public figure as Muffy presents, she also shared a side of herself that struggles with self-esteem. Even as she is preparing to talk to a large audience, she is wondering if she is good enough, pretty enough, accomplished enough of a speaker. In our interview, she told me that her anecdote to these habitual doubts is Jeff. She sees Jeff as someone who naturally thinks highly of himself, although not in an egotistical way. He can laugh and joke about his faults without having it turn against him. He feels very secure that who he is, is enough.

How does Muffy's work constitute peacemaking? When someone loses use of their limbs, it can feel like being condemned to a prison of immobility, with gravity as one's jailor. At the very least, they have lost their freedoms that they formerly had, freedoms that other people in their world have and often take for granted. It is easy to feel subordinated to those who are "abled" because of the habitual beliefs of oneself and of society as a whole. Muffy and Jeff are spending their lives opening these prison doors by example, by talking, and by teaching.

When I asked Muffy what advice she might give a burgeoning Peacemaker, she advised them to:

> *Strike a balance between being selfless and selfish. You can't be a good Peacemaker unless you take care of yourself, but at the same time you have to look outside of yourself and see*

what is needed that you can offer, and then learn how to serve that need.

When asked if she could turn back the clock on history and not be disabled, Muffy says that she wouldn't do it, because being disabled has taught her so many things. One of the most important is that there are so many ways to accomplish one's goals. She had a goal of being an Olympian, and she has earned seven Paralympic medals. She wanted to serve people by being a doctor, but has found a richer way to serve humanity as a motivational speaker. She is a strong advocate of never giving up your goals, but never getting attached to how you reach them.

Epilogue

Sun Valley now has a ski run named Muffy's Medals. It is nestled between Gretchen's Gold and Christin's Silver.

By her own description, the accomplishment she is most proud of in her life is giving birth to Glenda Noelle Davis. Elle was born to Muffy and Jeff just before Christmas of 2008. Motherhood is by far the best of all her adventures.

Muffy won three gold medals in the London 2012 Paralympics, in a sport that was new for her, hand cycling, which she began after the birth of her daughter, Elle, as a way to get back in shape.

Muffy has retired from Paralympic competition, but was recently elected to the International Paralympic Committee's Governing Board, where she is honored to work to further progress the movement that gave so much to her life. Additionally, she has served on the Paralympic Women in Sport Committee for eight years, working to improve the status and opportunities for women with disabilities in the Paralympic Movement.

In 2018, Muffy began a new career as a member of the House of Representatives in Idaho, where she aspires to improve the collective future of thousands of Idahoans.

CHAPTER EIGHT

Educating Girls to Save a Nation

Sister Mary Vertucci

• ARUSHA, TANZANIA •

Peace Work:
Educating Maasai girls to come into their potential
and save their people from vanishing

Metaphor:
I am a bridge between cultures.

*The fastest way to change the world
is to mobilize the women of the world.*

—Charles Malik

Reaching Out With Solar Education

While my children were growing up, we lived in Carbondale, a small town in western Colorado. One of the distinguishing things about our town was that for many years it was the home of a technical school named Solar Energy International, commonly known as SEI. Here, men and women came to learn how to install solar, hydropower, and wind alternative power systems.

To their credit, the founders of SEI realized that in the U.S. these skills were proactively wise, but for many other places in the world, these skills were desperately needed. These were often places that never had the resources to be a petroleum-based economy, or places where the traditional fuel supplies, such as wood, were already depleted.

To address this need, SEI offered their courses to many students from developing countries. Even though the school worked hard to secure scholarships to cover the tuition and travel, it wasn't unusual for such students to arrive in Carbondale without any arrangements or funds for housing during their summer courses. SEI appealed to the people in our town to offer free housing for these students. Our family offered our home to many SEI students. We did so not only because we believed what the school was doing was good, but also because it was our family's way of getting to know about different cultures around the world. Around our dinner table with these students we learned about Navajo traditions and the plight of women in Bangladesh and the diminishing fuel supplies in African countries.

Two Maasai Houseguests

In the summer of 1997, our household was blessed with the presence of two Maasai, Lukas Kariongi and Seela Sainyeye, a young man and woman from Tanzania who were attending SEI classes. All I knew of the Maasai before meeting our guests was that when they danced the women wore stiff beaded necklaces that clacked up and down as they moved, and the men's dances including jumping contests. Clearly our family knew nothing of the culture gap these two brave young adults were bridging.

My first clue was the blank look on their faces as I showed them the stove and dishwasher so they could prepare and clean up from their meals. The workings of the bathtub and shower were mysteries to them. When I took them to the grocery store, they were amazed at its size, that it could stay open after dark because of its electric lights, and that there was so little "food" to eat in such a large space. Lukas picked up a can of tuna fish and said, "You mean if I could figure out how to open this thing, I could eat something out of it without cooking it?"

Later I understood that the main elements of the Maasai diet were the milk, blood, and the meat of cows and goats. Their cooking, which they called "burning," was done over open fires, much like we might cook a hot dog on a stick. They were just beginning to introduce corn and beans into their diet. Water was a rare commodity hauled over many kilometers in the sun-baked dry lands that the colonial governments of Tanzania and Kenya had allocated to these Indigenous people.

I soon realized that the best way to learn about their culture was to listen to their questions about our culture. For example, when I told Lukas I was driving my car to Denver, he asked why I needed a car. When I explained that Denver was 150 miles away, he still didn't understand. I learned from him that it was not unusual for a Maasai warrior to walk that far. Each day brought a new revelation for how wide the gap was between our cultures. I started researching everything I could find about the Maasai.

My research told me the Maasai had a long history of being proud warriors, one of the few tribes that never became slaves. Their spoken language was Maa, even though they lived in countries where Swahili was the primary language. Their culture was highly patriarchal. They were pastoral people who live in northern Tanzania and southern Kenya.

Pastoral means they followed their herds of cattle and goats from grazing ground to grazing ground, rotating the herds to keep from overusing the pasture feed. Each night the animals were herded into an enclosure of thorn bushes where the families lived in order to protect them from leopards and other predators. Cows were revered. When I made the mistake of taking Lukas and Seela to a rodeo, it pained them greatly to see how the cows were treated. They were even more pained to learn that in the summertime, we leave cows in large herds in the mountains, unprotected from the predators.

Not only were cows the standard of currency in Maasailand, but their meat, blood and milk were primary source of sustenance. During certain seasons, the cows were "tapped" by puncturing a blood vessel, which provided blood when needed, and then plugged with mud when not needed. This provided a valuable source of protein without sacrificing the life of the cow.

Cows were the primary basis of both Maasai social and economic systems. They were owned by men, and the size of a man's herd spoke to his perceived wealth. When a man married, he gave cows to the wife's father as a dowry. Hence the primary value of a girl was linked to the number of dowry cows for which she was traded. Traditionally, the Maasai men were polygamous, having anywhere from two to three wives, and sometimes as many as fourteen.

The role of the Maasai male was herding, marketing animals, planning, and decision making regarding family resources. Fathers made the decision about when and whom their girl children would marry. Girls were promised to marry at young ages, sometimes even before they were born. Generally, the young boys did most of the herding. The teenage boys, after undergoing their circumcision ritual, wandered the land until it was time for them to settle down in their community. If a father died, his herds and his girl children belonged to the deceased's brothers.

Lukas

Lukas was the younger son of a large family. He had entrusted his cows to his mother while he was in the United States. It spoke to his connection with his mother, for not many women in the Maasai culture were put in charge of cattle. Lukas was uncharacteristically short for a Maasai, but he lacked neither skill nor courage and he had a heart of gold. He was the champion spear thrower among his peers, and he had killed a lion with a knife, as was the custom at that time for a young Maasai man coming of age. He had married Maria shortly before leaving for his solar training in the United States. Even though his father had several wives, Lukas made sure to tell me that he would take only one wife in his life, something he had adopted from the Lutherans that had recently come to his area.

Lukas was on the cusp between the traditional Maasai male role and the new uncharted role for a Maasai male. I realized it was amazing that he had secured himself a scholarship to travel halfway around the world to learn a skill that was unknown to his fathers and grandfathers.

Seela

If it was amazing that Lukas showed up at my home, it was a downright miracle that Seela did the same thing.

The traditional role of Maasai women included building the mud houses, which have to be rebuilt when weather ruins them or if new grazing grounds were sought. The women were also responsible for all aspects of birthing and raising the children. Their jobs included caring for the sick and aged livestock, milking, and preparing milk products. Women were in charge of collecting the scarce firewood, and the collection of even more scarce water for human use, which often was kilometers away. Amidst this prodigious workload, the woman traditionally had little apparent decision-making power in the culture.

The only person with traditionally less rights than a Maasai woman was a Maasai girl. She assisted her mother with all her tasks up until she was ten to twelve years old. She was not to get pregnant before she was clitoridectomized (where the clitoris is removed by cutting), which often happened prior to her first menstruation. After this ceremony, she was usually promised to an older man as his wife, or one of his wives, in exchange for cows, where the circle of traditional Maasai life began again. Because of the need for her work at home, and the scarcity of anything resembling a school within walking distance, Maasai girls rarely received an education.

Seela was married and had a new baby boy named Lepapa. Both she and her son had come down with a resistant strain of malaria a few weeks before she was to come to the United States. The opportunity to learn to be a solar technician was so strong in her that she got out of her hospital bed to go to the airport to fly to the United States. Her mother was caring for Lepapa while she was away.

Seela credits her mother for helping her break out of the mold of the traditional Maasai female. When Seela's father died, his brothers showed up at the door ready to claim the daughters and all the cows for their own purposes. Her mother told them she was too overcome with grief to part with the girls at that time. She used the same excuse on several future occasions, until all of her daughters had found their own partners, and all the cows were gone. Seela's mother also saw to it that Seela went to school, learned both Swahili and English, and somehow developed an interest in working with solar power. As I said, a downright miracle.

At the end of their training, Sella and Lukas asked me if I could find some employment for them in our town so they could each earn enough money to purchase a solar panel to carry home. They wanted to install these panels on their mothers' houses.

The more I learned about the Maasai, the more I realized how unique and courageous Lukas and Seela were in their culture. I was also left with a deep feeling of unease about their future, and the future of all their people. It felt like two solar technicians trying to swim upstream in a river whose current seemed to be rapidly washing their entire people toward extinction.

By the time these two pioneers from Maasailand left to return home, a strong bond of kinship had been forged between them and our family. I vowed that I would find the means to go visit them in their homeland.

Visiting Maasailand

I kept my promise to visit Maasailand. In 1999, two years after Seela and Lukas returned home, my college-aged son and I flew to Arusha, Tanzania where Lukas and Seela met us and took us on a seven-hour dusty, roadless drive to their home villages to meet their families. We were treated like royalty. Much of what they had tried to tell us while staying in Colorado now came into visual perspective.

In preparation for the trip, I made contacts to interview four women Peacemakers while we were in Africa. One of these women was Sr. Mary Vertucci in Arusha, Tanzania. While my son was on a walking sojourn with some of the Maasai men, I returned to Arusha, where Sr. Mary graciously accepted my invitation to hold our interview. In meeting her, she gave me answers to many of my questions of how dire the plight of the Maasai was. I also got a glimpse into what might turn the tide for these people in the future.

Mary Vertucci Growing Up

Growing up in Somerset, New Jersey, Mary had known she wanted to be a nun from the time she was a little tyke in primary school. But not like the nuns that taught her in Catholic school; she wanted to be a Maryknoll nun.

The Maryknoll Sisters of St. Dominic are a group of Roman Catholic women founded in New York in 1912. The sisters devote their lives to doing service abroad. They currently number close to four hundred members from diverse cultural backgrounds, serving in a variety of fields including medicine, communications, education, agriculture, social services, and spiritual formation. The sisters serve the needs of the people where they are sent to missions in about twenty-four different countries around the world.

When I asked Sr. Mary what led her down her current path rather than some other path, she partially credits her grandmother, who immigrated to the U.S. from Poland when she was sixteen. Even more so, Mary credits her mother. Mary's family never had much money, given that there were five children, but generosity was high on the family's list of values. Her mother also was interested in the world and taught her children to work for others rather than work for one's self. As a result, Mary became a Maryknoll nun, another sister worked for the Mennonite Central Committee, a third worked with mentally disabled adults, and a fourth sister worked with people who had AIDS.

Sister Mary's Unique Gifts

Mary has a unique gift of empowering young women to discover themselves and follow their dream. She cares deeply for each girl she teaches or mentors. Her goal is to do more than simply give a girl specific academic skills, but to help the girl discover what calls to her and then come into her own potential of following that path.

She also has a unique pace that she sets for herself. She calls it one-on-one, day-by-day. As a result, she never appears to wear out. She tackles the next task in front of her and focuses on whoever is in front of her, without ever losing sight of her overall goal.

Sr. Mary spent her first twenty-six years as a nun, teaching. After finishing her training, she was initially assigned to Tanzania where she taught math, physics, and chemistry at a girls' school. During her days of teaching, she had opportunities to get to know the Maasai as acquaintances much more than just being known to them as a professional. She could sit around and drink a beer and eat goat with some men from the village like one of their peers. She showed me many pictures of a white haired, fair skinned, bubbly Sr. Mary surrounded by several tall, dark-skinned, serious Maasai men with hair no longer than a quarter inch. Mary feels building this kind of informal relationship with the Maasai was foundational to the trust some of them have given her in her later work.

After spending some interim time working with young women that wanted to join the Maryknoll Sisters back home in the United States, Sr. Mary was reassigned to Tanzania in 1987.

Sister Mary's Research Reveals a Dismal Situation

A turning point in her life came when she was asked to be a research assistant for a Maasai Pastoral program. As she gathered information about the current Maasai people, she began to realize the vulnerability of their entire culture in today's world. This was especially evident as she researched the status of education among them. The results of her research revealed a dismal situation, especially for Maasai women.

The Tanzanian Maasai were aware that much was changing beyond their control, but they were not sure what to do about it. Some of the men went to work in the Tanzanite mines and some became security guards in towns and cities, which suited their warrior nature. It was the women that were sensing the need for major change, but without having much power to effect that change.

Mary's research revealed one of the most inhibiting factors was the lack of educational opportunities for the girl children. In 1996, from a population of 500,000 Tanzanian Maasais, only two or three Maasai girls were selected to go to government secondary school in nearby Arusha each year.

In recent years, the Maasai pastoral culture has been greatly threatened by various forces. A primary force has been the governmental policies that have forced the Maasai out of their historical grazing ground with the establishment of national parks, not unlike what happened to the Native Americans of the Unites States. Droughts have been another devastating factor. Agribusiness concerns and even small non-Maasai farmers have impinged on the dry and rainy season pasture grounds, squeezing the Maasai herds into smaller and smaller feeding grounds and resulting in overgrazing. Several sources described the Maasai as being at a crisis point in their history.

A Maasai Girl's Odds For Getting Educated

And yet somehow in 1997, Seela Sainyeye showed up at my doorstep speaking English, married to a man of her choosing and having won herself a scholarship to come to the United States to study solar power.

Let's look closely at the odds a Maasai girl would have to overcome to accomplish such a thing. In Tanzania, even though primary school, grades 1–7, was nationally mandated, it often simply didn't happen in Maasailand. Secondary school, grades 8–12, happened even more rarely, as there were so few such schools in the rural areas.

129

A girl might have to walk twenty kilometers to get to the nearest primary school. And once she arrived, the teacher might not have shown up because teachers' pay was abysmal, and if she did show up, the teacher might not have more education than a primary education herself. She would teach you in Maa, which meant that somehow you would have to learn Swahili to understand what was going on in the education system, and English if you wanted to compete to get in a secondary school in an urban area of your district.

And if you miraculously passed the entrance exams to get into a government school in a nearby town, where would you live and sleep at night? Your family would be seven or eight hours away, if the weather co-operated. If it was the rainy season, the roads, if there were any, were impassable.

And what about your family? If your father was alive, he badly needed to trade you as a wife to an older man, in exchange for needed cows in the dwindling economy of livestock. If your father was no longer living, your uncles would make the same claims upon your future. You would be lucky if your male family members hadn't bribed your teacher to dismiss you from school so they could garner cows. Worse yet, perhaps AIDS had taken one or both of your parents, and your future had become open game for whomever needed cows.

And your mother, if she were alive, worked her fingers to the bone, and needed all the help you and your sisters could give her. And wouldn't you be lonely if you went away to secondary school? After all, you have been through your genital cutting ritual just like most of your friends, many of whom are now pregnant. Wouldn't it just be easier to do what girls had done for decades and repeat the traditional life cycle?

But from her twenty-six years of teaching and befriending the Maasai, Mary knew there was much more needed than some tutoring and a few uniforms. She felt the Maasai were on the verge of extinction. Something major had to change in the lives of this age-old culture, and she was convinced it must start with the girls.

Giving Birth to Emusoi on a Wing and a Prayer

And so, on a wing and a prayer, a prayer that came from the soul of a Maryknoll nun and the heart of a woman who believed in the potential of young women, Sr. Mary launched Emusoi in Arusha, the closest small town to many of the Tanzanian Maasai.

Emusoi is a word in the Maasai language of Maa that means "awareness or discovery." Sr. Mary had a dream of Emusoi being a hostel, or a center where a Maasai girl could come to have a safe, fair chance at getting educated. If she had been lucky enough to make it through one of the sparse rural primary schools, she could take exams to get into the secondary schools in Arusha. If her skills fell short of the exam requirements, she could get assistance. If she didn't know enough English to negotiate the secondary classes, which were all taught in English, she could learn English at Emusoi. If she needed a safe place to sleep and be fed while she was attending school, Emusoi would provide that also.

But even beyond that, Sr. Mary wanted Emusoi to be a place where the Maasai girls could answer the questions, "How do I balance going to school in this town with my life in the village of my family?" and "How do I understand what is happening to my people and what role I might play in making a difference for them?" Emusoi would be a place where girls could talk about these questions, not only among themselves, but also with the few educated Maasai women Sr. Mary would bring to the Center as speakers, mentors, and role models. She wanted the girls to get an objective picture of the path of their Maasai people. She planned to bring in both males and females from other organizations that had insights and wisdom to help inform these girls. Sr. Mary was confident that these newly educated girls would become a part of the new future of their Maasai people, for she had learned that the women were at the heart of the Maasai life. Sr. Mary even envisioned that Emusoi would eventually be run by Maasai women.

Mary started Emusoi in April of 1999. When I visited her five months later, she had rented a four-room house that provided a classroom, a library, a kitchen, and a dorm room. At that time, she only had enough bunk beds to sleep four students, so her first six students slept two to a bed, head to toe. There were four staff members: herself, a cook, a night watchman, and a Maasai woman, Anna Shinini, who together with Sr. Mary did tutoring, recruiting, transporting, hand holding, and everything else that was needed.

Somehow, Sr. Mary begged, borrowed, or bought a Toyota Land Rover, which was essential for transporting the girls to Emusoi from their villages many hours away. Sometimes these trips happened under cover of night with Sr. Mary at the wheel, as a Maasai mother entrusted her daughter to a whole new life path. These mothers knew full well the next morning they might encounter wrath from their husbands feeling publicly embarrassed and robbed of the dowry of cows they were supposed to receive at their daughter's planned marriage on that day.

She told me in our interview that many people had been contacting her about getting a girl into Emusoi. My comment was, "Very soon this building will become too small."

Mary's response was an enthusiastic "Yes!" Her dream included Emusoi having property and a building all of its own. She could envision it!

How To Fund a Dream

When I asked her how she was funding her dream, Sr. Mary looked me directly in the eye and said with a chuckle, "Whew!" I didn't know if this meant, "Whew, you should see all the money rolling in for us!" or "Whew, I never know from day-to-day!"

It turned out to be the latter. She spoke of a grant proposal to a Dutch nonprofit organization that had been turned down. She had written personal letters to everyone she knew. A woman who had been her classmate before becoming a nun sent her request out in their school alumnae magazine. Another friend was the headmistress of a school in Connecticut and offered to have her students be pen pals with Sr. Mary's students, which opened up other avenues of connection. I was sorely tempted to give her every dime I had in my wallet. Years later, my youngest son would volunteer to teach English for a few weeks at Emusoi.

Most of the funds to support Emusoi did indeed come from Sr. Mary's personal requests. Twice a year she wrote a letter describing what was happening at Emusoi and requesting funds. These requests were invitations, not cajoles or pressured sales spiels. For example, she wrote:

> *If you educate a woman, you educate a whole nation. Investing in the education of girls can be one investment with the highest return in the developing world. We invite you to participate in this investment. You will be helping to change for the better the lives of many young women and in turn to help a whole people.*

Then she would tell a story about one of the girls, thus educating potential donors about the heretofore unknown Maasai. I've kept these annual funding requests, as they chronicle what is happening with Emusoi as well as with the Maasai people over these years.

Day by Day, Girl by Girl

Day by day, girl by girl, Emusoi happened. By the fund letter for year five, Sr. Mary wrote that they were putting on the roof sheets for the new building Emusoi owned. She was now supporting 160 students, which needed a $25,000 budget. Mary wrote that she still needed about $100,000 to complete the construction of the hostel, the matron's house, the garage, and guest quarters and to furnish the buildings. "Keep this project in your prayers," she requested.

By year eight, the modern building was complete and two students were entering university or working on a professional level. One student, Neema, was selected to speak at the UN Session of the Commission on the Status of Women in New York City, and was subsequently asked to go to a Peace Camp in Zanzibar. Mary's annual letter said:

> *I thank you all for your support and I ask you not to get tired of helping us. Your support keeps us going. This month, I will start paying the school fees for second term. These payments will be over $50,000. It would be wonderful if we could have a sponsor for every one of our 430 girls. Many of these girls are finding ways to bring their newfound skills back to their home villages.*

Sister Mary's Definition of Peace and Advice to a Young Peacemaker

During our interview, I asked Sr. Mary for her definition of peace. Her ensuing silence was thoughtful and I could tell she took the question very seriously. Her answer is one I have chosen to read several times because it paints a beautiful picture of what peacemaking is capable of doing:

> *For me, peace is a dynamic harmony among all creation. Dynamic in the sense that there is constant movement, change, give and take, development, growth. Harmony is the blending of diversity into a pattern of beauty, cooperation, mutuality, and equality, but without the loss of identify of the various diverse elements.*

When I asked what advice she might give to a burgeoning Peacemaker, her answer came more quickly because it was in sync with everything she had been doing in her life. She answered:

First I would ask the young Peacemaker what path he or she was drawn to. And then I would encourage that person to move down that path that was beckoning. I would warn them they will meet obstacles, sometimes be hurt and discouraged, but whatever you are drawn to … keep seeking. And you will not only do the work, you will have much greater knowledge of who you are. If you really seek who you are in a mutually loving way, the path will open out. I would encourage you as a Peacemaker to move in that direction, and you will find happiness in what you are doing.

Sr. Mary's metaphor for herself as a Peacemaker is a bridge between cultures. Day by day, girl by girl, Mary built that bridge between herself and the Maasai. The image I get of Sr. Mary's bridge is one with a Maasai girl walking across a bridge. On one side is her mother, perhaps in tears yet determined, stretching out her arms to launch her daughter into a better life than the tradition-bound, vanishing life she herself has had. On the other side of the bridge is Sr. Mary, smiling with outstretched arms, ready to help this girl discover herself and, in doing so, return to her village as a skilled agent of change.

Childless yet with Many Children

As a Maryknoll nun, Sr. Mary purposely chose a path in life that would preclude having children. Yet she has given birth to a whole new future for hundreds of young Maasai girls, whom she knows as intimately as if they were her own children. She has faced daunting hurdles, yet she got up each morning and recommitted herself to doing the work she had started, never losing sight of her goals and never getting attached to how she got there. And in the process of doing so, she has become a pivotal force in the transformation of an entire culture of people who were on the brink of vanishing.

Epilogue

Seela

Upon returning home from her SEI training, Seela became a solar technician and installer for her pastoralist organization. Although she was quite talented at these skills, the pastoral hierarchy was unable to have a woman in such a position. Later she worked as the head of the Gender Department for a nonprofit organization in Arusha named Community Research and Development Organization, CORDS, whose focus is to work on achieving sustainable pastoral development, and curbing the trend of further marginalization and impoverishment of pastoralists.

Besides Lepapa, Seela had two more children, after which her husband left her for another wife. In 2008, Seela's beloved mother died. This left Seela a single mother, an orphan, and living in the city away from her traditional birth community. The challenges of keeping a roof over her children's heads, food in their mouths, and giving them a good education have been steep.

To top it off, after a reorganization of CORDS, Seela lost her employment. She is currently working with an organization that helps women obtain microloans. She is also determined to somehow provide her three children a college education.

Lukas

Three decades later, Lukas is now a progressive village leader in Maasailand and the father of seven beautiful children with his wife, Maria. He recently founded and is the Managing Director of a community-based NGO called the Rural Community Support Organization (RUCOSUO). This Tanzanian grassroots nonprofit strives to enhance sustainable development throughout the Simanjiro District.

Lukas's broad activities are directed at coaching community leaders, training youth as solar technicians, helping organize youth educational programs and supporting women's cooperatives. Maria teaches classes to Maasai women in building and using solar ovens. RUCOSUO's goals are directed at reducing poverty by creating employment and entrepreneurial opportunities for the youth. Specifically, Lukas's accomplishments include: starting a training school for Maasai boys and girls that features hands-on practical solar training and computer/IT skills; initiating a solar-powered, community-owned and operated radio station; working as a trainer installing solar power in remote rural health clinics and village schools; and teaching local youth entrepreneurs how to sell and install solar home systems.

Emusoi

By 2008, Emusoi's ninth year, ten girls finished advanced level studies, one started medical school, one was studying banking, another laboratory technology, and a fourth was ready to become a secondary school teacher. The class that was coming right behind them had students in social work, teacher training, community development, hotel management, agriculture, and office management. And Emusoi had forty-eight new secondary school graduates ready to follow their own paths of education to help their people.

On January 15, 2015, Emusoi's sixteenth year, the *Arusha Times Weekly Newspaper* printed the following article:

> *In a rare move, a local tour operator has made a lifetime commitment to offer the Emusoi center, popularly known as pastoralists' girls' safe heaven, a Tsh 100 million support annually.*
>
> *Willy Chambullo, Managing Director of Kibo Guides and Tanganyika Wilderness Camps issued that package to sponsor vulnerable pastoralists' girls through Emusoi Center effective later 2014.*
>
> *"This commitment will continue for the rest of my companies' lifespan," Mr Chambullo said during a form four graduation ceremony for 65 young girls under the center patronage, where he was the chief guest.*

A month later when I emailed Mary congratulations on this donation, she answered back: "Yes, there is a big revolution brewing in Maasailand among the women!" Even though this donation gives her a good base for operating costs, she still needs to reach out to cover the schooling-related costs of an ever-growing number of girls that Emusoi serves.

In 2016, Emusoi's seventeenth year, Mary wrote of how blessed Emusoi was to have her original students returning to mentor and support the new incoming students. She also sent the following message in her letter:

136

Emusoi was begun with the aim of helping Maasai girls get access to secondary education. But we were always open to accepting girls from other pastoralist groups and also from some of the hunter/gatherer communities. Girls from these groups also were severely disadvantaged with regard to access to secondary education. We have girls from the Barbaig, Taturu, Ndorobo and Hadzabe communities.

Two years ago we accepted 3 Hadzabe girls. The Hadzabe are considered to be the last hunter/gatherer society in Africa. They are related to the San Bushmen living in the Kalahari Desert in Namibia. It is estimated they have been living in Tanzania for as long as 50,000 years. At present, they number only about 3,000 and farmers and hunters are encroaching on their traditional lands. Life is difficult for them as they are being forced to surrender their land and lifestyle to pressure from more developed societies. They are facing extinction and they need help to fight for their rights. Your help to Emusoi is very far reaching.

In July 2017, Sr. Mary wrote of the death of a beloved student from tuberculosis, a disease that continues to take a toll in Tanzania. In addition, she shared the following story:

Just today I heard about one mother, Mama Agnes, who has been beaten and despised by her husband and sons because she wanted to educate her daughter. She didn't care what happened to her, but she wanted her daughter to have an education. She also sent her granddaughter to us.

Unfortunately, both girls did not do well in secondary school, but moved to vocational school after 2 years. Now they are both working in hotels in the kitchen and sending money to their mother/grandmother. They put a tin roof on her house and added a solar panel. Their mother earns money when people come to her to charge their cell phones with her solar! She has been able to farm and has enough food and now she is even gaining weight. Mama Agnes was always so thin and dressed in rags; now she looks so good and even has new clothes because of the help of her children! You all have helped.

In 2018, Emusoi is now staffed by three former Maasai students. They are supporting 250 young women students from the Maasai, and other pastoralist, hunter/gatherer communities.

One of my favorite messages from Sr. Mary is the following one:

As I watch the world news each day, I become very sad to see all the death, destruction, hate, war that fills our TV screens. I ask myself what can I do to bring peace and healing to the world. At this Christmas season, we remember the baby born in Bethlehem and what He brought to the world. Can we imitate him in some way to bring a positive influence to our broken world?

When I see our students blossom and grow during their year with us, I believe that we are adding to peace in the world. Girls who come to us frightened, unsure of themselves, having no idea of their beauty and worth change into confident young ladies who laugh and play and develop their minds and their gifts. Surely this energy helps to heal our world. When you contribute to us, support a student, pray for us; you, too, participate in this healing.

CHAPTER NINE

Make a Little Peace, Make a Little Dinner

Chona (Encarnación) Ajcot
And Myra Maldonado

• SAN LUCAS TOLIMÁN, GUATEMALA •

Peace Work:
Bringing opportunity to oppressed
Mayan people, especially women widowed by the genocide

Metaphor:
I am a rabbit hopping from house to house.

It is said that our Indigenous ancestors, Mayans and Aztecs, made human sacrifices to their Gods.
It occurs to me to ask: How many humans have been sacrificed to the Gods of Capital in the last 500 years?

—Rigoberta Menchu Tum

An American Visits Guatemala

Living in the United States during the 1970s and 1980s, I had vaguely learned from the American newspapers and magazines I read that Guatemala was undergoing a civil war. Sometimes it was called "The Violence," or *La Violencia*. I was busy raising a family at the time, and it seemed far away, beyond the attention I needed to attend to my current life. In the late 1990s, as I entered graduate school and began to focus on peacemaking, Guatemala became more relevant for me. I was delighted when an opportunity to visit this beautiful country came my way.

During my travels through Guatemala, I found myself drawn to visit San Lucas Tolimán, a town near Lake Atitlán. There was a sense of easy, bustling activity about the town. Clearly, the hub of the activity seemed to be in, around, and through the Catholic church and Mission. There was also an enticing smell of newly baked bread in the air. Having not eaten breakfast, I decided to follow the traffic and the aroma of the bread. I found myself greeted by a cheerful white-haired Anglo fellow as I entered what seemed to be a community hall. He introduced himself as Father Greg and asked how he could help me.

I told him of my search for a woman Peacemaker in the Mayan area. I showed him my hands cupped as if to catch water, in an "equal respect" position; I told him this represented peace. I moved my hands apart, indicating a dominant and subordinate situation, or un-peace. As I slowly moved my hands back together toward the "equal respect" position, I asked if he knew of a Mayan woman working to make "peace" happen.

Without a moment's hesitation, he answered, "Yes, I do! And her name is Chona. Come back in about an hour and I'll see if she can meet with you." What I didn't realize was that Father Greg would figure greatly into the story that Chona would tell me later that afternoon.

Interviewing Chona

As I sat across from Chona for our interview, I was taken by her natural beauty. I realized that her Spanish, being her second language after her native Mayan Tz'utujil, was both well-paced and well-pronounced. With my halting command of Spanish, I could understand some but not all of her answers to my questions. I could tell by her face that she understood most of my questions spoken in English, but was reticent to answer with her limited English. We were both grateful to have a young woman named Myra Maldonado act as our translator.

I once heard someone say that if you ask a Mayan a question, they will give you the answer they think you want to hear. I wondered if this was a habit learned from their decades of servitude under the Spanish elite or if it was an innate characteristic of the Mayan culture. When Chona answered my questions in few sentences, Myra would fill out the answer when translating. Chona was very humble about her life. Myra was both proud and respectful of Chona's contributions to the Mayan community in San Lucas Tolimán, so she added just enough to her translations to help me ask better questions. This let the story of Chona's life at least partially unfold before me. After I returned home to the U.S., I learned more about Chona's life from other people's observations of her, and from reading talks she gave about her life at the Mission.

Myra

Translators have a tricky job. Strictly speaking, their job is to translate exactly what is said into a second language. But an interview about peace-making is very enticing. Sometimes Myra wanted to contribute her own answer to a question. She always asked my permission first and then explained to Chona what she had told me. I welcomed her contributions. Chona was fifty-three; Myra was thirty. They each offered different perspectives about living through the period of genocide of the Mayans by the Guatemalan government known as *La Violencia*.

Paradoxically, interviewing Chona was both a heartbreaking and uplifting experience. It was also a redolent adventure into the tastes and smells of the Mayan culture. No matter what question I asked, her answers nearly always had some reference to food. When I asked about her birth family, she told me what her mother cooked for her impoverished family of thirteen. When asked how she helped the widows of San Lucas Tolimán, she talked about the food she brought to their gatherings. She described how the coffee was picked and roasted. And to top things off, the interview took place in the large room adjacent to the San Lucas Tolimán Mission kitchen. The smells of warm bread and the delicious lunch being prepared by Chona's helpers—whose job it was to feed the large daily crowd of workers, visitors, and volunteers at the Mission—kept wafting past our table. It all made my mouth water.

Growing Up Chona

Born in 1950, Chona described her rural Guatemalan childhood as very poor and very happy. She was one of eleven children, two of whom died in infancy, in her Cakchiquel Mayan family. She played with a stick of coffee as a doll when she was a little girl, and she used the empty skins of avocados as little dishes to serve imaginary meals. She ground her pretend corn on the adobe bricks. Only two of her siblings received any education, and then only through the second grade. Chona remembers her mother as a very, very good mother:

"My mother used to take care of us, and we always had beans, corn, and a little chirmol (salsa). When she had just two eggs, she would put in things to make the meal bigger. And also we used to have the beans with chipilín and other herbs."

When she was twelve, Chona went to live with an aunt so she could earn enough money to buy her own clothes. At thirteen she went to work at the Sisters of Notre Dame convent in San Lucas Tolimán. The nuns became her mentors and taught her how to clean house and wash windows, all new skills for someone who had lived with a dirt floor and no windows in her family home. They also taught her Spanish, a brand-new language for a child who had only spoken Tz'utujil at home.

When Chona turned fifteen, the people at the parish gave her a Quinceañera, a celebratory party honoring her role in the parish and her passage from childhood to womanhood. She remembers this with great fondness, as girls raised in poverty never heard of such celebrations, much less became the recipient of them.

She worked for the nuns for four years. Then she helped clean the house of Father Gregory, cooking his food and baking his bread and cakes. Over time, Chona worked in the orphanage, worked with malnourished babies and the disabled, helped set up the school, and ran the Mission kitchen. If Father Gregory was the father of the Mission, Chona became like the mother. When I interviewed her in 2003, she had been there for thirty-eight years.

Father Gregory Schaffer

Gregory Schaffer was born in 1934 in St. Paul, Minnesota. He was one of ten siblings who grew up in a household fed by its own garden, and with the smell of homemade bread ever present. He attended St. Paul's Seminary, and in 1963 at the age of twenty-nine, he received an assignment that would change his life forever. He was sent to the Mission in San Lucas Tolimán in Guatemala, a country of which he knew very little, where they spoke a language that felt foreign to him. The original assignment was for five years, but like Chona, it became a life-long commitment. Little did Father Greg know that within twenty years, he'd be living the beginnings of *La Violencia*, which would put him to the strongest of tests.

When Father Greg arrived in 1963, he proved to be a strong advocate for bringing justice to the poor and oppressed. He practiced one of the basic Catholic social teachings known as Preferential Option for the Poor. What better place to practice this liberation theology than in the impoverished town of San Lucas Tolimán with its twenty-two surrounding communities of Mayan people who had known poverty and subordination for centuries.

When he first arrived, Father Greg, by his own description, knew nothing about the Mayan culture, nothing about the politics of Guatemala, nothing about the needs of the people. Besides being known as a man of huge compassion, one of his main gifts was that of listening. He listened in the confessional, in the coffee fields, on walks, at the market and sitting at the communal meal table in the Mission. As he listened, the Mayan people began to trust him enough to tell him what they needed to rise out of their abject poverty.

At the time Father Greg arrived, San Lucas Tolimán was the poorest community around Lake Atitlán. Only two percent of the population was literate, and almost none of the Mayans owned their own land. In fact, overall in Guatemala at that time, two percent of the population owned ninety-eight percent of the land. This spoke of the both the economic poverty and the cultural poverty, because in the Mayan culture, land is one's identity and corn is everything. The Mayan saying goes, "without tortillas we die, and corn grown on one's own land tastes better and is better for us." Most of the Mayans worked on farms, or *fincas*, owned by the wealthy elite descendants from the Spanish conquerors and sometimes owned by large American companies.

The People of New Ulm

Father Greg had a special asset—he had the people of New Ulm, Minnesota, his former diocese, who strongly believed in social justice and wanted to help. Year after year, Father Greg brought them to the Mission as volunteers to work so these heart-centered Americans and these people of the noble, if impoverished, Mayan culture could get to know each other.

The task Father Greg and the New Ulm Diocese undertook was to enhance and enrich the whole of every person—spiritually, intellectually, and physically, as well as to fight the immediate effects of poverty and its underlying causes. He brought new spiritual life to the Catholic community and helped build churches in the neighboring poor villages. A medical and dental clinic was built, and local Mayan people were supported to train as doctors, dentists, and natural healers. An orphanage was established for the children who lost their parents in the period of violence. An elementary school, which began with three students and grew to 625, was built. The Mayan teachers taught in their native language. A library was built, as was a Woman's Center. Several agricultural initiatives were started, including a coffee cooperative for the coffee raised by the local Mayans and sold in Minnesota.

Most transforming, Father Greg purchased land from surrounding land owners. Initially, this was done with money raised by Father Greg with the help and collaboration of the New Ulm Dioceses (sometimes as much as a million dollars in a year). This land was then freely given to the Mayan families in small plots. In this way, land ownership was created for nearly four thousand Mayans around San Lucas Tolimán.

One condition of owning land was that a house with a bathroom must be built for the family living there. Since the men mostly knew only farming skills, new skills in construction, plumbing, and electrician trades were taught to them, skills which fathers then passed on to their children.

Each plot of land had enough room for a garden to grow food for the family, and a second plot for growing coffee. Half of the coffee crop was purchased by the Juan Ana Coffee Cooperative, named after Father Greg's parents, John and Ann Schaffer, whose inheritance to their son became the seed money for the cooperative. The coffee was then sent to Minnesota where New Ulm Diocesan volunteers filled orders across the United States for this unique, fair trade coffee. This, in turn, provided the first modest income the San Lucas Tolimán Mayans had ever known.

When I asked Father Greg if the plots were given to the Mayans, he replied that each owner signed a letter of promise to repay the funds. Without him saying it, I realized this eliminated the humiliation of a handout.

When I asked if the funds were able to be repaid, he smiled and said, "Yes, some."

Feed their Bellies

The goals that Chona took on were quieter, more understated. It was to feed the bellies of those doing the work with her cooking. And eventually her work would provide opportunities for the most hidden victims of *La Violencia*: the women, the children, and the disabled that remained behind to cobble together a way to raise their families after the maelstrom of genocide had blown through their lives. She was tending to their exhaustion, their battered self-esteems, their absence of joy, and their terrified souls that had experienced betrayal, helplessness, and hopelessness.

The Double-Edged Sword of Owning Land as a Mayan

At this time, land ownership for the Guatemalan Mayans was a double-edged situation. On one hand, owning one's own land offered Mayans something they had long desired, a way out of the oppressive poverty, which was becoming intolerable. On the other hand, it woke up a lion in the government who primarily represented the two percent wealthy landowners that felt threatened at the idea of losing their position of power and dominance, something they had enjoyed for decades as farm *(finca)* owners using Indigenous cheap labor.

The average coffee picker earned two to three dollars a day on a quota system. If their quota was not met, they received no pay. So rather than sending their children to school, they put them to work to help meet quotas. Food and necessities could only be purchased at the expensive company store, which eventually created enough debt for the Mayan family to entrap it in the cycle of poverty. To complicate matters, some of these large farms, such as the United Fruit Company, were owned by North Americans.

The idea of Mayans owning their own land and growing their own small crop of coffee threatened every aspect of this system. As Chona put it, "We wanted houses and land; instead we got death."

The seeds for this period of violence were sown when the Spanish colonists arrived in the 1500s, not only claiming the lands as theirs, but claiming the Indigenous people, including the Mayans, as their slaves or indentured servants. This began the "otherization" and "less than" status of the Mayan people. Without the education to read the documents of

146

their slavery, Mayans did not realize that the period of their indentured service could last longer than their lifetime. In Chona's words:

> *The Mayans are more noble than the Spanish but more innocent and therefore easy to take advantage of. The people in power would tell lies and "manage the minds" of the Mayans because they were not formally educated in the colonists' language.*

La Violencia

The tension of *La Violencia* started in the 1960s. As it smoldered, the oppressed *finca* workers formed guerilla forces. Their oppressors rallied the government military power to crush them. It began as a force to disallow land ownership by the Mayans. By the 1970s and 1980s, under the leadership of two successive rampant dictators with some alleged help from the United States' Central Intelligence Agency (CIA), it grew into a concentrated genocidal effort to "eliminate, exterminate, and annihilate" the entire Mayan culture in Guatemala. The conflict lasted until 1996. The worst of it, occurring between 1981 and 1985, was the same period when Chona was coming into womanhood, wifehood, and motherhood at the Mission.

Often people living in the capital, Guatemala City, had no idea what was going on, but the rural Mayans were living in constant terror, especially, as Chona told me, at night when the raids happened. Somewhere between forty to fifty thousand people, including men, women, and children, eighty percent of whom were Mayan, were "disappeared," or killed, often being dumped in mass graves. Those that survived, especially the women, often faced even more dire consequences.

Women were thrice endangered because they were poor, they were Mayan, and they were women. The UN Rapporteur on Violence against Women describes *La Violencia* as "a war between men fought on the bodies of women." She estimates that over 100,000 women, mostly Mayan, were the victims of violent rape, often repeatedly, and sometimes in the presence of their children.

It was 1990 before peace talks finally began, and 1996 before cessation of the violence known as *Firma de la Paz*, was finalized. Although the genocidal terrorizing had stopped, there was nothing in the peace agreement that addressed land ownership reform, or that addressed the structural underpinnings of the poverty. Nothing was mentioned that would provide an avenue for creating justice for the deep and massive harms that had occurred in this thirty-six-year genocidal program.

In my interview with Chona and Myra, I began to grasp what it takes to loosen the long fingers of genocide, even years after the negotiated peace.

Disappeared

Chona married a man whom she dearly loved. He became the secretary of the Mission and a valued member of Father Greg's efforts to provide the Mayans with land. Together, she and her husband had three children who were four, six, and seven on the day he "was disappeared." It was December 1, 1981. He was taking legal documents regarding the land ownership for some Mayans to the nearby town of Sololá.

He never returned.

Years later, as Chona and I interviewed together, she was unable to keep tears out of her eyes or voice when describing what it was like for him to simply not return home, and to never know what happened to him.

His disappearance sparked a period of terror for Chona and her children, who moved from home to home so that the authorities would not come to kill them. She fled in the dark of night, hardly ever sleeping. She had heard stories of the government army torturing people by slicing the soles of their feet and then making them walk. There were many stories of children witnessing the torture and murders of their parents.

After five long months of hiding and searching for his body, her husband came to Chona in a dream. He told her to look for him no longer. He also told her to take good care of herself because she was very valuable to their children.

I had heard this phrase "being disappeared" before, especially in my growing knowledge of *La Violencia*. But when I thought deeply about it that night after my interview with Chona, the wicked impact of what it must mean to a family began to seep into me.

What would it mean if my father had been disappeared in the United States when I was a child? Did that mean he was dead? Or still alive but being tortured? Do we go look, or just wait? Do I cry or hold out hope for when he will return? How long do we wait to begin to adjust to such tragic news? Clearly we must do all the work the disappeared person used to do, but just for now? Or forever? Who will bring home the money for our family provisions? Whom can I run to and hug when he comes home every night? Can we honor his life with a church service if we don't have his remains? Who did this? And why my father? Does someone go to Heaven when they have been disappeared? Does the person that disappeared them go to Hell?

Muy Duro

I gingerly asked Chona to speak of *La Violencia* and how she felt about it. She used the words *muy duro*, or "very hard," over and over again.

The guerrillas were fighting on behalf of the Mayans. But if a Mayan family aligned itself with the guerrilla forces, it became a source of suffering and death. Chona explained: "The government army had ears everywhere. If you were for the army, the guerillas would kill you. If you were for the guerillas, the army would kill you. The army killed the most people."

She thinks her husband was a target because he helped get land for the poor Mayan people, exactly what people in power wanted to crush. He was one of thousands of Mayans killed from San Lucas Tolimán and the Lake Atitlán area.

When I asked, "by whom?" she answered, "By the military soldiers."

When I asked where the soldiers came from, the answer was they were a mixture of men who came from all over, and they were placed everywhere.

"But a Mayan boy would not volunteer to be a soldier, would he?" I asked.

"No," said Chona. "The rebel guerrillas would come offering money for the boys to fight. But the government came to kidnap them."

And then Myra asked permission to speak to me with her words.

> I remember when I was a child, the trucks came here to San Lucas Tolimán with the military and they caught the village boys like fish and the kids were running. And sometimes they would fall in the street, and the mother was screaming and running. And then they had to go and look for him in Sololá and show them that he was studying. And they didn't believe them. They just took them like cows. They just put them in trucks. They were catching every kid that was Mayan. And

149

then they trained these boys to be soldiers. They came back and killed their own people. That was just terrible.

She translated what she had said to Chona, who nodded her head in agreement. As difficult as it was to recall these events, these two women needed the world to know what had happened to their people.

At Thirty, the Mother of Eleven

It was a miracle that Father Greg and Chona were not "disappeared" by the military, given their ongoing aid to poor Mayans. Chona tells a story of Father Greg hearing from the priest in a nearby village named Quiché. The military had come at night and broken into the homes of two Quiché families with a total of eleven children. The parents were killed in front of their children. The military was now looking for the children to kill them because they had seen the faces of the murderers. The priest asked Father Greg to bring the children to the San Lucas Tolimán Mission. Clearly, had Father Greg driven to retrieve the children, the army guards at one of the three military checkpoints would have killed everyone, including Father Greg. So Chona went instead, recruiting a driver and a van. Petrified, she concocted a story that she was the mother of all eleven children (even though she was only thirty years old) and they were returning to San Lucas Tolimán after visiting friends in Quiche. At the first checkpoint, the traumatized children were crying, but finally calmed down by calling her "Mother." So the soldiers let them pass. At the second checkpoint, the children calmed their crying by sucking on the sweets Chona had brought in her purse. At the third checkpoint, Chona and the children were busy saying the Rosary. When they finally reached the Mission, Father Greg had set up an orphanage house for them called Casa Feliz, or the Happy House. Today, three of the children still reside in San Lucas Tolimán with their own children and grandchildren.

Peace and Forgiveness

I asked Chona to give me her definition of peace. She spoke for a long time and when she finished, Myra said, "She didn't give her definition, but the point is that there is no peace here because the people that have the power always have been oppressing the Mayan, never letting them go on, never letting them have opportunities. All the Spanish people and even the Latina women consider themselves above the Mayan women. They have learned this through the generations ever since the Spanish discovered Guatemala. Chona said that peace for her was 'opportunity.'"

When I asked Chona if she felt that she worked to make "opportunity" happen, she replied:

> *Yes, especially because Mayan women don't have the opportunity to have social connection or to feel like they have value. They don't have confidence in themselves and often believe they are less than other people. By being the cook for the parish, and helping them raise money, and helping Father Greg, I set an example for them of how they, too, can be of value.*

My next question was whether Chona felt forgiveness was an important part of peacemaking. Of everything that happened during *La Violencia*, I knew Chona got the most upset thinking about what so many children had to witness. As I waited for the translation, I could tell by the softening of Myra's eyes that Chona's thoughts were wise and beautiful.

> *If you have love for God, you have to forgive the people because you need to have peace in your heart in order to forgive and to give happiness to everybody. Because if we have love for God, you have a better life. And thanks to God, I am like that right now. I have no anger. I suffered a lot but I couldn't go on that way. And I couldn't help my kids. And I received help from Father Greg and other people, but I feel happy right now and I am helping widows. There are many, many to help, so I want to have peace in my heart.*

Chona Fiestas

Myra told me that Chona had a group of widows that she was helping:

> *One hundred widows. She began with twelve women two years ago. And the main thing she wants to give them is that they can go out of their houses. They have a monthly meeting. Someone is always having a birthday. Wherever Chona goes, there is sure to be a party. She also has a group of fourteen physically handicapped people. She shares good food with*

151

them like beans, and sugar, and rice—whatever the parish pantry has at the moment. And they have a really good time sharing. They tell each other about their problems. And that is how Chona hears what they need. These Mayan women have been alone in their homes, just trying to survive and raise their kids. She has contests and sometimes they dance. Every time at a party there is a piñata. We give presents and gifts. We do special parties for Mother's Day and Christmas Day. People refer to them as Chona fiestas.

Listening to this account, two things dawned on me. First I realized that Myra was more than just a translator; she was Chona's assistant in these activities. Second, the idea of a birthday party as a peacemaking tool struck me as stunning.

People with financial means offer their money and expertise as a way to help people suffering from poverty. Poor people offer their time, attention, and friendship, things that money can't buy, as a way to honor and overcome the loneliness of poverty. Both kinds of assistance are needed. Both can be effective if offered in dignity. And, as Chona taught me, why not have a party in the process.

"This is such a good example of peacemaking!" I said.

"There's more," Myra said.

She goes to the homes to help. Or they come here all the time asking for help. Somebody is sick; they need clothes; they need food. They need help with one of their children. Or often they need to talk. They need help solving a problem. They respect her when she goes to talk to someone. Chona also wrote a book. Well, not actually wrote the book because she cannot write, but she felt that people in the Minnesota home parish needed to know what good things Father Greg was doing for the Mayan people down here. So she 'talked' the book while she was cooking all our meals, and someone else wrote it down.

Rabbits and Sunflowers

Chona's metaphor for herself was a rabbit, hopping from house to house. When I suggested that she was like "Madre Teresa," she laughed heartily and said, "No, no. I'm just that rabbit hopping around."

My next question was, "If a young man or woman came to you and said they wanted to help make peace for the Mayan people, what would you tell them to do?" Even as the question was coming out of my mouth, I suddenly realized Myra WAS that young Peacemaker. Just as the Guatemalan mothers teach their daughters to weave, Chona was teaching Myra to assist the Mayan women in overcoming the isolation and grief of their situations. While Chona was a role model for the older women, Myra was a role model for the younger women who watched her step into a position of value in the parish.

I asked Myra her metaphor as a Peacemaker. She answered that she was a sunflower, "because with the bright light from Chona, she gives me the opportunity to be part of the changes in my community." Myra's definition of peace was "where respect and equal opportunities exist between all people, from different races, especially countries like Guatemala, which are pluricultural and multiethnic." This definition means even more because Myra considers herself part of the Spanish-Latina population often known as the oppressors of the Mayans.

Father Greg and Chona learned by osmosis. He learned from the Mayans by being in their midst; she learned from the Minnesota parishioners that came to volunteer. They learned from each other. As Father Greg's knowledge of what the Mayans needed deepened, Chona's administrative skills increased, but always in Mayan style. And in this organic, subtle process, like two trees whose branches share the same sunlight and wind, this man and woman of different cultures, different economic status, and different levels of formal education forged a heart-guided team, a partnership that operated collaboratively in the service of this burgeoning uplift of the Mayan people.

Someone asked Father Greg if the current government was leery of the Mayans in his parish owning their own land. After all, there had been a brutal crushing of the Mayans by the government over this very matter in the recent past. He quipped that whenever the government looked at the Mayans in San Lucas Tolimán, they saw people who were much too busy to form rebel troops. In fact, for his accomplishments in San Lucas Tolimán, Father Greg received the Order of the Quetzal, the highest award given by the Guatemalan government for the accomplishments at the Mission.

No such public award was ever presented to Chona. Yet Father Gregory knew. The Mayans in San Lucas Tolimán and the parishioners from Minnesota knew. And, most importantly, as humble as she was, Chona recognized the difference between the subordinated, terrified, and poverty-stricken Mayans of the 1980s and the property-owning, educated, and secure Mayans of the first decades of the twenty-first century. In her heart, she knew she had much to do with the peacemaking partnership between herself and Father Greg.

Neither could have accomplished alone what they did together: Father Greg with his parishioners, his heartfelt listening, his farsighted planning skills, and Chona with her motherly tending, her cooking, her rabbit hopping and piñata parties, and her role modeling. The award for this was the lasting gratitude of thousands of Mayans.

Make a Little Peace, Make a Little Dinner

The day Father Greg was presented the Order of the Quetzal award, Chona cooked a huge traditional American Thanksgiving dinner with turkey, dressing, and mashed potatoes for everyone, including the Minnesota parishioners that had come for the ceremony. The President of Guatemala, Óscar José Rafael Berger Perdomo, arrived in his black helicopter, surrounded by his guards, to make the presentation. After a brief speech, the President said he had to leave before the dinner to meet other obligations. Chona told him to come to the kitchen on his way to the helicopter. There, the woman whose husband had been disappeared by the men in these very same power positions, flying in the same kind of helicopter, handed them turkey sandwiches she had made for them to eat as they flew to their next task. Make a little peace, make a little dinner.

Epilogue

Chona's three children all have advanced degrees and have grown up to be an anthropologist, a social worker, and a lawyer, respectively. Her adopted daughter is currently newly married and working as a secretary at "IMAP," the Institute of Mesoamerican Permaculture.

The largest meal Chona ever prepared at the mission was for the memorial service of Father Greg in 2012. During the prior two years, while he was receiving treatment for his lymphoma cancer, Father Greg's need for health care kept him in Minnesota. He guided the Mission by remote control, while Chona and the other Guatemalan Mission project directors became the on the premises overseers of affairs.

With tears, Chona still remembered Father Greg's last words to her before he died. He began by thanking her for her help because without her, he wouldn't have been able to work as long as he did in San Lucas Tolimán. She asked for forgiveness for their occasional arguments over the years and he as well asked for forgiveness for his errors. He then blessed her. And despite the tears that welled up in Chona's eyes as she relived this difficult final farewell, she, of course, had to mention the last meal that Father Greg ate: beans and tortillas. And through the tears, she smiled.

Cauldrons of Food

On the day Father Greg's casket arrived in San Lucas Tolimán, Chona knew there would be throngs of people coming to pay their respect to the memory of their beloved *"Padre Gregorio,"* so she made cauldrons of food. Indeed, throngs appeared. Father Greg's casket was passed from hand to hand along the forty blocks teeming with the Mayan people whom he and Chona had served, until it reached its destination at the mausoleum. And Chona served a huge meal.

After fifty years of service, Chona retired from the Mission in San Lucas Tolimán, but continues to give her talks with groups who visit the Mission, with the intention to keep Father Greg's memory alive. She now has ten grandchildren and is happy to have the free time to dedicate more of her attention to her family and in fighting her chronic illness with diabetes.

Amidst her busy retired life, Chona still finds time to help poor children and widowed women … and, every once in a while, prepares her special meals for visitors, and her famous Christmas party that she hosts for poor children once a year.

Chona is thankful for the opportunity to share her story and is grateful for those who collaborated with Father Greg's work, who is now an angel in Heaven for the Mayan people of Guatemala. She prays that the seed of peace and love that was planted will never die.

*Do a little bit of good where you are;
it's those little bits of good
put together that overwhelm the world.*

—Desmond Tutu

CHAPTER TEN

From Renaissance To Refugee

Inge Sargent / Thusandi

• HSIPAW, BURMA •

Peace Work:
Helping a rural region attain
modernized healthcare and education

Metaphor:
I am a drop in the ocean.

Bullets cannot be recalled.
They cannot be uninvented.
But they can be taken out of the gun.

—Martin Amis

Meeting Inge

Three different people had given me Inge's name as a candidate for my book. From them I learned only a few details: she had lived somewhere in Burma and contributed mightily to the improvement of the medical and educational facilities there, he had two grown children; and she was now living in Boulder, Colorado, an easy driving distance from my home. In phone calls, Inge was gracious enough to accept my invitation to interview her for my book.

As I rang her doorbell, the door was opened by a woman with a warm smile, her long, black hair wound into an unusual bun on the top of her head. I had no idea that the story she would tell me would let me accompany her through a romantic, almost fairy-tale beginning, to a dark, deeply difficult middle, to her current place of dedicated service.

Setting the Stage

Before launching into Inge's tale, it might be helpful to provide a cursory summary of geopolitical underpinnings that are the stage for this story of peacemaking. Burma is a country in Asia where many very different ethnic nationalities are living within one national boundary. This boundary was drawn more by outside political forces than by internal similarity. These ethnic groups include the Burmans, who live in the vicinity of Rangoon. Other ethnic groups include the Kachins, Karens, Kayahs, Chins, Pa-Os, Palanungs, Mons, Myanmars, Rakhines, and Shans.

These people differ from each other in their historic origins, their languages, their religions, and their cultural practices. They also differ in the topography of the land they inhabit. Some live in lowlands rich in agricultural soil upon which things such as rice or poppies grow. Others live in hill country rich in mineral deposits and trees.

In the 1930s, twenty years prior to Inge's arrival in Burma, the Shan states comprised roughly seven percent of the population of Burma. Each Shan state was headed by a lineage of hereditary leaders who functioned as princes in a feudal-like governing system. Each leader, or *saophalong*,

159

was responsible for the governance and law enforcement of his state, including having his own armed police, civil bureaucracy, and judicial system. The British colonizers of Burma who were primarily interested in the area near the capital, Rangoon, rarely interfered with this distant, quiet section of the country.

In 1942, as Burma's desire to gain independence from British rule was growing, China and Japan waged a bitter war for domination of the northwest section of the country, where the Shan states were located. The bombings from both sides devastated some areas of the Shan states, much like the devastation seen in Europe after World War II. The Burmese government had built up a sizeable military force during this time, both to vanquish the invaders and to quell any efforts by the northern states to secede from the Burmese union. This would play a role in Inge's story.

As British rule was eventually restored in the area, the nationalist party who had spearheaded the movement for independence from British rule for all of Burma, began to gain momentum. The emerging leader of this movement was General Aung San, the father of today's leader of Burma, Aung San Suu Kyi. He encouraged the frontier people to join Burma in negotiating this transition, which took place in 1947, hence the current boundary lines of the country.

Importantly, the Shan and other states received the right to secede from the proposed Union of Burma after a ten-year period, ending in 1958, if they found this partnership unsatisfactory. This right was granted to them in the new Burmese constitution.

Burma's peaceful independence from British rule was set for January 4, 1947. Tragically and unexpectedly, six months prior to this date, General Aung San and five others leaders of this movement, including a Shan prince, were assassinated by a political rival during an Executive Council Session. In addition to the personal losses this caused, it left the country without the skilled leadership to lead the new nation. What did remain intact, however, was the strong military force that had been built up in the previous years.

Inge Growing Up

Inge was the eldest of four children born into the Eberhard family in Wiesenau, Austria. As a six-year-old, she watched the Nazis invade her small village, interrogating children and taking away her neighbors. Her mother was arrested and released three times.

160

For several years after World War II ended, Europe reeled from the devastation of the war years, so Inge set her sights across the Atlantic for her higher education. She was one of the first people to be awarded the Austrian Fulbright Scholarship, and she was chosen to enroll in Colorado Women's College in Denver, Colorado.

While there, she attended a gathering of international students from several of the colleges in Denver. She found herself attracted to another student who was an engineering major at the Colorado School of Mines. His name was Sao Kye Seng, and, to her delight, the attraction was mutual. Their love for each other grew in the wonderful playground of the Rocky Mountains and they decided to marry. But Inge was obliged to return home for a year after her American studies before she could marry. During that time, Sao learned some German so he could ask Inge's father for her hand in marriage when he visited her home in Austria.

Sao had known for years he would marry a foreign-born woman. His family's astrologer had foretold it. Sao tried to tell the truth to Inge's father about his station in life, but between Sao's fledgling German and her father's non-existent English, it never quite happened. Even so, the permission to marry was granted. The couple returned to Colorado for their "ecumenical wedding ceremony," so called because on that day in March, 1953, Sao the Burmese Buddhist was married to Inge the Austrian Catholic by an American Methodist minister in a private home service, attended by a best man who was Coptic from Ethiopia and a bridesmaid from Hong Kong who followed Confucius.

Sao's Surprise for Inge

Then Sao and Inge set sail with two dozen other people on a small ship bound for Rangoon. Many days later, as their ship approached the dock, Inge noticed several small boats paddling directly toward them, filled with people in brightly colored clothing, singing and throwing flowers into the water. As she wondered who in their small passenger group warranted such a charming welcome, Sao drew her away from the railing. Inge wanted to stay at the rail to watch the fascinating entourage, but Sao was urgent about speaking with her.

Then he looked directly into her eyes and told her the boats were meant for them. When she questioned why a mining engineer might deserve such a celebration, he admitted that he had not revealed everything about himself. He apologized deeply when he saw the hurt in her eyes.

These people had come eight hundred miles to meet this boat because he was their saophalong, the prince of Hsipaw (pronounced See-paw), one of the Shan states in northern Burma. And, more to the point, she was now a Shan princess. Her first shocked comment was that she wished she had dressed in something other than her hand-woven Austrian dress.

Sao told her that in public, tradition dictated that she could no longer call him Sao; she had to call him Saopyipha. When she asked the meaning of the word, he told her "older-brother-who-is-the-ruling-prince." This made them both laugh, taking the edge off of Inge's consternation at the news he had withheld from her. He further explained that he could no longer call her Inge in public. He was to call her Thusandi, the name predicted for her by the family astrologer.

As Thusandi descended the gangplank, she suddenly had one week in Rangoon to transform herself into a princess.

Instant Princess

The best silks were selected to be sewn into longyis and aingyis, the traditional long wraparound skirt and blouse of Thusandi's new culture. She traded her Colorado hiking boots for new velvet slippers. Precious gems were purchased and made into royal jewelry. She learned how to arrange her long, black hair in the traditional bun atop her head, something she continues to do today.

Once she and Sao had settled into the palace in Hsipaw, she began learning both Burmese and Shan, two very different languages. With the help of her beloved attendant, Moei, Thusandi learned much about the Shan culture, and the Shan people eventually came to accept her and love her. In due time, they called for the ceremony that would officially make her their Mahadevi, or Celestial Princess. With the bestowal of this title, she felt thoroughly accepted by these people whom she had grown to love very much.

Sao's Legacy for his People

Thusandi was not the only one embarking on a new life and a new way of thinking. Sao's family had ruled Hsipaw as feudal lords since 45 B.C. Sao was the first Shan prince, or Saophalong, in this long line of feudal rulers to even think about giving his people some rights and responsibilities over their own destiny.

Shortly upon his return to his country, he gave ownership of the royal

162

family's rice paddies to the farmers who cultivated them. He abolished the practice of kneeling before him. He ordered tractors and agricultural implements and taught his people how to use them, making their use free to those who would clear the land for new crops to be grown. He planted experimental orange groves near the royal palace.

Sao had attended the Colorado School of Mines to help investigate mining possibilities, knowing his Shan state was rich in minerals. He established the Tai Mining Company and also started a salt mine. Any profits were turned back into research and development so all people in his Shan State could eventually share the wealth of the gifts in this land they loved. And, unlike some of the earlier rulers, Sao was honest and not corruptible.

His far-reaching goals for his state were to bring Hsipaw, which had been a British colony during his childhood, into democracy. But the closer he got to realizing this dream of democracy for his people, the more he upset the growing Burmese military forces that were gathering power in the country.

Although there was less fanfare about it, Burma gained its independence from the British Empire at the same time India gained its independence. The ten-year transition arrangement General Aung San had brokered for the Shan States gave Sao the opportunity to launch his ideas of democratic governance within a Federation of Indigenous states. However, this potential for self-governance became increasingly threatening to the Central government of Burma. The Shan States were the Rice Bowl of the country, and they had mineral and agricultural resources, including limited but highly valued opium products, all of which contributed significantly to the tax base that went to the capital, Rangoon. Losing control of these resources and income meant a loss of power. The Burmese Army became the primary enemy of Sao's ideas of independence, and under the leadership of its General Ne Win, it committed countless heinous acts of violence and power-grabbing throughout the country.

Inge's Legacy For Her People

While Sao's dreams of democracy for his country during those experimental years had been far-reaching, it did not take Thusandi long to realize there were similar opportunities that begged for her touch. The Hsipaw health care and educational situations were in need of attention. The people of Hsipaw sought her out to assist in these areas, but she was hesitant, as she had no experience in such things. Sao's confidence in her gave her the boldness she needed to accept the requests. As their Mahadevi, she proceeded carefully, introducing her knowledge of Western ways while showing respect for their long-established Shan traditions.

For example, Moei, Thusandi's personal maid and beloved companion, did not show up for work one day or the next day. Thusandi inquired about her and was told by the village headman that Moei was quite ill, but could not die until Thusandi gave her permission to do so. Quietly, without appearing confrontational, Thusandi knew she simply could not give her permission for this. Privately she went to the hospital where Moei was in a feverish coma. Reaching out to hold her hand, Thusandi whispered to Moei that she must live, as Thusandi did not want her to die. Moei did indeed live, and continued to lead a thriving life. After this, the local respect for Thusandi and her ways increased.

One evening as Sao and Thusandi were having their ritual late afternoon cocktails together on the veranda of the palace, she mentioned to him that two doctors and the chief Minister had been to visit her that day. They asked her to organize the Maternity and Child Welfare Society of Hsipaw. She told Sao that she couldn't say no because she knew three out of four babies died before the age of four, but she couldn't say yes because she had no training in such matters. Sao told her she had the basic ingredients: common sense, care for the people, and perseverance. He assured her everything else needed would follow.

With his vote of confidence, the next day she recruited the help of an Anglo-Burmese woman named Maggie, and together they called a gathering of thirty-seven women of all ages, both Shan and Burmese. Thirty-five of them knew the pain of losing at least one child. They elected Maggie as their secretary.

On the following day, Maggie and Thusandi unobtrusively paid a visit to Hsipaw's only birthing center, a modest one-story building. They were met by Nang Noom, the tiny head nurse who was dressed in her blue cotton longyi and white aingyi. Despite their efforts to keep their profiles low, Nang Noom recognized them and was honored to show them around the birthing center.

The delivery room was spotless and filled with natural light. It contained a wooden delivery table, a stand with a washbasin, and a small cabinet containing what looked like a pair of forceps and a pair of scissors. There was nothing else in the room, neither water nor electricity. An average of thirty babies were delivered here each month, as most of the

Burmese women delivered their children at home. The bulk of these births occurred around the full moon, taxing the two available midwives. They were sorely in need of a third midwife during these times, but they knew the neighboring doctor could not spare any of his nurses. When Thusandi asked about pre- and post-natal care, Nang Noom looked puzzled, not sure what the words meant.

Three rooms contained a total of twelve narrow beds, each with a small crib beside it. Seven beds were occupied, but only six of the cribs held tiny babies. When Thusandi asked if she could hold a baby, the mother giggled with glee to know that the Mahadevi would hold her lucky baby. When asked the baby's name, the mother replied that she did not know. Maggie explained that naming Shan children often took months. Astrologers and older relatives often made the selection. The day of the week on which the child was born dictated the beginning letter of the name. Thusandi felt a surge of maternal love as she held this newborn baby. Little did she know as she was holding this child of the Shan mother, she was also carrying in her own womb the first of two children she and Sao would have together.

Realizing that most of the babies were born in the villages, Thusandi took a "field trip" to the village of Moei, her maid. She wanted to know how the women lived, worked, became mothers, and nurtured their children.

Her first task was to greet the *bumong*, or headman, and then diplomatically ask if he might leave his house so she and his wife and some of the village women might talk "women's talk." Women and girls of all ages filled the home for the afternoon, enlightening Thusandi about their daily lives.

From the age of four or five, girls took care of their younger silblings while their mothers cooked, washed clothes, or gathered food. Sometimes the mothers worked at the cottage industries, weaving baskets, making paper, preparing food, or farming. The girls usually married in their mid-teens and lived in the home of one of the parents. They frequently bore children soon after their marriage.

During their pregnancies, they never saw doctors or nurses, as the village midwife assisted at the births. Newborn babies were bathed daily. They offered the breast whenever the child was hungry. The mothers rarely let their babies out of their sight. No vaccinations, no medical care, and no sustenance other than mother's milk. These children usually thrived until about the age of eight months when the mother became pregnant again, at which time their milk dried up. The infants' diets abruptly changed to soft, white rice. Most were never given any fruits or vegetables, which were believed to cause stomach disorders and other diseases. On rare occasions, a spinach-type leaf and a mild pumpkin might be mixed with the rice. The once thriving infant became sickly and malnourished until the new baby was born, when they might be lucky enough to receive any milk that was in excess of their younger sibling's needs.

It was clear that the Maternity and Child Welfare Society had at least three agendas that needed attention. The first was to upgrade the Birthing Center; the second was to invite and encourage the use of the Birthing Center; and the third was to do village outreach to improve the chances of children reaching their third birthday in good health. To this Thusandi added another agenda: that of getting buy-in from the general population.

Although she could easily have used royal funds to finance the Society, she instead solicited the financial assistance of several of the wealthy members of the community, including the tea broker, the rice mill owner, the meat contractor, as well as her husband. She also involved ordinary citizens by organizing community fund raising events such as movie showings, soccer matches, and music competitions.

A huge crowd gathered for the ribbon cutting ceremony for the up-graded birthing center with its electric lights and its staff of four midwives. There was an outpatient area for mothers and children. A cheer went up as the faucets in the delivery room were turned on for the first time, de-livering hot and cold water.

If They Don't Come To Us, We Will Go To Them

But almost no one came to use the services in the ensuing weeks, es-pecially not the village women. So the Maternity and Child Welfare Soci-ety went to them.

Several of the women on the committee joined Thusandi in making the first village call. It took some convincing for the first pregnant woman to come to the head villager's house for an exam by the midwives, but she was then followed shortly by others. Thusandi, Maggie, and other So-ciety members worked out of their vehicles, showing the women how to give vitamin drops to their toddlers. They demonstrated how to sprinkle milk powder over the traditional rice cereal, rather than to take the risk of stirring it into the water that was rarely boiled in the villages. Thusandi tasted the mixture herself, which delighted her onlookers. Gifts of vitamins and milk powder were passed out with the invitation that more could be obtained by coming to the new clinic.

Within six months, the clinic had doubled its number of births. Hundreds of children received vaccinations, and thousands of pounds of milk powder had been given out. As a result, infant mortality decreased significantly in Hsipaw.

Beloved Royal Leaders

Thusandi's popularity spread and matched that of her husband, who was bringing enlightened governance to Hsipaw. When the couple then gave birth to two beautiful daughters, three years apart, the admiration for them grew even stronger. As their oldest daughter reached school age, Thusandi applied her talents to the local school situation, just as she had to the local health situation. The citizens of Hsipaw noticed the quality of their health, their lifestyle, and their children's education was increasing, and they were grateful.

The young couple's popularity continued to grow to almost magical proportions. It was not uncommon to place the wedding picture of Sao Kya Seng and Sao Thusandi beside images of the Buddha on the family altar.

People in Asia likened Sao to the beloved king of Thailand. Westerners might liken the couple's popularity to that of President Jack Kennedy and his beloved wife Jackie in the United States. Both couples led their countries into new practices during the late 1950s and early 1960s. Both couples had two children of similar ages and allowed their countrymen to share in the delights of their family life. Older citizens of both countries continue to look back on the eras of their beloved leading families as a kind of Renaissance.

And, tragically, within twenty months of each other, both women became widowed by the political assassination of their husbands.

The Dark Times

For Jackie Kennedy, the loss of her husband was immediate, shocking, and very public. The country grieved with her as she walked, veiled in black and holding the hands of her two young children, in the memorial parade that carried the casket of her beloved deceased husband. All of

America shared her grief as they watched their televisions that day, and they will never forget it.

For Thusandi, it was slow, confusing, and lonely. Sao simply did not return when he was supposed to from a parliamentary meeting in a nearby town, or the next day, or the next. The military under the command of the ever-more-arrogant General Ne Win staged a coup, arresting any leader who opposed him in philosophy or in action, and Sao had been high on this list of those he wanted to eliminate. He felt Sao's democratic ways of returning ownership of the land to his countrymen robbed the central government of income and valuable resources. Sao's thinking was too innovative to suit the authoritarian practices of the military. Sao's integrity and popularity posed too big of a threat for General Ne Win, who Thusandi later learned was under psychiatric care for a mental disorder. On March 2, 1962, Sao was taken prisoner and never heard from again. The following day, Thusandi was put under house arrest.

Rumors reached Thusandi that Sao had been arrested and was being detained in a small bamboo cage. For the next two years, she pursued every possible channel, official and informal, to gain information about Sao. To this day, neither she nor her daughters have ever received official word from the Burmese government that they abducted or killed Sao.

Thusandi carried on parenting and making official decisions as best she could under such circumstances. The strain of not knowing Sao's fate was tremendous. In the worst of times, her vision would go double and she couldn't think clearly.

Sao had told her early in their marriage if he ever disappeared, she should wait two years and then leave the country. So at the end of that time, she and the children left their beloved Hsipaw, taking the long train ride eight hundred miles to the capital Rangoon. During her months of continued semi-house arrest in that city, Thusandi embraced Theravadan Buddhism, which helped restore her calmness and clarity of thinking.

In 1964, with the help of friends and the Austrian embassy, and with only a three-hour notice, Thusdandi and the girls were secreted away from Rangoon in a plane that took off in the night. Each of them had one suitcase of belongings, all the material goods that were left from their life in the Shan States. But their hearts were filled with the memories of the blessed years of enlightenment in Hsipaw during Sao and Thusdandi's time of leadership. A cheer went up from the passengers as the plane flew out of the airspace dictated by the cruelty of General Ne Win and his military forces. And with that cheer, Thusandi once again became Inge.

Inge, Once Again

Inge and the children stayed for two years with her parents in Austria, and then moved to Colorado in the United States, where she and Sao had fallen in love. Keeping a low profile for the safety of the girls, she took a job teaching German in a high school to make ends meet. All that was left of her time as a Shan Princess were the memories, her long black hair, which she continued to wear in the traditional Shan bun, and constant nightmares of running with the girls as bullets flew past them.

Inge and Tad

During that time of teaching, Inge met Tad Sargent. Tad and Sao had much in common. In fact, Inge sometimes wondered if Sao had not sent Tad to her. Both men were excellent parents to the girls. Both men fully supported Inge in her endeavors. Inge and Tad were married at the end of 1968.

After the girls were grown and living elsewhere, Tad encouraged her to write a book about her experiences in the Shan States. This would involve Inge coming out of hiding and exposing herself to the world. In 1994, she published *Twilight Over Burma: My Life As a Shan Princess*. When the book was published, her nightmares ceased. Moreover, as well as exposing the brutality of the military under General Ne Win, her detailed accounts are known as some of the best historical information of the Shan States prior to the military coup.

During the time between her escape from Burma and the publication of her book, things had changed dramatically in Burma under the military dictatorship. The name of the country was changed from Burma to Myanmar (a word Inge refused to use). It was no longer known as the Rice Bowl of the world, but had become one of the major suppliers of opium and heroin in the world. The average annual income in 2001 was $107 per year, and most children received no education beyond the fourth grade, unless they were children of the military, in which case excellent schools and health care were part of the benefits.

During this time, Aung San Suu Kyi, whose father had been assassinated thirteen years prior to Sao's disappearance, returned from her exile in England to care for her ailing mother. As Aung San's daughter, she became a lighthouse for the unrest that was developing under the military dictator-ship. On August 8, 1988, there was an uprising that was brutally quelled, paralleling the violence of Tiananmen Square in China.

Threatened by Suu Kyi's popularity, the military placed her in house arrest. Two years later, her party won eighty percent of the vote in the elections, while the military candidates won only two percent. The military immediately declared the elections null and void and continued their brutal ruling of the country.

When I asked how two percent of the country could remain in rule when eighty percent of the country wanted otherwise, Inge's answer was quite blunt: "Because they had guns and they shot people." Three years later, in 1991, Aung San Suu Kyi received the Nobel Peace Prize in absentia for her nonviolent leadership of her people. Her son accepted the award on behalf of his mother, who was still under house arrest.

As the military continued its governance by dictatorship, homes, land, and livestock were confiscated by the military. Rape, torture, imprisonment, forced labor, slavery, and ethnic cleansing had become common practices, earning Myanmar its rank as the country highest in human rights abuses around the turn of the twenty-first century. Five to six million people were internally displaced, with families running from place to place in the jungles, with no security, and inadequate food, water, education or medical care. Countless people were murdered.

During this time, over one million Burmese escaped the brutality by fleeing to Thailand, and hundreds of thousands more fled to Bangladesh. The refugee status of the Burmese in these two countries created ripe conditions for clothing industries to set up sweatshops using their labor to make cheap clothing to sell to consumers throughout the world.

Peacemaking From Afar

It was to these refugees that Inge turned her attention from the United States. If she could not help her people up close, she would do it from afar. She described this to me as the time when she actively became a Peacemaker. By my definition, Inge's work in Burma also qualified as peacemaking. She specifically stated that she is not a "political Peacemaker" but rather is doing her work "to help people survive the oppression, survive the violence, to return home and choose their own way of life."

Inge's definition of peace is: "The absence of international conflict, national conflicts and absence of violence in the home; freedom to choose, to make daily decisions; freedom from sexism or any kind of slavery; the absence of any coercion."

She and Tad founded Burma Lifeline, an organization that collects funds in the United States and sends them to trusted relatives who disperse one hundred percent of the collected funds to provide food, water and medical care for the refugees. Inge raises the money any way she can, including giving talks to audiences of all sizes, telling them about the joys of her days as a Shan Princess, as well as about the contemporary situation in Burma. Inge writes a personal thank you note to every donor. She also participates in protests against companies such as Pepsi and Halliburton, who have continued to support the economy of the military regime. Each time she examines why she chooses to spend her time and energy in this way, she reminds herself: "I am connected to these people. I've lived with them—and lost my heart there. How can I not help them?"

Epilogue

In 2008, Burma Lifeline established the Sao Thusandi Leadership Award. It has been given annually to a young woman or man from the Shan States who is committed to the pursuit of a democratic and peaceful society in their land. This prestigious award, given at a public ceremony, includes a cash prize and great honor. It has already been bestowed on ten outstanding women and men who will carry on the work that Inge and Sao began many years ago.

Inge and Tad ran Burma Lifeline for more than eleven years and raised more than a million dollars. The two of them did most of the work of raising money and administering the funds. It was clear that neither one of them could manage the organization without the other. When Inge became eighty years old, they turned the remaining funds over to Partners Asia. Since then, Partners Asia has continued to support some of the relief groups that Burma Lifeline funded.

In 2015, the Colorado School of Mines posthumously conferred on Sao the Distinguished Achievement Medal in recognition of his outstanding professional achievements as an alumnus of the school. Inge and their two daughters received the award in Sao's name.

Every year, without fail, Inge and her daughters write letters to the Burmese government asking about the fate of their husband and father. Their letters have been met with profound silence.

Look Them in the Eye... or Not

Shahla Waliy Al Kli

• IRAQ •

Peace Work:
Village Reconstruction and Development
of Civil Society Programs

Metaphor:
For Iraq, I am just a drop in the
ocean, but a drop that has made important ripples.

I like to believe that people in the long run are going to do more to promote peace than our governments. Indeed, I think that people want peace so much that one of these days governments had better get out of the way and let them have it.

—Dwight D. Eisenhower

Meeting John Barbee

I'm not sure what possessed me, but I found myself on a sunny Sunday morning driving twelve miles to a nearby town to attend a Unitarian Universalist meeting. As I drove, I was reminded that hundreds of other Americans were attending church services dressed in camouflage with their military units in Iraq.

Beginning in college, I explored several religions; Transcendentalism, Quaker, Jewish, Baha'i, Buddhism, to name a few. But I had never attended a Muslim or a Unitarian service. What I remembered from that Unitarian morning was there were lots of friendly people, not very much ceremony, really good snacks, and a fellow named John Barbee who was the main speaker for the morning. As John stood at the front of the room, he wasn't preaching or lecturing. He was quietly yet vividly describing a situation in Iraq he had recently left. It made that war very real, not in gory military details, but in compassionate stories of what happens to citizens in war, to towns and villages, to a country's sense of hope and hopelessness.

At the end of the meeting, I went up to tell John of the research I was conducting on women Peacemakers and asked if he knew of a woman Peacemaker in Iraq. John looked at me with his kind, blue eyes for quite a while. In hindsight, I believe John was sizing me up to see if I had the necessary integrity and respect to handle the information he was about to give me.

Then he said, "Why, yes I do. Her name is Shahla Waliy."

Everything Going Against Her

Looking through one kind of lens at Shahla, she had everything going against her. She lived in Iraq, which had undergone three wars by the time she was thirty years old; she was a woman living in a country infiltrated by extreme religious terrorists, which made being a woman very dangerous; she was a Kurd, living in a country where the president had killed many Kurds with mass chemical genocide; and the president was Saddam Hussein, who had turned on his own people with a wicked revenge for an attempt to unseat him. Hussein was also seen as an international threat, which placed a devastating set of sanctions onto Iraq that nearly decimated the economic, educational, and health conditions of the citizenry. When Hussein persisted in being a threat, the superpowers moved in with a military wrath that destroyed the physical environment and killed massive numbers of innocent civilians all around Shahla. Underneath all this chaos and ashes was the tiny seed that would become Shahla's peacemaking work.

Dinner with Shahla

I knocked on the door of Shahla's Massachusetts apartment where she was living while studying at Tufts University. Even before she opened the door, the delicious aroma of the spicy stew she was cooking wafted its way into the hallway. She met me with a warmth that put me instantly at ease.

Shahla began our interview with some very specific things she wanted me to know. She showed me several pieces of jewelry. As she brought out each treasured gem, she explained that a Kurdish woman from a good family will come with much jewelry of her own, which speaks well for her in the eyes of prospective in-laws. And then it is the role of the husband-to-be to buy her more jewelry, usually of 21 karat gold or better to add to her collection. In fact, Kurdish women often refer to the amount of jewelry they have in terms of kilos.

Shahla also showed me other treasures she had brought with her from Iraq to America: a set of clear rosary beads known as a *sebha*, a picture from Dubai of her girlfriend, a box with inlaid wood from Egypt, a candle with Zoroastrian symbols on it, a leather purse made of fine Baghdad leather, which she fondly referred to as her "friend." Then she showed me an Iraqi flag and had me listen to the ringtone of her mobile phone, which was music from a popular Iraqi singer.

I began to get three impressions of Shahla through this half hour of sharing. First, I realized she came from a very good family. Second, I learned that Kurds have their own unique culture. And third, I had a strong feeling she was homesick.

Shahla is the oldest of four siblings born to her Kurdish parents. When I asked her to give three adjectives that described her mother, Shahla answered, "Very intelligent, very confident, and I don't know what the word is for bigger than kind." Describing her father she said,

"Very emotional (like me), very strong, and he sacrificed everything for my education."

For twelve years, the United Nations had placed an embargo on Iraq to curb Saddam Hussein's bellicose behavior, making it very difficult for middle and upper class families to educate their children. Many of the educated citizens left the country, and of those that remained, one in ten of them left their cities of origin where the violence was escalating and moved to other parts of Iraq.

This was the third war Shahla had lived through in her country. She was in second grade when the war with Iran commenced; she had just graduated high school when the First Gulf War broke out. And at thirty-two, she was now living through the Second Gulf War. When the war was at their door, her family, like many families, fled to a neighboring country. Ironically they returned just before the bombing began. It was then that Shahla realized that, unlike the other wars, this time her beloved Baghdad was to be left in utter ruins. The sight of it happening cast Shahla into a depression. Her family agreed she should go to her sister's home in Northern Iraq to heal her soul. While she was there, she saw an advertisement in the paper.

And that was the beginning.

From Depression to Peacemaking

The advertisement Shahla answered was placed by Counterpart International, an American non-governmental organization (NGO). At this time, there were many NGOs with billions of allocated funds that had set out to help rebuild the damage in Iraq, even as new damage was occurring. Counterpart differed from most of these organizations in one important respect: their goal was capacity building. They rebuilt the capacity of the local people to help themselves, rather than rebuilding for them. Counterpart was adamant that whatever projects they undertook would be run by locals, the projects would be identified and requested by local recipients, all labor would be by local people, and whenever possible, all materials were to come from local sources. From their experience, this had been the most successful way to jump-start a beleaguered economy.

It was also the best way they knew to both build trust among the locals, and build back the self-esteem in their leaders that oppression so often steals. The skills and trades that were reacquired while rebuilding the community infrastructure then became sustainable sources of future income for previously unemployed citizens. Counterpart also differed in that everything they did was made transparent to the local citizenry, not only what they were doing but where every dollar came from and how it was being spent.

When Shahla answered the ad, she had no previous experience in this kind of work to recommend her. She had worked for the Iraqi government as a translator and as an accountant in big fancy offices that offered elite training trips to Dubai and Jordan. She had also worked for a private company that dealt with the medical equipment allowed in through the Oil-for-Food Programme. She had worked with programs, but she had never worked directly with people who were devastated.

Going to work for an "organization" was an act of courage in itself. Under Hussein, there had been no such thing as non-governmental organizations (NGOs), or nonprofit organizations. Everything was run by the government, including the unions, whose officers were always high members of the Ba'ath Party. Hussein considered everyone that was not part of the Ba'ath Party to be spies, foreigners, and wanting to destroy his country. The concept of self-determination for a community was unheard of.

First Assignment in Erbil

Shahla's first assignment with Counterpart was a pioneer program in Erbil where she had gone to live with her sister. Her job was to go to the hospitals and schools and ask them what they needed. She then sent their wish lists to Counterpart, who gathered these goods in the United States and shipped them back to Shahla. They asked for school supplies, books, beds and mattresses for the hospitals, but never medicine, for they knew medicine was disallowed by the embargo. Shahla's job was to deliver these goods. She describes the experience as:

> *What's this type of work? We were directly working with the community, feeling the impact of the work directly on the face of the people who were receiving these supplies. For me, it was a new experience, a marvelous feeling. I never felt like this before.*

Shahla's depression quickly disappeared and after a year, she found herself applying to run another Counterpart project in the Al Anbar region in western Iraq. The first person selected for the job left. The second person turned out to be a poor fit. So Shahla was taken on temporarily until they could find someone else.

But they never needed someone else. Perhaps it was Providence. Perhaps it was Shahla's ability to learn quickly and her dedication to the same principles that were foundational to Counterpart that resulted in what she calls "the biggest opportunity of my life." And learn quickly she did. As she put it, "Believe me when I tell you that I developed within six months as much as I had developed in four years after I graduated from college."

New Assignment in Ramadi and Fallujah

The new assignment was in Ramadi and Fallujah. No longer was she in the relative safety of her ethnic Kurd relatives in Northern Iraq, nor in her familiar streets of Baghdad. She was now in the heavily Arab section of the country where the Allied military invasions were ongoing and brutal and political chaos reigned. This project carried with it much more responsibility and much more danger. Shahla described the situation as:

> *The terrorists were mainly Saudis who entered Iraq through Ramadi and Fallujah because Saddam had opened the border for them, not to be used against the Americans. He wanted to use them against us, the local people, because he was afraid that the uprising of 1991 against him would occur again. These terrorists were the Al-Qaeda branch. Its name in Iraq is* Tawheed wa Aljihad. *It was considered to be the most scary faction within all terrorists or insurgency groups. They were really scary.*

The good news about her new job was that it brought into Shahla's life a Counterpart trainer and mentor named John Barbee. John was an American male but cut from different cloth than the other camouflage-clad American soldiers known to Iraqis at that time.

John Barbee

John and his wife Nancy had been in the American Peace Corps in the 1960s. It was there they learned the idea of what needs to be done to help any area should be determined at the grassroots level, at the family level, the village level, the neighborhood level, but never by outsiders. If there was an identified need for a missing resource, such as funds or skills that needed to be learned, this was an appropriate role for foreigners, such as Americans, who were fortunate enough to have such resources to share.

John and Nancy also realized that people who have been beleaguered by war and embargoes are in a difficult position to determine their own needs. They were likely to be in need of things such as hope, self-confidence, a sense of accomplishment, and even more, basic safety and sustenance, before they could rebuild their material world. They knew it was as important to build these things as to build schools and new health clinics. An important goal was to foster improved communication among the people with whom they were working, and to help build trust between them and their leaders.

The relationship between Shahla and John in the coming months created a field of mutual trust, admiration and a mentor/mentee bond that changed Shahla's life forever. Shahla referred to John as her godfather.

Shahla became a sponge for John's tutelage. Not only did it fit with her hopes for her war-torn country, but John also helped her organize her prodigious skills in a way that overcame numerous financial, religious, gender, and cultural hurdles. The way Shahla put it was, "John empowered me to empower my fellow countrymen and women."

The Counterpart International assignment to Shahla in Ramadi was fairly straightforward: find office space, secure a staff and train them, find out from the local communities what they need, and meet those needs using local labor and materials whenever possible. Easier said than done given the cultural and wartime restrictions surrounding the project. All this was to be accomplished in four months' time.

The first thing Shahla had to do was employ her brother to be her male escort. Otherwise she would not have been allowed to set foot on the Al Anbar Province streets alone. The second thing she did was find an office space for her project that was on neutral territory, not affiliated with either the local government or with the American military. Her second hire was Ezzedeen, the doctor son of the governor. Besides being both kind and helpful, Ezzedeen's place in the community spoke well for the project. Together they then hired twenty-six more men and three women.

Co-leading Two Valuable Trainings

During March with John's backing, Shahla provided two extensive trainings for this staff, one in helping communities determine their own needs and one in conflict resolution. She also used this month to go to the local community leaders to ask them what projects they needed in their communities. Then it was *"Hallas!* Everybody get to work!"

So Much Accomplished in Four Months

By the end of the four months, beginning with nothing, Shahla and her team completed twenty-six reconstruction projects, a list which, when I thought about it, made me wonder how these communities had managed without such services before Shahla and her team appeared.

It was clear rehabilitating buildings that had been destroyed would involve replacing windows that had been blown out by artillery. In order to accomplish this, the glass factory—which had also been destroyed—had to be rebuilt. They installed drinking water networks and completed four garbage collection projects.

The team also supplied technical equipment for three health centers, rehabilitated three community gardens, and reconstructed several schools and a mosque, reviving the community's ability to meet their own basic needs for body, mind, and spirit.

When a surge of refugees arrived, her team built not ramshackle tents, but fifty-two straw bale homes for them. When news arrived at the office that the American forces had inadvertently cut off all access to food supplies for a large area of the city of Fallujah, Shahla and her team prepared and miraculously delivered six hundred paper bags of food supplies to residents, under the crosshairs of the military gunfire that never abated.

When I asked Shahla to give me a metaphor for her peacemaking work, she answered, "For Iraq, I am just a drop in the ocean, but a drop that has made important ripples." The "ripples" from her four months of directing the reconstruction projects for Counterpart International were not only important and deep, but also far reaching.

More Valuable Than Buildings

When she was done, 1,400 new jobs had been created in the governorate, quite a gift to a country with a sixty to seventy percent unemployment rate. More importantly, the people with whom she worked felt a sense of ownership in their work and pride in pulling themselves up by their bootstraps. She also left them with new skills in community self-determination and in conflict resolution. She had shown them a partnership between Iraq and America that was positive and constructive. The concept of Civil Society once again had roots in this war-torn country.

How Shahla Accomplished Her Peacemaking Tasks

As phenomenal as this accomplishment was, it was not *what* Shahla accomplished that qualified her for being a Peacemaker; it was *how* she did it. One reason Shahla succeeded where others had failed was because she purposely kept herself and her team under the radar of the American military, the insurgents, the terrorists, and Saddam Hussein's Ba'ath Party, even while she was becoming well known and trusted by the people whom she was assisting. Although the entire staff knew their donor was Counterpart International, an American-run NGO, all their project vehicles carried the name *Alnatheer*, the Arabic translation of Counterpart. In this sense, her style of working exemplified the often necessary "hidden side of peacemaking."

Shahla was mindful that the relationships that were built during the four-month period were as important as the physical projects themselves. She related to her team as their manager, not as a woman, because in the beginning it was culturally awkward for these young men to take direction from a woman. In the training period, she took her new team members to her former work site in Erbil so that the Arab young people of the Ramadi team could become acquainted with her former Kurdish team in Erbil, thus creating the first intermingling of the two groups since Hussein's 1991 ban on Arabs entering the Kurdish section of Iraq. It is remarkable that two of her Erbil staff fell in love and got married in the office during the four-month push to accomplish the work.

Perhaps the hardest relationship of all to build was that between herself and the tribal leaders. She described it:

> So, it was pretty amazing when I went to the first community meeting. Basically it was simple. It was in a tribal leader's house, and he was inviting all the local figures, people who were considered to be important people, twenty to thirty of them, and it was amazing how they were listening to a woman talking, even though I wasn't talking to them as a woman, but as a project manager.

They had so much to lose and yet so much to gain by trusting her. Her philosophy was to see things from their way of understanding and then elaborate it, explain it, and develop it to the end when she added her own message. She spoke quietly to them as a fellow Iraqi, as someone, like all of them, who had suffered under the dictatorship of Hussein, whose family members and heroes had been killed, whose children had been denied educations, whose communities had been ravaged by the sanctions and the occupation, and who had been isolated from the international communities. She invited them all—Sunni, Shia, Kurd and Christian—to start taking back their futures and rebuild their communities. She simply suggested they identify projects that were needed in their community and then give her and her team three months. If they did not like what they saw at that time, she would pack up the project and leave.

In the end, she was trusted by both her staff and the tribal leaders, and she felt the same about them. She cited the example:

> *They respected me, and protected me. I got sick there. My whole staff of twenty-five young men from conservative tribal Sunni families, took me in three cars to the hospital, and the doctor was like, "Who is this?" But they wanted me taken care of. I really started to love them. Love them in terms of respecting their family. I respected their protection. They were protecting me even against their own community, and I was the stranger. Iraqis are so passionate, whether Sunni or Kurdish or Arab or Shia. When they love you, they love you.*

When I asked what advice Shahla might give to a young person wanting to become a Peacemaker, she simply said: "Be honest." As she worked, she was very transparent about what her staff was doing and about how every penny was being spent.

She chose her first project to be one that yielded visual results, as well as demonstrating this transparency. This was especially important because so many other reconstruction projects in Iraq at that time failed to be transparent about where their money was being spent.

> *If we did the right work in the beginning, we would impress the staff with themselves. Because for the first time they witnessed the spending of the money in front of them and the procedure, how you openly select the contractor, how you pay the contractor. They didn't see the boss taking the money in between. The decision about who was going to get the contract was very open.*

> *So my first project, it was my most critical project there be-*
> *cause it was donor, it's community, it's headquarters, it's John*
> *Barbee, it's team. We started with the most primitive area to*
> *work because my idea was when you succeed, when you have*
> *something touchable ... then people are talking about us. We*
> *chose the glass factory to do first. The glass factory had its*
> *own apartment for employees. This apartment was built in*
> *the 1980s. The sewage system, the gardens, everything was,*
> *like, very disgusting, very bad. So if we should renovate this*
> *area, first, it would be a great thing for us in Ramadi. Second,*
> *we would impress our donors.*

Shahla worked very hard and was constantly out in the field, an unusual thing for a woman in Iraq at the time. Sometimes she was managing
ten projects at once. She rarely took any time off. One of her main teaching tools was role modeling. She describes the first training session in the
following way:

> *I gave the training, and John was, like, backing me up. I gave*
> *the basic lecture, and the second hour he would give more in-*
> *depth information, and I was translating. I was the trainer*
> *and being trained, all at the same time. John listened a lot*
> *and he was so careful. They would see, he's a big old man*
> *and I'm like the young woman and they saw this like father*
> *and daughter. And we were so in harmony. Without knowing*
> *it, we were really impressing people and transferring the mes-*
> *sage that an Iraqi can get in harmony with an American.*

Look Them in the Eyes ... Or Not

Shahla knew how and when to employ her soft side and her tough
side. For example, when she went to the homes of the tribal leaders, she
wore a scarf and avoided direct eye contact, as was the custom. But when
she got word the Americans troops had surrounded a section of Fallujah,
cutting the citizens off from all supplies, she and her team packed six hundred paper bags with food purchased from the local market and drove the
convoy of eleven trucks to the border of the town. She looked the American commander directly in the eye and convinced him to allow her convoy into the town. Moreover, she learned from him what streets to take

once in Fallujah to avoid heavy fire. She had to send some supplies to families via the Euphrates River, while other supplies were driven to their destination via side streets, as too many bullets were flying on the main traffic arteries.

Never Let Go of Your Goals, but Never Get Attached to How You Accomplish Them

Shahla, like other women Peacemakers, never let go of her goals, but always realized there were many ways to accomplish them. For example, $200,000 of Counterpart funds was allocated to go for a microfinance program. Shahla knew that in the Muslim culture, it is not allowed to earn interest on money that is loaned.

> *There is one part in Islamic banking called* Rabahat. *That means I take this money from you. If I lose, you have to lose with me because this is what is different. Our belief is capital cannot earn money. Always. When I make a profit, you share. When I lose, you also lose. You are not saying I am giving you one hundred dollars, and in three months I will have it back as one hundred twenty-five dollars. This is not allowed. We just don't put fixed interest rates.*

So Shahla did not collect interest on her microloans. She explained instead that the paperwork to keep track of the loans called for the work of an employee, and that employee had to be paid. The loan recipients were more than happy to pay an administrative fee to cover the salary of this person, there being a good chance that it was a person they knew. The microloans were given to trade groups of five people and were secured by verbal tribal guarantees. As no one would want to embarrass their tribe, there was a zero percent default rate. In the end, Shahla returned Counterpart's $200,000 and had covered all the administrative costs to boot.

The Dangers of Peacemaking

Although it might seem like Shahla was too busy to notice the dangers surrounding her, every day of her work was an act of bravery. At times the rate of civilian deaths where she worked was around one hundred people per day, and she was in an area that was a magnet for military firepower, suicide bombings, and increasing insurgent violence.

185

Her mother recognized the dangers. On the rare occasion when Shahla went home to visit her family in Baghdad, her mother would talk to her continuously on her cell phone the entire trip to and from her office, just to make sure she reached her destination alive. Shahla felt that everything she accomplished was due to the sacrifices and the support her family gave her. In the end, brave or not, it became too dangerous, for both Shahla and for her parents, for it was not uncommon to punish someone by kidnapping or killing their family members. At the completion of her time with Counterpart, she decided to leave the country for the time being.

When it was all over, John quietly went back to Colorado to resume his life with Nancy.

By the time I interviewed Shahla, she was in Boston at Tufts University on a Fulbright Scholarship earning a second master's degree, in the joint fields of law and diplomacy. She was safe but sorely missing her family. It was her first Ramadan away from home.

Epilogue

John Barbee passed away at his home in Glenwood Springs, Colorado on December 30, 2016 in the company of his wife, Nancy, and his family. John was seventy-five. Nancy received letters of condolence and remembrance from multitudes of people with whom they had worked throughout the world.

Shahla, in 2016, became a PhD Candidate at the Fletcher School of Law and Diplomacy/Tufts University. Given her Kurdish origin, her subject of study was Transnational Communities, Their Roles and Their Impact on the Middle East. She was examining the role Kurds played in hosting 1.5 million Syrian refugees, as well as being a beacon for democracy by providing boots on the ground in fighting ISIS forces across the Kurdish areas of Iraq, Iran, Turkey, and Syria. In 2019 she earned her PhD. in International Relations from Tufts University, receiving an award for her outstanding scholarly work in her dissertation "Decentralization and State-building in Iraq."

CHAPTER TWELVE

She Might Wait, But She Will Not Quit

Somboon Srikamdokkae

• THAILAND •

Peace Work:
Improving working conditions in factories

Metaphor:
I am a heart and a stone.

War is capitalism with the gloves off.

—Tom Stoppard

An Unusual Location for an Interview

Normally I would not have chosen a restaurant as a setting for an interview with a Peacemaker. Restaurants are full of noises that you don't want on your recording device, often drowning out the conversation. And they don't feel private. The busy Bangkok restaurant where I interviewed Somboon Srikamdokkae was chosen by a Thai woman, Karate, who had recommended Somboon to me as a Peacemaker. Karate also served as the interpreter for this interview. The two women were also accompanied by a young man, who introduced himself and then remained silent for most of the interview. As the interview proceeded, I got the feeling the public place and the young man might have been consciously chosen for Somboon's safety. After all, was I just an American woman interviewing women Peacemakers for a book? Or might I have been somehow linked to Somboon's former employer, whom she and her fellow workers were suing for negligence in the workplace?

Somboon sat across the table from me, and Karate sat to my right. At first I found myself confused about where to look when asking my question. Should I look at Somboon who answered the questions in Thai, or to Karate, who spoke the answers to me in English? Before long, it all worked itself out. I let the English float into my ears, but kept my eyes on Somboon who spoke a great deal with her eyes, her face, and her hands. And this is the story I gathered.

Growing Up Somboon

On May 10, 1976, immediately after graduating from high school, Somboon went to work for the Bangkok Weaving Factory. She remembers noticing how robot-like the workers looked. She also remembers fainting on that day. Her first task was to go to the spirit house and make a vow to be honest and hardworking and abide by the rules at her factory. Little did she know this vow would lead to a life or death choice for her. Somboon would eventually choose life ... barely.

She grew up in one of the fifty districts within Bangkok. Her mother was a farmer and her father was a soldier in one of the lower ranking positions of the military. In this time of the mid-twentieth century, Thailand was working its way up into a place of economic viability in the global economy. It had a history of producing beautiful textiles. It also had an abundance of cheap labor, as more and more people were moving from the countryside into Bangkok. Putting these two assets together, Thailand found its niche in the global economy by mass-producing textiles, primarily cotton. Somboon was one of thousands who sought to improve their lives by going to work in the textile factories.

Poor Work Environment

The workplace environments for this new industry were notably poor. Employers were more focused on their profits than the health of their employees. Two years prior to her beginning work in the Bangkok Weaving Factory, the worst industrial accident in history occurred at the Kadar Factory, also in Bangkok, where stuffed toys were made by mostly female employees to be exported to America. A fire started in the factory, which locked its employees into the building, killing 188 workers and injuring five hundred.

Somboon found herself working in the spinning and ironing rooms of the Bangkok Weaving Factory. The room where she worked was very noisy, dark, hot, and dusty with fine and gross cotton particles floating in the air. Ventilation in the room was notably poor. Every time the factory inspection officers came to check, the conditions were covered up during the time of the inspection.

Somboon was a good employee and she gained respect from her fellow workers. During this time, she met the man she would marry. He also worked at the Bangkok Weaving Factory.

After twelve years, Somboon found herself having increasing trouble breathing. The factory doctor confirmed that she was sick but did not give her a specific diagnosis or any explanation of the underlying causes of her breathing problem. The doctor did reassure her that her symptoms had nothing to do with the work place. On seven occasions, it became serious enough for Somboon to go to the hospital. Going to bed each night, she was so afraid she would not wake up the next morning.

Not the Only One with Symptoms

Somboon began to realize that other workers were also having breathing problems, as well as other symptoms such as hearing impairment, damaged eyesight, and signs of toxic chemical exposure. She made repeated requests of her employer to improve the safety of the working environment with masks, improved ventilation, and other methods. Every time her requests fell on deaf ears.

Her symptoms continued to worsen. She, like many others, was constantly irritated by dry and sore throats with phlegm as well as fevers and chronic coughing. The coughing escalated until pain was felt in her ribs and more pangs of pain occurred when inhaling. Sitting, standing, walking, or sleeping, Somboon always found her breathing uncomfortable.

She finally became ill enough to take time off from her job for five months. Somboon began to suspect her condition was related to working in the textile factory. Her employer certified that she was, indeed, sick, but adamantly denied that her condition was work-related. This meant she did not qualify for Workman's Compensation Fund monies while she was unable to do her job at the factory. She tried working odd jobs to help meet her family's financial needs. Her health improved during her time off, but began to fail again immediately once she returned to her workplace.

Byssinosis

Eventually, Somboon found her way to Dr. Oraphan Methadilokku of the Ratjavithi Bangkok Hospital. After visiting several other doctors, this was the only doctor in Bangkok who would finally provide her with a confirmed diagnosis, and provide treatment for her symptoms. Finally, in 1992, sixteen years after she began working at the Bangkok Weaving Factory, Somboon learned she had byssinosis, a disease caused by inhaling fiber dust from cotton, hemp, or flax. By this time, her husband had suffered similar symptoms for years and was given the same diagnosis. Oddly enough, their daughter also began to show the symptoms, even though she did not work at the factory. The treatment for byssinosis was a dose of thirty pills per day.

Byssinosis, sometimes known as "brown lung," is common among textile workers throughout the world. It is characterized by breathing difficulties, tightness in the chest, wheezing, and coughing. In the beginning, these symptoms often occur at the beginning of the work week. After weekend days of respite from the cotton fibers, the symptoms come on only strongly, hence the nickname of "Monday fever." Over time, the asthma-like symptoms occur strongly every day of the week. After several years of exposure to cotton dust, byssinosis causes chronic, irreversible obstructive lung disease. In Somboon's case, by the time she was diagnosed, it had destroyed forty percent of her lungs.

Byssinosis is not a new disease. It was first named in the seventeenth century. It occurs in the historical records of various developing countries that are in the process of creating a favorable gross national product by producing clothing for world markets with the use of cheap human labor. It was a common occurrence in the United States during its industrial revolution, especially in the case of child laborers working in textiles mills or factories. Today, due to labor laws and environmental regulations in the U.S., there have been only an average of eight byssinosis fatalities per year in the last decade of the twentieth century in the United States.

Treatment Options

If caught in the early stages, byssinosis can be mitigated. If left unidentified for a long period of time, the result is often fatal. In Somboon's case, the wait before she received a diagnosis and began treatment left her with only sixty percent of her lung capacity. On two occasions, she nearly lost her life. The first was when she was asked to attend the Bejing Women's Conference, but the air quality in Bejing was so poor for her limited lung capacity, two of her fellow travelers had to physically carry Somboon to a hospital during the conference. A similar life-and-death situation occurred when Somboon was asked to make a presentation of her situation at a conference in Australia.

The typical solution for byssinosis is to change the environment of the affected person, either by cleaning up the dust from the work environment, using protection to prevent the inhaling of the fibers, or by the person seeking another kind of employment. It would have been so easy to quit, to go work somewhere else away from the cotton dust that had destroyed nearly half of her capacity to breathe, but Somboon realized this situation was not just about her, it was about other workers subjected to the same conditions, some of whom were, indeed, dying. It was about employers who denied any responsibility for having unsafe workplaces. It was about a medical system that failed to identify the condition in a timely way for effective mitigation of symptoms. It was about a government system ineffective in holding its entrepreneurs accountable for providing safe workplace conditions.

So Somboon chose to take up the traces of this huge systemic problem and lean into the task of creating forward motion that would improve the safety for all employees in the garment industry. She continued to work at the Bangkok Weaving Factory.

The Classic Example of Patient, Persistent, Nonviolent Peacemaking

It is important to note that during the interview for this book, Somboon did not come across as a rabble-rousing troublemaker. Rather, in classic woman Peacemaker style, she came across as quietly determined, positive, fair-minded, bright, and infinitely patient. She never advocated violence of any sort to achieve her goals. She blended her advocacy work with raising her daughter and sharing a good marriage with her husband, as well as doing what was necessary to maintain her health. She was determined to do whatever she could, taking as long as necessary, to establish accountability of her employer and create better working environments for future workers in Thai textile factories.

When asked to give a metaphor for her work as a Peacemaker, Somboon thought for a long time. Finally she said, "I am a heart and a bird. The heart stands for justice, and the bird stands for freedom."

Back at work, she was re-elected as chairman of the workers' union. She continued to ask her employer to provide masks, ventilation systems, and other means to lower the amount of cotton dust, still with no results. In 1994, she and seven other workers formed WEPT, the Counsel of Work and Environment Related Patients' Network of Thailand. Each of these workers was suffering illnesses from their workplaces and had been denied Workman's Compensation Funds because their employers denied their illnesses were work related. Many of them she met in the waiting room of Dr. Methadilokkul.

Finally, in 1996, her employer fired her. She was just too much trouble. Soon thereafter, he fired her husband. With a twinkle in her eye, Somboon said, "He was thinking that I would go away and be quiet if he fired me. Little did he realize that it simply gave me more time to organize people."

And organize she did! Even though more people were joining WEPT all the time, she realized their numbers were too small to win a fight with the big and powerful employers.

Joining Forces

She asked permission of the WEPT members to join forces with the

Assembly of the Poor (AOP), who were organizing mass demonstrations. Such actions were very new at the time and Somboon had to convince her co-workers in WEPT of the greater potential for justice. With this permission, the byssinosis workers joined twenty-five thousand other workers in staging a ninety-nine-day demonstration in front of the Government House in Bangkok. As a result, in 1995, two hundred workers with lung afflictions qualified for receiving funds from the Workman's Compensation Fund, in spite of the employers continued efforts to block such action.

This brought some compensation for wages not paid, but it did not bring justice or lay the groundwork for other afflicted workers in the future. The process for receiving compensation was still arduous, expensive, and daunting for many ill workers.

A Historical Lawsuit

Somboon led thirty-seven of the two hundred compensated workers in pursuing justice by filing the first law suit against the owners of a textile factory ever to be filed in Bangkok. They hired lawyers who helped them file a case on May 9, 1995, asking the negligent employers for 1–2 million bahts per worker. The amount was calculated to reflect the cost of treatment (2,000–3,000 baht per month), the loss of opportunity to earn a livelihood (5,000 baht), assistance in caring for their children and their parents (3,000 baht per month), and the invaluable permanent loss of lung capacity. They waited for the court's decision.

Eight and a half years later, the court finally ruled on Somboon's lawsuit.

Her description of what it is like for this population to wait for eight years for the court ruling is detailed and heartbreaking:

> Meanwhile most workers started to suffer worse conditions. Some had to take refuge in the temples. Others had to eke out their living through hired work. Despite their frail health, they had to struggle to earn their living to support their young children and their old parents. Fearing discrimination, they had to pretend they were not ill and would not let anyone know about the ongoing court cases.

Somboon never wavered. She kept up not only her own spirits, but also those of the other plaintiffs.

And the Verdict Is…

Finally, all their waiting seemed to have paid off. They won their suit! The employers were found guilty and charged to pay the workers 60,000–200,000 baht, plus back interest at the rate of 7.5 percent per year. The workers were jubilant!

Immediately, the employers appealed the case to the Supreme Court, denying immediate compensation to the plaintiffs, whose health was continuing to worsen. The jubilant workers descended into ever-deeper despondency.

Eleven years later, the Supreme Court told the workers they had not provided enough information to the court. They were required to provide more inane information. For example, they were asked if the employer required the employees to have masks on during their work and did the employees comply with these requirements? Tears rolled down the face of the workers, many of whom could hardly stand by this time.

The aggrieved workers, now substantially more sick, had to undergo continual tormenting experiences to prove their employer's guilt. Many had been laid off. Somboon described the impact of this setback:

> *The workers began to suffer more from complications from byssinosis, including suffering from chronic cold, high blood pressure, cardiovascular diseases, diabetes, and most importantly bone diseases, all problems which have been experienced by most of us since we have been taking the medicine for a long time. The malfunctioned lungs have made us vulnerable to diseases.*

> *Apart from suffering from the physical impacts, many of us have been affected mentally. Some began to isolate themselves, getting more depressed, getting easily irritated, becoming insomniac, and being forgetful and blurred. Being unable to work, they have incurred a lot of debts. Some even thought about taking their lives, to run away from this vicious world.*

No Spare Parts for Human Bodies

Somboon looked poignantly at me across the restaurant table and summed up the disregard given by the employer for the employees by saying, "When an engine is dysfunctional and declining, we can still fix it and find the spare parts. But when our human body is getting sick or dysfunctional, then we can't find any spare parts for it."

Twelve years later after the suit was filed, on May 30 of 2007, the court ruled the workers again had won their case! The required compensation amount was half of the original award, but by this time the ill workers were so frail they simply wanted justice at any cost.

But again, their euphoria was short-lived. The employers, once again, appealed their case. Somboon had to maintain the compassion in her heart for those victims of the poor working conditions, and at the same time operate like a rock that kept steady pressure on the court system over time.

A Revised Metaphor

Her metaphor for herself had now changed to "I am a heart and a stone," reflecting her double-pronged approach. The heart still stood for justice, and the stone stood for perseverance.

By this time, several of the workers felt truly depressed and many resigned from the court case, saying they felt too helpless to continue. Somewhere during this time, the plaintiffs were notified that The Bangkok Garment Factory was filing for bankruptcy. The company asked them to settle out of court by paying each worker 100,000 baht, one-tenth of their original request, if the workers would withdraw their case. The workers voted to turn down this offer. Soon thereafter, the bankruptcy court announced that The Bangkok Garment Factory was not actually going bankrupt.

Never Give Up

Somehow, through all this, Somboon never gave up. When asked what she would tell a young man or woman who wants to become a Peacemaker, she replied, "You must love the people you are working for and you must have patience."

No kidding, I thought.

During all the arduous years of waiting, Somboon and WEPT did everything to keep up the spirits of these dispirited workers whose dignity had so often been crushed by their former employers. Somboon also kept her eye on the whole system of violations committed by the short-sighted and self-serving employers. She helped communities in other parts of Thailand that had been affected by industrial hazards and polluted environments.

In the beginning of her struggles to hold her employer accountable, Somboon was often asked, "How can small people like us win a fight with a big and powerful company?"

Her answer was, "Either we fight or we do not fight; either way we suffer, so it is better to fight."

Finally, on November 8, 2010, fifteen years and six months after the suit had been filed, only one of the thirty-seven defendants in the case against The Bangkok Weaving Factory received a quiet notice to come to court to hear the final verdict. That one person was not Somboon. Once she got word of it, Somboon and WEPT quickly circulated the news for all the defendants that were physically able to appear. By this time, they were ready for just about anything. As Somboon worded it, "They simply wanted the case to reach a final end so that they could die with their eyes closed."

The court upheld the earlier ruling. The employer was found negligent and in the wrong.

Justice Delayed is Justice Denied

The amount of compensation was reduced to a fraction of the original figure requested, but the workers were relieved the court had publicly recognized they really were suffering from work-related injuries. Their dignity had been restored. And more than that, they had set a precedent to help fellow workers realize their due rights. This time the ruling was not appealed, not overturned, and not undermined. The workers could, indeed, finally die with their eyes closed.

Did Somboon feel she and her coworkers got the justice they deserved? She used another metaphor to describe her answer to this question. "The affected workers are like fruits whose sweet and fragrant meat has been eaten up by worms, throughout this time they have to go on with their living until their last breath." Although relieved, she feels justice delayed is justice denied.

Epilogue

In the meantime, WEPT'S membership has grown to over one thousand members. It is a thriving organization that acts as a self-help network for people afflicted with occupational illnesses and as a lobbying group to draw national attention to workplace issues that have thus far been considered taboo in Thai society.

Somboon has remained the chairperson. Understanding the importance of joining forces to accomplish big tasks, WEPT, with Somboon as its leader, has increased their circle of influence to help other "small" people in Thailand harmed by the practices of large employers. WEPT was one of over one thousand signatory parties to eliminate the production and export of mercury products from Japan.

In 2011, Somboon wrote an article describing her journey with byssinosis and The Bangkok Weaving Company. In it she included a poem that reflects her philosophy:

A bunch of feeble sticks may pry a log
Small power may overcome massive power
With perseverance,
No strong power shall withstand
All the small sticks come together bravely
With the two hands of a worker,
Any force shall crumble.

CHAPTER THIRTEEN

Peace Begins in the Womb

Theo Colborn

• PAONIA COLORADO, USA •

Peace Work:
Providing accurate scientific information about
petroleum-based chemicals that undermine the
health and potential of humans and animals.

Metaphor:
David, as in David and Goliath.

It isn't enough to talk about peace.
One must believe in it.
And it isn't enough to believe in it.
One must work at it.

—Eleanor Roosevelt

A Unique Kind of Peacemaker

While the work of some women Peacemakers might look like teaching children in improvised classrooms, Theo Colborn's peacemaking work often looked like slogging through streams in fishing waders. It also looked like storming the offices of U.S. Congressmen and women, as well as cajoling scientists who rarely talked to each other to actually sit elbow-to-elbow studying each other's research findings. While some women of the "older generation" seem befuddled by computers, Internet, and the digital age, Theo, as an octogenarian, found a way to embrace it, recognizing it as one of the most valuable tools for her work. While some Peacemakers do their work with adults, Theo targeted another population: fetuses and their caretakers.

Are you concerned when you read that the Centers for Disease Control and Prevention states the incidence of autism in children born in the United States increased 120 percent between 2000 and 2014 and continues to climb each year? Have you ever found yourself asking why so many people today have diabetes when it was so rare during the time our grandparents were growing up? Why is this? You might have some theories or some good guesses as to the answers, but Theo Colborn has gathered the scientific facts about it.

Interviewing Theo

I interviewed Theo when she was eighty-three years old. It was more like taking a cram course in graduate school than an interview. She answered my interview questions and she had ever so much more to say. Theo never missed an opportunity, even with an audience of one, to spread the impassioned message she learned from her lifetime of research. When I left the interview, I knew I would never forget Theo, and I would never be able to ignore her message as long as I lived.

The conversation took place in her modest, comfortable home in Paonia, Colorado. Theo was dressed in blue jeans, a turtleneck, and a red pile vest. She lived there alone, her husband having passed away over three decades earlier and her children now adults leading lives of their own. Theo and I both live in Paonia, a unique town in western Colorado that boasts a diverse population of coal miners, ranchers, organic growers, artists, and writers. It is also the home of one of the earliest independent public radio stations, a famous environmental newspaper, *The High Country News*, as well as thirty-nine churches. It is the dancingest town I've ever known in my life. Theo is a brilliant, valued colleague in the international scientific community, as well as a beloved heroine in our local community. Somehow, she found the comfort of this small town a safe niche from which to conduct the later years of her campaign to wake up the world to the long-term dangers of living in a world full of petroleum-based chemicals.

Growing up Theo

Theo was born in New Jersey in 1927. Take your imagination back to what it was like to be a bright, incessantly curious young woman on the East Coast of the United States in the 1930s. The heroines of those times were Eleanor Roosevelt, Amelia Earhart, and Jane Addams. The Model T car was being replaced by the Model A. The Great Depression, World War II, the Korean, Vietnam, Gulf, Iraq, and Afghanistan Wars had yet to express themselves in history.

Even as a child, Theo was fascinated by water. She was raised in a family where children were to be seen, not heard. So, she listened a good deal. It was not common for a young woman to pursue higher education, although Theo describes her parents as people "who would do anything for education." Perhaps this is why she eventually acquired a bachelor's, a master's, and a doctorate degree.

While earning her bachelor's degree in pharmacy at Rutgers University, she met Harry Colborn, also studying pharmacy. She and Harry later married and had four children together. They worked at the drug store owned by his father and expanded into several other locations. But Theo became disillusioned with the field of pharmacy, as she did not like prescribing drugs with unknown side effects.

The Colborns decided to move their family to western Colorado, where they began raising sheep. Theo, ever attuned to her environment, noticed that a number of local people were suffering from poor health, possibly, she wondered, from drinking water that was downstream from coal mines. During this time, her husband passed away and, in time, her children made their own way into the world.

A Whole New Direction in Midlife

In 1978, at the age of fifty-one, Theo decided to enroll in a master's degree program at Western State College in Gunnison, Colorado to study fresh water ecology. Her field research at the nearby Rocky Mountain Biological Laboratory proved that an aquatic insect, the mayfly, could be used to determine heavy metal pollution from industrial development near fresh waterways. As she waded in the streams taking samples of the water and the fauna, Theo realized the wildlife that ate and drank from these waterways would also have high levels of cadmium and molybdenum in their systems. Equally important, Theo proved the level of heavy metals in the aquatic insects was a more accurate measure of these metals than the standard testing measures of the toxicologists of the time. This is when Theo began to question the field of toxicology.

She went on to the University of Wisconsin to obtain a doctorate with her fresh water research, but this time, Theo decided to study several different disciplines simultaneously. Her major was in zoology and her minors were in epidemiology, toxicology, and water chemistry. This allowed her to look at problems through a variety of lenses. Observing a situation from a whole-systems perspective became a guiding theme in Theo's life. The findings in her research with stoneflies from the Wisconsin waterways scientifically confirmed that toxins accumulated in the bodies of those who came in direct contact with the contaminated water. She also proved the same was true of those who consumed animals contaminated with these toxins. At this point, Theo might have gone down the route of linking this knowledge to the incidence of cancer. But she took a different path in the road.

Washington, D.C.

In 1985, at the age of fifty-eight, Theo sought out a U.S. Congressional Fellowship with the Office of Technology Assessment (OTA), and subsequently was hired by the Conservation Foundation, a think tank in Washington, D.C. It was here she learned the ins and outs of how regulation and legislation worked in the U.S capital. She began working there as Ronald Reagan became president. This was two years before many of the laws and regulatory agencies created during the Nixon administration began to be reversed by the Reagan administration.

She found an apartment that was on the fourth floor of an old nunnery that had also served as a whorehouse in one of its eras. It was funky and tiny, but it had high ceilings, parquet floors, and a closet made into a kitchen. She slept on a futon on the floor. Out her window, she looked at the dome of the United States capitol. She often invited a friend to go to concerts or the museums. Since she was a long-time birder, she joined the Audubon Society and often went on birding expeditions. Theo loved living in Washington, D.C.

Besides working at OTA, she also received grants to do additional research. Her target this time was the Great Lakes drainage basin. Notably, effects were occurring in the parents and the offspring of wildlife that lived in and around the Great Lakes. Problems included reproductive failure, birth deformities and altered metabolism, behavior and hormone function. Both the Canadian and the American governments were her funders.

It was during this time Theo took a very important turn in her career that would later become her trademark. She combined doing her own research as a first order researcher along with being a second order researcher, where she extensively reviewed the findings of other scientists. She and her team reviewed somewhere between two thousand scientific papers and five hundred government documents from research projects taking place in and around the Great Lakes ecosystem. They found, among other things, that many wildlife populations were disappearing in this area.

Theo and her team published a book entitled *Great Lakes: Great Legacy?* The emphasis was on the question mark in the title, because the book identified multiple environmental problems, including the deposits of chemicals like DDT in sixteen different species of wildlife. Their research verified the profound impact on several generations of wildlife from man-made actions and decisions. They also documented the deterioration of the water quality in eighty thousand small lakes due to acid rain and the loss of wetland ecosystems. To further magnify the reality of the situation, they identified the costs of solving these problems.

Being Awake When the Opportunity Floats By

One night when she had nothing else to do in Washington, Theo went to a talk given by a man named J. Peterson Myers. He was the Director of Research for the National Audubon Society in New York. He knew all the migratory bird populations and was famous for his photos of them. In his talk, he spoke of the Sanderling, a small darting shore bird, and how it had disappeared. By the end of the talk, Theo felt she had some information from her research that might be useful in explaining the disappearance of the Sanderling, but there were so many people wanting to talk to him, she finally went home. But she didn't give up.

She decided she would call him. As she put it, "It takes a lot of nerve for me to cold call someone. I'm not like that. But I called him, and got him directly." She told him she was at his talk and there was something about the disappearance of the Sanderling that he should be aware of. She started talking about her findings in the Great Lakes. Before she got a third of the way through, he said, "Wait a minute! You hop a plane tomorrow. I'll cover your expenses. Get up here!"

Two days later, she found herself in New York, taking a shuttle to his office, an easier transit than she had feared. She talked to Pete and his staff informally in a crowded office. Before she left, he said, "Would you like to come work here?"

"Oh, God," Theo thought. "Do I have to live in New York City?"

But she chose to be awake at the moment Providence threw this offer in her pathway. At age sixty-four, she took a new job that would open incredible doors for her. The day before she was due to show up for work, she drove to her sister's house in Point Pleasant, New Jersey. The next morning, she took the train into New York. She remembers it being "one of the coldest days of the year. Oh my God, it was cold. I was dressed like Nanook of the North and I was carrying all this stuff I had brought to show him." She arrived just as the office Christmas party was underway.

Pete met her at the door and whisked her into his office. "Never mind the party," he said. "Have you ever heard of the W. Alton Jones Foundation?" When Theo told him no, he blurted out that he had just accepted the directorship of that foundation and that he wanted her to be part of his acceptance package. His job came with eighty million dollars a year that he could dole out in research funds. He wanted Theo to take a Chair there for three years and do nothing but continue her research! Here was an offer she could not turn down.

The Wingspread Conference

In 1990, Theo's research had come to the attention of a man from the Wingspread Conference Center in Racine, Wisconsin. He asked Theo what she was going to do with her impressive findings. Theo told him what she had discovered and what she really wanted to do was bring scientists together from all different disciplines who were doing related research. "I want to get them all together in a place where they can't have a telephone, and keep them locked up for a couple of days so they can ponder what I have seen, what I have discovered, no interruptions."

"That's just what we can offer at Wingspread—a conference venue where we can put them all together," he said. "Write me a proposal."

With this offer, Theo was able to play an instrumental role in making her dreams come true of cross communication between high-level scientific researchers in her field.

This woman who did not like making cold calls started making lots of them to scientists in numerous different disciplines. Most of them she had to argue with to convince them to come to such a multidisciplinary kind of meeting. They would rather talk to the researchers in their own field. Theo simply said, "It's very important. Please come."

Her strongest playing card was to get Howard Bern from UC Berkeley to come to the conference. Bern had long been studying the impact of years of American and Japanese doctors prescribing the drug DES (diethylstilbestrol) to prevent miscarriage in pregnant women. Bern's reputation was a draw for many other scientists.

All in all, Theo brought together twenty-one scientists from the fields of anthropology, ecology, comparative endocrinology, histopathology, immunology, medicine, law, psychiatry, psychoneuroendocrinology, reproductive physiology, wildlife management, tumor biology, and zoology. Theo had carefully invited those experts in each field that she deemed to have the most critical research findings as well as those scientists who were held in high esteem by other scientists. There were seventeen disciplines represented, herself included, all doing some kind of research on the effects of what this team of scientists would eventually label as "endocrine disruption."

Most of the scientists that attended were individually focused on studying the effects of petroleum-based chemicals in their specific species. But not until Theo locked them together for three days and two nights in a room at the Wingspread Conference Center and made them listen to and look at slides of each other's findings did the bigger picture rise up before their eyes. The cross-fertilization of their research took on a life of its own.

Theo describes what happened as such:

> *The fish biologist would show a slide from a fish that had been exposed to DES from the industrial effluents in the Great Lakes region. And the human biologists yelled out, "That's not a slide of a fish! Where did you get that? That*

looks just like our work with Japanese scientists showing cancer in human beings. Why are you using a human slide?"
And the fish biologist retorted, "No, it's not a human slide.
These are Great Lakes fish!"

A Turning Point for Scientists and for Science

Light bulbs started going off at ever increasing rates. Excited cross conversations went on through both of the next two days and nights. This conference was truly a turning point for both the scientists and for science. Today it is simply referred to as "The Wingspread Meeting," and is recognized as the beginning of the field of endocrine disruption. By the end of the meeting, they felt compelled to issue a statement to members of the U.S. government to make them aware and urge them to take action. They wrote a consensus proclamation before they disbanded, carefully selecting each word. In essence it stated:

> *Many compounds introduced into the environment by human activity are capable of disrupting the endocrine system of animals, including fish, wildlife, and humans. The consequences of such disruption can be profound because of the crucial role hormones play in controlling development.*

These scientists mandated Theo write a book about their discovery, to which each of them would submit a paper. The result was a textbook entitled *Chemically Induced Alterations in Sexual and Functional Development: The Wildlife/Human Connection*. By this time, the Republicans and corporate lobby forces that were in power in Washington were beginning to catch on to Theo and her work. And they did not like it. The Chemical Manufacturers Association did what they could to thwart the publication of the book, but Theo found an alternative way to get it published.

She felt strongly that the public should know about this threat to their mental and physical development, so she wrote a popular version of the Wingspread findings, in collaboration with Dianne Dumanoski and John Peterson (Pete) Myers. The title of the book is *Our Stolen Future* with the subtitle *Are We Threatening our Fertility, Intelligence, and Survival? A Scientific Detective Story*. It makes for both fascinating and frightening reading. It quickly became known as the contemporary counterpart to Rachel Carson's famous book, *Silent Spring*.

Theo told me the format of *Our Stolen Future* reads like a detective story with her as the investigator of a crime. The list of victims is enough to make one cry: eighty percent of Florida's bald eagle population became sterile; the Great Lakes mink population slowly failing to be able to reproduce; sixty percent of the male population of alligators at Lake Apopka in Florida found with abnormally tiny, dysfunctional penises; the death of 18,000 harbor seals in the North Sea of Europe; the death of 1,100 striped dolphins in the Mediterranean Sea; and in the human species, between 1938 and 1990, a fifty percent drop in sperm count in human males across several continents, accompanied by a rise in testicular cancer.

The closing paragraphs of *Our Stolen Future* implored an enlarged global community from scientists to chemical companies, government regulators to environmental groups, parents to philosophers to give serious consideration to their findings. They called not for finding substitutes to do the work of the dangerous petrochemical-based substances upon which we had become so dependent, but rather for redefining the problems differently and redesigning new solutions accordingly. This would take courage, they warned, but since the stakes were so high, we owed it to our children.

Theo stormed the halls of Congress, the truth of her findings making her unafraid in the face of the Republican and corporate forces that were building against her. The result was that within five years of publication of the Wingspread consensus statement, miraculously, laws were being drafted to detect and regulate endocrine disrupting chemicals in the United States. It is no surprise that Theo's favorite quote is from Goethe, who wrote, "Whatever you can do, or dream you can, begin it. Boldness has genius, power, and magic in it."

Exactly What Is Endocrine Disruption?

At this point in the interview, I asked Theo to explain what, exactly, "endocrine disruption" was. She started by giving me a brief history lesson.

In the '30s and the '40s we had toxins that we always knew were dangerous going up the smokestacks of our coal-fired power plants. Then we got the cracking of the crude oil that provided fuel for our war efforts. Right after World War II, we began producing all sorts of products from natural gas and crude oil, including the plastics and the resins. Fifty percent of the natural gas that is produced today does not provide energy. It goes into plastics, pesticides, glass, and fabrics. It even coats the paper receipts we get from using our credit cards. In the '70s we began to see the increases in all of these population disorders that were formerly rare.

"Glass?" I asked incredulously.

"Glass," she replied. "Remember when glass used to break in big shards? Today much of our glass is shatter-proof. And the shatter proof material is the resin in it; that toxic resin is full of bisphenol."

"Fabric?" I said.

"Clothing." Theo replied, catching me looking at the bright red pile vest she was wearing. "I know. I wear it all the time. What can we do?" she said. "I'm always cold. It keeps me warm."

Credit card receipts felt like the last straw in my ignorance. Apparently the shiny paper receipts that you can mark with your fingernail are coated with BPA, a synthetic estrogen. The chemical easily migrates from the paper onto people's hands and their groceries and wallets, and gets into their bodies through the skin and mouth … I wondered how many hundreds of these flimsy little papers I had held in my fingers in my lifetime.

The original research done by toxicologists told us what levels of these petroleum-derived chemicals were lethal for an adult human. But none of these early studies considered the effects of these chemicals on fetuses. We now know that doses of thousands of times lower than what is toxic to an adult can substantially alter the physical and mental development of a fetus if it occurs in the mother's womb or through her milk.

The endocrine system is an exquisitely balanced master signaling system, which drives the timely production and delivery of hormones that regulate such functions as body growth, response to stress, sexual development, production and utilization of insulin, and rate of metabolism, as well as intelligence and behavior. Theo went on to explain:

Think of a lock and key situation. Each molecule of a hormone such as estrogen for example, is a key. This hormone travels to a specific site in the body such as the uterus, which has cells that are the perfect molecular shape, or the lock, to receive this estrogen molecule. Under normal circumstances, the natural key fits into the natural lock at just the right timing. However,

209

when we introduce man-made substances that can mimic these hormones, they fill or block the keyholes with synthetic molecules. This interrupts the cascade of events that turn on and off developmental growth, resulting in any number of distorted outcomes. As we do more research we realize there are many more ways the endocrine system can become undermined, and more and more widely used chemicals have been shown to be endocrine disruptors.

We Are Losing Our Humanity

The research has shown that the disruption happens not only in the physical development of humans, but also in the mental development. One of the earliest researched areas is how exposure to the petroleum-based PCBs undermine intelligence. One especially vulnerable part of the developing brain is the hippocampus, where humans send and receive emotions such as love, compassion, and empathy. Also affected is the function of the brain to do consequential thinking, where we reflect on an action before taking it.

"I feel," Theo said, "we are producing fewer and fewer what I call leaders in our society today, people who have compassion and who think beyond themselves." Theo's voice lowered as she spoke these last sentences, signaling me that it was an area of deep disquiet for her. "That's the big concern. We have done this without realizing. We are losing our humanity."

I Look At All These Beautiful Babies Born...

One of the most troubling messages from Theo's research is that it takes an infinitesimally low concentration of one of these fossil fuel based chemicals getting into the womb environment to alter critical things for both current and future generations; infinitesimally low as in one drop of water in twenty swimming pools of water. Some of the damage done is discovered at birth, some shows up later in the life development of the child, and some shows up in the offspring of the grown-up child, and in the offspring of the offspring.

"In animals," Theo told me, "it takes one or two generations to create major population disruption, such as the inability to reproduce or the disappearance of a species. In humans, it continues for some generations. We are currently in our fourth generation of living with petroleum-based chemicals. I look at all these beautiful babies born, and I worry so about what's going to happen in third grade, fourth grade, fifth grade. Where and when are these characteristics going to show up?"

Painful Consequences of Her Own Research

Although one might mistake Theo for a little old lady in tennis shoes, she has the energy of a dynamo. She has worked every day of the week nearly all her life, and she also meditates every day. She does not hesitate to identify problem areas, and will speak openly and honestly with others. She has definitely made things happen. Many find her sense of humor delightfully mischievous. What was not so obvious was Theo was living with a very painful consequence of her own research.

On a trip home to Paonia from Washington D.C. in 2002, her two daughters accompanied Theo to a doctor's appointment to find out why it was getting harder and harder for her to get around. Before the neurosurgeon showed the women the results of her X-rays and MRI, he asked Theo, who was seventy-five years old at the time, what she still wanted to do in her life.

"Well," she said, launching into the dreams for her future work, "I want to get some legislation passed. And I would like to see an international cooperative research effort established where corporations around the world would all put money in a pot for totally conflict-interest-free research, with which we would tackle this endocrine disruption problem, similar to the way we did the atom bomb. We need another Manhattan Project."

"Let's look at your pictures," the doctor said. When the three women saw the pictures of Theo's skeleton, her veterinarian daughter exclaimed, "Oh my God, Mother. When I have an animal whose skeleton looks like that, I put him down!" Theo's bones were slowly crumbling. The cadmium that she had found in the bodies of the mayflies and the aquatic life while she was wading in the fresh water streams in Gunnison, Colorado, had deposited itself in Theo's skeleton and was now eating away at her own bones.

"Truly, you can't go back to Washington to work," the doctor told her. "You are going to have difficulty walking and getting around on the streets. I just don't see you going back."

Theo's daughters looked cautiously at her, wondering if she might cry. Instead she threw up her hands in a gesture of relief, and said to the doctor, "Thank you! Will you write me a letter?"

Relocating But Never Missing a Beat

Theo literally did not go back to work one more day at her office in Washington. Her staff packed up ten thousand pounds of research papers and files and shipped them to Paonia where Theo, at the age of seventy-six, set up a new office one block from her home. Prior to her trip to the doctor, she had been awarded half a million dollars for research from Japan, which she added to her other grant money, so there was hardly a blip in her forward motion of reviewing the research on endocrine disrupting petrochemicals. She established the nonprofit organization The Endocrine Disruption Exchange, more commonly called TEDX.

Theo began to gather a new staff in Paonia. Some started out as volunteers because they believed so much in the value of what she was doing. Many women Peacemakers I have interviewed understand their work will not be completed in their lifetime, but Theo was aging just as the urgency of her findings needed a platform, a rooftop from which her message could be shouted out to the world of legislators, health workers, activists, scientists and parents … before it was too late. She couldn't afford to let her age rob the world of her message.

Serendipitous Coming Together

In an intuitive moment, Theo agreed to interview a woman who lived in Paonia. Her name was Carol Kwiatkowski. She, her husband and two small children had moved to Paonia after living in the hinterlands of the Colorado mountains. Carol had read Theo's book *Our Stolen Future* while nursing her youngest child, but it's impact had gotten swallowed up by the pressing job of raising children. And now Carol was looking for a job to balance out her parenting. She knew little about the field of environmental health, but the three-hour interview with Theo turned out to be serendipitous and pivotal for both women. Carol was hired on a probationary basis for ten dollars an hour for sixteen hours a week. It was, as Carol puts it, "not much more pay than working at the local grocery store, but definitely more interesting."

The intuitive part of offering Carol a job was that Carol's background was in statistics, and her PhD was in cognitive psychology. Not only was she someone who could make sense of the data as well as communicate the research to multiple audiences, she was also just gutsy enough to push Theo to continually clarify technical details.

Carol described one staff meeting as:

I was yelling, "I don't get it!" to Theo who spun on her heel and glared at me under knitted brow. She would have grabbed my shoulders and shaken me, but at eighty-two years old and only 110 pounds, she didn't take those kinds of risks. "It's two benzene rings!" Theo shouted back, her laser-keen eyes boring holes right through me. Like a defiant teenager, I stomped my foot and threw my hands up in the air. "That doesn't explain anything to me!" There was a missing link in Theo's story and since my job was to translate the research findings to the public, I aimed to get Theo to clarify it.

By the time Theo held her interview with me three years later, Carol had moved up to the position of Executive Director, and Theo described her as "fantastic and brilliant, someone who loves her job and what she is doing; she can read the health journals and she understands the messages." The relationship between Theo and Carol was the best kind of symbiosis: Theo shaped Carol's future by giving her a unique career, and Carol gave Theo the gift of knowing her legacy work would continue on in the best possible hands.

Accompanied into the Digital Age

Carol took over management of the office and staff, hiring highly qualified scientists and support staff. She accompanied Theo into the digital age, developing a website to electronically present Theo's information to the world. The TEDX website, which stands for The Endocrine Disruption Exchange (not to be confused with TEDx Talks), is one of the most informative and utilized scientific websites on endocrine disruption. It contains a wealth of information, including an interactive chart entitled Critical Windows of Development, which uses animal studies to show the impact certain petrochemicals could have on development of a human fetus at different weeks of a pregnancy. On this page, the reader finds links to citations for hundreds of peer-reviewed research articles that form the scientific foundations of the information.

The website also contains a wealth of other information about endocrine disruption, petrochemicals, oil and gas development, advice for living in a world full of chemicals, and about Theo herself. On this website, TEDX hosts public teleconference calls with endocrine disruption specialists.

The Septuagenarian Launches a Fourth Career

It seems Providence may have had a hand in getting Theo back home to Paonia. In 2012, the oil and gas industry announced their plans to drill multiple gas wells on thirty thousand acres of public lands in the North Fork Valley that surrounds Paonia. They proposed drilling locations that were adjacent to schools, in reservoirs that irrigated the organic farms, and in creeks that provided the drinking water for the local towns. They declared they were going to use hydraulic fracturing, known as "fracking," to extract the raw material. Little did they know this industry had provided Theo with her fourth career as a septuagenarian, which was to stand up to the fracking industry with her scientifically based ardor at its well-honed best.

The TEDX team had been gathering data on every aspect of the fracking process since 2004. How did it affect the environment? How did it impact the water quantity and quality of the area? What kind of air pollution was created by the fracking? How did the industry protect their employees from negative health consequences? What would be the social, economic and structural impact on the community of multiple massive trucks on the roads every day? What federal legislation and regulations had the oil and gas interests eliminated so they could economically and efficiently proceed with the drilling and the fracking? And of course, most dear to her heart, what kind of endocrine disrupting chemicals were used in the fracking procedures?

The oil and gas industry said the chemicals they used were proprietary, and they could not, therefore, reveal their contents. By using lawful yet very creative means of gathering of information, Theo and the TEDX team, working with many local volunteers, identified over six hundred chemicals used in the fracking process, over a third of which were identified as endocrine disruptors. TEDX obtained funding from the U.S. Environmental Protection Agency to make a forty-five-minute long video entitled "What You Need to Know About Natural Gas Production," which explains the impact of gas development in language that is calmly delivered and understandable to everyone from scientists to school children. Copies of the DVD are distributed for free to anyone who is facing a future with fracking, both in the United States and abroad.

As Theo's message now reached more and more people she found herself less and less popular with the giants in industry. I asked her if she ever felt unsafe.

"Oh, pfff," she replied. "We had to quit worrying about that a long time ago." When I asked if her information system was safe, she looked me directly in the eye and said, "You can't imagine how many backup systems one can have."

David and Goliath

My metaphor for Theo as a Peacemaker is a modern rendition of David and Goliath. Goliath is a faceless, multimillion-dollar corporation that knowingly produces products and by-products that disrupt our endocrine systems. David is Theo, a tiny woman pointing her finger and glaring at the corporation. Only Theo is taller than the corporation because she is standing on a huge pile of scientific papers. In her hand is a slingshot that is loaded not with a rock, but with the TEDX database.

When I asked Theo what kind of compensation she got for her work, she answered the privilege of doing the work was her primary and enduring reward. I asked if she had a message for young Peacemakers. Without a moment's hesitation she declared,

> I would tell them to get a degree in endocrinology. We know more about the moon than we do what goes on in the womb. We need chemists, we need biologists, we need endocrinologists, we need people who can get into that womb environment and understand what goes on there. We need as much focus on inner-space research as we are putting into outer space research.

You might ask how does Theo's work constitute peacemaking? Remember that peacemaking is about narrowing the gap between oppressors and oppressed. In this situation, the oppressors are those that are putting petroleum-based products into our environments and bodies, in the form of, for example, construction materials that surround us in our homes, or chemicals sprayed on the food we eat, or the waste ponds of fracking sludge. It is one thing if the "oppressor" is doing this naively. But when the evidence of the danger of their actions becomes scientifically proven, and yet they continue to do so, then their actions clearly constitute oppression. It is, in my opinion, no longer an uneducated mistake, but an intention driven by greed, entitlement, and misuse of power. And when the oppressor turns to tactics of secrecy or lobbying to eliminate the laws

215

that control their processes, or shutting down the regulatory agencies that are the watchdogs of their actions, it becomes a deadly form of bullying.

And who are the oppressors in this situation? The most obvious answer is the corporations that are continuing to put petroleum-based products into our environment. And it is the same corporations that are dismantling any regulatory hurdles that get in their way, and that lobby for the closing of the labs that are researching the effects of their chemicals on the endocrine system and human development. It seems Theo's concerns about the lack of empathy, consequential thinking, and intelligence in today's leaders is, indeed, a compelling wake-up call.

The less obvious answer is the oppressors are the consumers that continue to make it lucrative for these corporations to realize profits by consuming their petroleum products. These consumers have our faces on them. Yours and mine. We do this knowingly by filling the gas tank of our car, or heating our house with gas or coal-derived electricity. And, we also do this in our choices of how to clothe, feed, and house ourselves, and how to keep our children healthy. Yet Theo has shown us that many of our choices to keep ourselves healthy are actually damaging not only ourselves, but our fetuses, and the fetuses of our fetuses. In this, we have become both the oppressor and the oppressed.

Interviewing Theo about her work and her findings changed my life forever. It is hard to go back to sleep or feign ignorance about life choices after spending three hours interviewing her. I rarely make choices these days without considering endocrine disrupting consequences. Of all the many words Theo shared with me, the five words I will never forget are: "Peace begins in the womb."

Epilogue

On December 14, 2014, at the age of eighty-seven, Theo died peacefully, surrounded by her family. It was as if a mighty oak had fallen in the forest of contemporary scientific research.

Carol invited all tributes to Theo to be submitted on the TEDX website. In doing so, it was almost as if Carol had created a virtual Wingspread Conference with the focus being: "How Theo Colborn made a difference in our lives." The diversity of the contributors speaks to the vastness of Theo's influence. Besides coworkers in the scientific realm throughout the world, comments came from European Union parliamentarians, environmentally sensitive people, fund grantors and fund raisers, students to whom Theo had given graduation speeches, activists, film makers, numerous non-governmental organizations, radio commentators, the Escher Fund for Autism, Greenpeace, The Environmental Working Group, academics, the National Birth Defect Registry, farmworkers, shrimpers, and childhood friends.

There were two groups whose comments could not be found paying tribute to Theo. There was a loud absence of comments from corporate entities engaged in extracting petroleum products and injecting them into our daily lives. And there was an unspoken absence of messages from those yet to be born, who would have to wait to speak their gratitude, until they grew up to be the third and fourth graders about whom Theo was so concerned.

In the four years prior to her passing, Theo developed many videos and webinars about the hazards of oil and gas development. They have become part of the vast information available at endocrinedisruption.org, which is updated regularly.

One of her last messages was a letter she wrote directly to First Lady and President Obama in which she identified the imminence of the danger from the endocrine disrupting petrochemicals for today's generation of children. She shared her vision for the formation of a council of scientists, including endocrinologists, who fully understood the environment of the womb and the far reaching negative consequences that even minute amounts of these chemicals posed. She urged that taking actions in this arena was even a higher priority than climate change. When she returned home, she said to Carol, "I've said my piece, it's up to the rest of you now."

Theo's legacy to Her Community

The citizenry of the North Fork Valley in western Colorado, armed with Theo and Carol's information and inspiration, have twice defeated the oil and gas industry's attempts to drill in their valley. Similarly, fracking has been banned in the state of New York, and in the entire country of France, to mention only two locations of many.

In the meantime, Carol has modernized TEDX into a virtual organization and opened an office in North Carolina's Research Triangle Park. Here TEDX is surrounded by three research universities and roughly one hundred organizations and laboratories that feed into and make use of TEDX's repository of information.

Theo must be smiling to know prestigious professional organizations such as the Endocrine Society, the American College of Obstetricians and Gynecologists, the American Society for Reproductive Medicine, and Federation of Gynecology and Obstetrics are now calling for preventative measures to avoid exposure to endocrine disrupting chemicals.

Together, Theo and now Carol have shifted the concept of endocrine disruption from a hidden concept that did not even have a place in our lexicon twenty-five years ago, to a cadre of awakened scientists, legislators, practitioners, parents, and consumers. Using today's modern technology, they have narrowed the gap between ignorance and informed action to protect the future of humans, animals, and our environment. It is a superb example of modern peacemaking.

CHAPTER FOURTEEN

I am Someone!

Yvonne de Mello
And Isabel Löfgren

• RIO DE JANEIRO, BRAZIL •

Peace Work:
Building self-esteem and
educational skills in street children

Metaphor:
I make a white revolution by educating the masses
so they have the tools to fight the inequality.

*It's time that we acknowledge
the wisdom women have acquired
by managing the chaos of daily life.
Women are realists,
the glue that holds society together.
They bring a reverence to life that's instinctual,
not just intellectual.*

—Teresa Heinz Kerry

Fortuitous Contact

One day when I opened my mail, I found my friend Marcia had sent me a clipping of an article she tore from the United Airlines' *Hemisphere Magazine* she had been reading on a recent flight. The attached note said, "This sounds like a Peacemaker to me." It was a brief article about Yvonne de Mello and her work with shantytown and street children of Rio de Janeiro, Brazil. At the end of the article was Yvonne's telephone number.

By this time, I had become accustomed to making cold calls to women Peacemakers all over the world. As I made the call to Yvonne, she answered the phone herself. In the ensuing twenty minutes, it became clear not only that she was a Peacemaker, but also a woman who hundreds of children would sorely miss if she were not working with them. Her daughter, Isabel, was graduating from a North American college in four months and she would be coming to New York for the ceremonies. We agreed to do an interview at that time. The added benefit of this arrangement was Isabel also joined us, adding an enriched generational flavor to the interview.

The interview took place in Isabel's New York City sunny apartment where she had lived while attending undergraduate school. Isabel sat shoulder to shoulder with her mother, whom she called Vonny. At times Isabel remained quiet while Yvonne described her work and her philosophy. Sometimes Isabel added to what Yvonne had to say, and still other times she spoke insightfully about herself. There was an easy flow between them as they answered my questions. Isabel knew her mother well, possibly better than Yvonne knew herself.

Yvonne is a no-nonsense, action-oriented and uniquely fearless woman. Isabel describes her mother as beautiful and intellectual as well as having large doses of both intuition and pragmatism. My own impression of Yvonne as we interviewed can be described in unlikely pairs of adjectives: huge heart in a small body; upper class but with little money; lonely yet surrounded by hundreds who love her; lives in an upscale neighborhood yet surrounds herself by poverty and crime on a daily basis, warm-hearted yet non-sentimental; both right brain and left brain firing full bore all the time. How, you might ask, can one woman embody so many enigmatic adjectives?

Life in Rio de Janeiro

Yvonne grew up in Rio de Janeiro, when Brazil was more often under authoritarian governments than democratic ones. Independent thinking and actions taken by individual citizens was a rare commodity during those times. She described Rio as a society that was stratified into classes: upper classes, middle class, lower class, and poverty, with big gaps between these classes.

At the time of our interview, only two percent of the Rio de Janeiro population earned more than $2,000 per month, but that two percent had substantial amounts of wealth. She described Rio as being divided into neighborhoods for each of these classes, with the poverty class comprising the largest neighborhoods that literally spilled into the streets. Yvonne is practical enough to know there will always be classes, but the big gaps between these classes results in misery for some. This is what Yvonne does not like. "It's one thing to be poor; it's another to be miserable," she told me.

When asked to describe her definition of peace, Yvonne said without hesitation, "Peace for me means equality. A balanced society. Justice among the classes in a society. Not too big gaps, because that's when you have the conflicts."

The poverty class children are divided into two categories: the shantytown, or *favela* children, and the street children. Yvonne filled me in on the difference between street kids and shantytown kids.

> *In the shanty towns, they are poor, but they live with their families in make-shift dwellings. The street kids, they have left their families. They leave their families because it is unbearable to live at home. When they are in the streets, they are, let us say, free. They start to put themselves into gangs. Often the only way they show they exist is by violence. That's their way of saying "Yeah, I'm here. I can't be an empowered citizen, but I can make a mess in your society." And they really can make a mess!*

Imposed on top of these stratified economic classes is the drug scene in Rio. Rio has a full-blown network of drug lords, drug dealers, and rampant users of heroine, marijuana, and cocaine. These poverty ghettos are controlled by the drug dealers. Yvonne describes them as a "pile of bandits." And the government does not make a showing there, so they make their own laws. There is a national constitution, but nobody knows about the constitution, so nobody cares about it or obeys it. Consequently, all of the classes live in their own kind of segregated ghettos and they all have their own laws. She told me:

> With the drug lords, it becomes submission of the masses. The drug lords live in the wealthy part of the city, but the drug dealers have taken over all the poor communities. It's like the Middle Ages. You have to do what they tell you because they have guns on their hips. It is ghettos ruled by gun barrels. And the people in the shanty towns are in a state of submission. Sometimes the government is afraid of coming in, so there are open conflicts between the drug dealers and the police every single day. So the people in the shanty towns submit. They don't know how to fight all that. And that's where I go in.

Yvonne's metaphor for herself as a Peacemaker is a White Revolution. "That means a revolution by information. That means that I inform the masses and give them the tools to fight against oppression themselves."

When I asked why they let her into the ghettos, Yvonne replied, "I don't know. Because I'm just like that. I think there may have been a reincarnation from another life when I was very poor and lived in such a place, because I am very at ease there. I am never afraid."

Not so for her daughter Isabel. When I asked if the work is dangerous, Isabel interjected, "Very dangerous! There's always shooting," raising her eyebrows to emphasize her point. "When I started going to work in the streets with my mother at age twelve, the first thing I learned was to duck and pray."

Yvonne works with a specific group of street children. She also works with children in two shanty towns, one of which overflows with twelve thousand people. Many of these children have never known their fathers, some have been raped and/or beaten at very young ages. I asked if she feels like she becomes a surrogate parent for some of the children. She was quite clear with her answer.

No, because I don't want to be a parent. I want to be more than that. If you are like a mother, you get sentimental. If you are sentimental, they are going to think that you are weak. So you have to be loving but not sentimental, because you see people getting killed every day. When I see a kid getting killed, I can't be sentimental because this one is gone. They respect me because I am strong. I can deal with situations every day. I see so many kids killed in front of me. I realize I couldn't save that one, but I have to think about the others. If you don't think that way, you can't do this job. Otherwise you would be complete gravy.

During the early days of her work, Yvonne accomplished what she did with the children on relatively little money. She contributed four to five hundred dollars a month of her own money, and friends provided another seven hundred dollars. She refuses to take government money if it means she must compromise what she knows the children need. She also doesn't want a large infrastructure because she doesn't want to sit in an office. She prefers to be on the street with the kids. She did receive funds from friends in other countries. Among them was an ex-Peace Corps volunteer who became a teacher in Eugene, Oregon in the United States. He has started a nonprofit organization called Students Helping Street Kids International. For several years the students in his Oregon school room raised money to send to Yvonne's efforts as a contribution to their "sister school" in Brazil.

Teaching Children They Exist

Naively I thought that Yvonne, the White Revolutionary, must teach these children to read and write as one might do in a traditional school. But there is absolutely nothing traditional about how Yvonne transfers information to these children. She intuitively identifies what each child needs on a moment-by-moment basis. She told me that her first objective is to teach them that they exist.

This phrase brought me up short and has haunted me ever since she said it. What is it like to not know that you exist? How did I learn that I existed? Yvonne is clear about her plan for teaching these children that they exist.

She begins by teaching them the mechanics of the society in which they live; what is a neighborhood, a city, a state, a country, and what are the laws in these places. That is very important because if they know the mechanics and the laws, they will know for the first time when a law is being broken. She tells the children to straighten up their homes and make the streets they live on safe for others to walk on them.

Perhaps one of Yvonne's most poignant ways of teaching "existence" is to take a child by the hand and stand out in the street, look up to the sky, and together yell, "I AM SOMEONE!!!"

I will never forget my reaction to hearing Yvonne say these words. Time stood still for that moment. I remember where the sun was shining on the floor, the smell of the pastries we were eating. This struck me as one of the most simple, powerful acts of peacemaking I had yet encountered.

Reading the Children's Code Together

Sometimes their reading primer is the Children's Code that identifies the rights of children. Sitting on the street with a child on her lap, Yvonne moves her finger along the sentences of the Code. She helps a child sound out the words. Together they read the code aloud and then Yvonne interprets what this means for them.

Yvonne gave me an example of a time when she knew this information was sinking in. The police had come to one of the shanty towns where she worked. They dragged a young boy into the bushes and beat him and put a plastic bag on his head. Immediately after the police left, Yvonne got a call at her home from one of the other shanty town students saying the police had not shown the required papers to enter the child's home. Yvonne took the boy and some of the children who had witnessed the event and went to the police station. She told the chief that ten policemen from his office were guilty of four crimes: kidnapping, torture, invasion of house, and abuse of authority. She pointed out that there were several witnesses to this act, and that she would sign the papers for his denouncement. The police chief was afraid and apologized in front of the shanty town dwellers. This was a rare happening in those times of police brutality.

I asked Yvonne if that changed things for the next time the police entered the shanty town.

"Ah," she said, "not yet. That is just one event. This is a shanty town of twelve thousand. Once you have one thousand people doing that kind of standing up for their rights, the police will begin watching their steps." The most important thing for Yvonne from the event was that the children realized they had rights, and that they had been violated. One has to "exist" to have rights.

On another occasion, in 1993, Yvonne was working with a group of seventy-two children in the shanty town of Rato Molhado (Wet Rat). It was late at night when she received a call from the children saying they were dying. She immediately went to the scene that would later be known as the Massacre of Candelaria, where eight children and adolescents were murdered by the police. She arrived quickly enough to see who the killers were. This information got her kidnapped twice, but with the help of a lawyer and international media, she not only gained her freedom, but also went on to bring the first trial in Brazil where the police were named as the accused for killing these youngsters. This event galvanized Yvonne's career into full time helping these at-risk children of her city.

Yvonne continues teaching children they exist by helping "build proudness" in them. All of these children are black descendants of African folk who were brought to Brazil as slaves. "I teach them Black history and let them know that slavery was only a small part of their heritage. When I show them pictures of their esteemed ancestors and tell stories about them, the kids feel better. They begin to realize that they come from somewhere."

Yet another cornerstone of helping the children understand themselves is to give them insight into their own behavior. She starts each day by asking each child how their night was. She told me:

> *Some days all things are set aside simply to deal with a trauma a child has experienced in the last twenty-four hours. With the street kids, every day it depends; depends on how was the night; depends on how drugged they are; depends on a lot of stuff. So we can't plan, sometimes they are so aggressive. I may take one hour just to calm them down. I say, "OK, what happened yesterday that you are so aggressive today?" Because I know that aggresivity is a survival tactic. We have inside us a little point that is the survivor point. So every time this point is touched, we do things.*

Daily Schedule Guided by Intuition

Yvonne rises at 6:30 a.m. By 8:00 she leaves home and distributes beans and rice to the street children, calling each of them by name. She then proceeds to the shanty town where she makes food enough to feed two hundred children breakfast. What happens next is guided by Yvonne's intuitive sense of what the children are able to learn that day. Pragmatically, she knows that learning must be tied to life skills. She also knows that the children's learning disabilities and drug addictions often mean they can only handle chunks of fifteen to twenty minutes of any lesson. When all is well, sometimes they do math, sometimes gymnastics, sometimes they learn trades like cutting hair. Sometimes it takes a whole year for a child to learn how to write or read. Yvonne has identified a few children with innate artistic talent. During our interview, she told me she is going to have a show of their art along with her own art. Her hardest task is to wean the children off of the drugs.

Yvonne and Isabel's Other Lives

Yvonne returns home every day at 2 p.m. to spend the rest of her day writing. She has written a book entitled *The Butcher and the Last Sheep*, a story about a child in the ghettos. She has also written a series of six children's books, depicting what life is like for a shanty town child. Besides her fiction, Yvonne writes newspaper articles and a personal journal. She speaks on the radio every day. She also spends a portion of her free time sculpting and creating art installations.

She and Isabel, who is a talented artist in her own right, collaborated on a huge four panel installation that was a memorial to a child that had died in the streets from overdosing. It told the story of how cocaine enters Brazil and how it affects the country at an international level, a national level, a local level, and a personal level. One wall of the installation was made of cocaine bricks. Another panel traced how marijuana entered from Colombia and spread throughout Brazil, the panel being smeared with dirt from the favelas and the blood of the dying children.

Marginalized Because of Her Work

When I asked if she had time for a social life, I learned that Yvonne's work with the street children has been looked down upon sorely by the men and women of her class. Isabel interjected that Yvonne's best friend is her computer. It has been lonely going for this creative woman. No publisher in Brazil will publish her books. The art installation created by the mother and daughter team was shown in the yard of a foundry, as no gallery was willing to risk showing the depiction of truth to their clientele of buyers.

Isabel continued to share her insights about her mother:

> *There is a big problem for Vonny because intelligent people, no matter how hard they try, can never come across as dumb. You cannot hide intelligence. I think she has a lot of problems in relation to other women, especially these society women. She outshines them. But not because she intended to. It's just because it is her natural self. Women who are intelligent and successful and as beautiful as she is have a problem with loneliness.*

Yvonne admits this has been a problem all her life. As a child, she tasted discrimination for being the daughter of a divorced single mother. Coming from a lower class and being in a school with girls from a higher class, she quickly learned it was not wise to come in first in all her schoolwork, so she began to purposely answer two questions wrong on all of her quizzes.

Advice to Young Peacemakers

When I asked Yvonne what she would tell a young person who wanted to be a Peacemaker, she replied:

> *First, you must love the people you work with. If you are motivated by interest or research or something other than love, you will never make it. If they do not see love in your eyes, they will never accept you. Second, you must understand and accept the situations of the children without pity. You have to be able to work under difficult situations, and you can't scream because you have to handle the children. Do not waste your time trying to educate the establishment, because their goal is to remain in power.*

Isabel, too, had advice about becoming a Peacemaker.

> *If you do a kind of freelance thing like my mother does, and if you aren't well with yourself, don't depend on institutions for your well-being. You must have inner strength. Do not be attached to images or to things, and don't forget yourself. Your last resource is yourself, so take good care of yourself.*

Isabel plans someday to work with the children and teenagers on the Brazilian streets, but in her own way as an artist. She is not sure she is ready yet. Once she has completed her architectural degree at Yale, she feels she has a lot to resolve in her heart. She wanted to discern what are her conflicts and what are the conflicts of other people in order to respond to situations genuinely and sincerely. I was impressed with this young woman's maturity.

The Role of Forgiveness

When asked Yvonne what role, if any, she felt forgiveness plays in peacemaking, she replied that acceptance is far more important than forgiveness. She also feels that every person has instincts upon which they act, and one has to analyze each situation when the instincts were acted upon to know if forgiveness is appropriate.

To illustrate this, she proceeded to tell the story of a young boy who had recently come to her explaining that he had knifed the companion of his mother because "the guy wanted to rape my little sister." His instinct was to "kill the guy." Yvonne talked with him about why he did it, and found out "the guy" wanted to kill his little sister. Yvonne chose to not turn him into the police. However, a serial killer, Yvonne feels, is a different matter. "If you build the society just on forgiveness, it's hypocritical. There is a reason for everything."

Influences in Yvonne's Life

In describing what influenced her own path in the direction of this work, Yvonne cited several things from her life that either initiated or supported her peacemaking. Her mother used to bring poor children to their home on the weekends. At age thirteen, her mother told her to find some means of working with people that were in need, so Yvonne began reading to the blind. She enjoyed this because she also got the benefit of the books. At fifteen, she began working with handicapped children. In the 1980s, she joined Solidarity France Brazil where she worked with young rape victims and helped start daycare centers for very poor children. She soon realized she wanted to do more than feed them, kiss them, and talk to them. She wanted to change their lives.

At the same time Yvonne was learning how to serve those less fortunate than her, her mother was doing everything she could to pave Yvonne's path from being a child of the middle class to being a member of the upper class. Her prayers were answered when Yvonne married a Swedish diplo-mat, which immediately landed Yvonne in the upper echelons of Brazilian society. Yvonne and her husband had three children in five years, Andrea, Gunnar, and Isabel, the youngest.

Once she had tasted the upper-class life, Yvonne didn't like it at all. "I didn't like it because if you are not born rich, if you are not a tycoon or made yourself very rich, you are not accepted. They think always you are not like they are. And you are not. They made me feel I was not from their class."

This marriage however did give her an opportunity to travel and see the poor in other countries and to study at the Sorbonne. At the time she was living in Sweden, the Swedish government had projects in several de-veloping countries, which she followed very closely. Some of these inter-national friends continue to help fund her work in Brazil today. During this period, she worked as an interpreter for an international aid agency. Her visits to Kenya, Tanzania, Ethiopia, Sudan, Angola, and Mozambique gave her repeated insight into the impact of violence on a child's ability to learn. This information became invaluable when she started working with the favela children in Brazil.

Influences in Isabel's Life

Isabel, on the other hand was born into the upper class. I asked if she felt at home there. She replied:

> No, not really. I mean, I have had an extraordinary educa-tion. I've traveled everywhere. I'm about to attend one of the best universities in America. I have a really fantastic resume and all that stuff, but I intend to use that upper-class thing towards helping these people in my work. But you know, as a kid growing up in Rio, I never found a group of kids that were on the same wave length. There is no transformation that will come about with people who are interested in keeping their bank books safe, because the people from the upper class do not question themselves.

Yvonne does not have an aggrandized view of her contribution to the world nor of the time it will take to start seeing different futures in the chil-dren with whom she works. She simply says:

I focus on the kids, hoping that from these kids we have some leaders someday. I'm not going to be the one who is going to make the changes. I'm one of the troops. But it takes time. Takes twenty to thirty years, forty years. I think that this is the role of generations. Normally when people are famous, they want to do things right now, because they want to be remembered as the one who did it. But it doesn't happen that way. One of them is going to make it, but normally 99.9 percent are the ones who make the way for that one. He makes it through because that is his destiny.

So has Yvonne's work as a "trooper" made any difference? Her assessment at the time of this interview in the late 1990s was "So far, so good." Of the 220 youth that she worked with over the four years prior to this interview, only one went to work for the drug dealers. One girl "made it out" and has become a housekeeper. Yvonne considers it ample compensation for her work that she has helped make Brazil a little better.

Epilogue

Yvonne's focus on educating the children of the favelas and the streets has never wavered. Her reputation and her work have blossomed in the years since my original interview with her. Yvonne and her second husband, Alvaro Bezerra de Mello, a Rio hotel magnate, live in an upper-class neighborhood. Yvonne, often known as "The Saint of Rio," continues to work with the street youth every morning.

Projeto Uerê
She has started Projeto Uerê. The name means Children of Light. Projeto Uerê is an "informal school" originally established underneath a bridge. The teaching methodology is custom-designed to each child taking in account his or her difficulties in learning. It includes three houses for those children and youth in the Mare and Vigario Geral shanty towns. The houses receive children and teenagers from local communities and from the streets. The project is staffed by a multidisciplinary team and regularly

receives volunteers from all over the world. In these houses, the children are offered help with their learning skills, their concentration and aggressiveness, and with medical situations such as early pregnancy or rape.

In fifteen to twenty-minute modules, the children also learn the alphabet, art therapy, drug prevention, sexual education, music, computer classes, ecology and health care, capoeira (Brazilian dance), and English. They make monthly visits to museums.

The Projeto Uerê Youth Force is a large program for teenagers aged sixteen to twenty-one who are at risk, often illiterate and marginalized in society. The offerings range from literacy to computer lessons. The Youth Force has its own newspaper. As of 2000, in partnership with the Brazilian Federal Government, two programs were offered as learning venues for these youth: one in making furniture with recycled plastic bottles, and another in telecommunications and electricity.

Projeto Uerê in Mare

By 2014, Projeto Uerê moved to Mare, a labyrinth of sixteen favelas where 130,000 people live. The children come for half-day sessions, broken into twenty-minute segments. The school has an open-door policy, meaning that the children and others can come into the school as they wish, something that follows the pace of life they have learned on the streets.

Currently, Projeto Uerê is now working with over four hundred children between the ages of six and eighteen. Yvonne's goal for the school is to make these little people with big problems strong enough to survive their everyday life and bring some hope for their future.

Respect for the Brains of Traumatized Children

Learning from her experience with Brazilian and the African children, Yvonne believes every child can learn, but the brains of children who have been in the presence of violence are traumatized and blocked up, and it takes a special kind of program to help unblock their minds. Projeto Uerê provides the children with what Yvonne calls necessary pre-learning.

The eighteen teachers, all from the surrounding area and familiar with the environments of these children, have professional qualifications and are specifically trained in the unique Projeto Uerê teaching methods. These teachers are paid the same salaries as the public school teachers, and are responsible for cleaning their own classrooms. The 300+ children are fed two meals a day and the cooks are trained in the same pedagogical methodology. The cost for running Projeto Uerê is less per child than in the public school, proving that this program can be both financially and educationally effective.

Neuroscience as Foundation

Yvonne believes all teachers should be trained in neuroscience. The goal is to eliminate blocks to learning by building new neural pathways. This way the child can begin to absorb information, concentrate, and learn at the rate the mainstream students are learning. This proves, in Yvonne's words, "Intelligence can be repaired, and we have found a way to do it."

Each child's experience is different, so the program custom designs each child's learning process. The process begins with gathering information from the student, their family and teachers to understand the student's current capacity to learn and their daily rhythm.

A detailed analysis identifies the exact moments of trauma for the child and looks carefully at the prior two years of the child's life, including medical history, family circumstances, and past and ongoing causes of trauma. Then the teacher designs a program that will help build trust with the child and create a strategy of learning, including games, books (some written by Yvonne), software, and individual and group activities. For example, a child might be taught to say basic words and count in five different languages, waking up the synaptic connections in his or her brain.

When evaluations show the student is ready, somewhere between six months and a year, Projeto Uerê then assists them in integrating them back into the public or private school setting. Uerê monitors their progress in social behavior, grades, mathematical and linguistic abilities, and their ability for being included in the job market. Yvonne guarantees that all the children at fifteen will find some work, paving the way for them to succeed and breaking the cycle of poverty from whence they come.

Far-Reaching Implications of Projeto Uerê

Yvonne's method of teaching is now known as the UERE-MELLO PEDAGOGY, which is both a method of learning and a method of classroom management. As of 2009, it has become an official public policy implemented in the network of public schools of the city of Rio de Janeiro.

In 2011, it began to spread to other Brazilian school systems. Not only have seven thousand children and adolescents benefited from personally being in Yvonne's school, but over ten thousand teachers of public and private schools of four municipalities have been trained, benefiting more the ninety-five thousand students.

Building Resilience, One Child at a Time

From her former days of being marginalized and alone in her work, Yvonne has now persevered in finding effective ways for hundreds of traumatized children living in poverty to develop self-esteem and acquire an education. For herself, she has learned the wisdom of not wasting her energies on trying to change the big systems of Brazil, like the drug problems, the violence, and the government policies. Instead, she keeps re-focusing on building the resilience and skills of individual children, one child at a time. As a result, the value of the work that has emerged from her beliefs and her hard work is now catching fire and greatly impacting the educational system in the favela Mare, in Brazil, and internationally.

CHAPTER FIFTEEN

Re-Limbing Youth

Elissa Montanti

• STATEN ISLAND, NEW YORK, USA •

Peace Work:
Helping children who are victims of war,
accidents, and disasters receive medical treatments,
surgeries, physical therapy, and prosthetic limbs and eyes

Metaphor:
I am a concert mistress.

*Peace is achieved one person at a time,
through a series of friendships.*

—Fatima Reda

My First Glimpse of Elissa

For several years, I have gathered with seven or eight women with whom I graduated high school. We meet in a different location each fall for a few days of hiking, cooking, and sharing with each other our travels and our undertakings. This group of women has been supportive of my authoring this book on Women Peacemakers.

At one of our gatherings, Dorothea Bonneau took me aside, saying, "I know you are well on the way with your book, but I want to show you something on my computer I think might interest you." She pulled up the website of the Global Medical Relief Foundation, or GMRF. After fifteen minutes of looking at the website and the CBS 60 Minutes news magazine program on Elissa Montanti, the founder and director of the foundation, I was more than interested. I wanted to meet the woman behind this organization.

GMRF is a nonprofit, non-partisan charity founded and operated by one woman, Elissa Montanti. Since 1997, she has helped over four hundred children all over the world who are amputees, burn victims, and children injured by war, accidents and disasters. At no cost to the child or family, the GMRF children receive medical treatments, surgeries, physical therapy, and prosthetic limbs and eyes, as well as housing, meals and transportation. They receive follow up care until age twenty-one. The mission is to assist these children in mending and healing both spirit and body so they can return to their families and homes and grow up to become productive, self-sufficient members of their own communities.

"How do you know her?" I asked Dorothea. "I'm writing the screenplay for the story of her life," she replied.

Answer on the First Ring

When I called Elissa, she answered her phone after the first ring, something that I would come to know as one of her hallmarks. I was coming to New York for Thanksgiving. She found a way to make time for our interview amidst dozens of doctor's appointments she had made for the children staying with her. She gave me the address to get from Newark Airport to the Dare to Dream House, where the children resided while they were in the United States receiving their medical procedures.

Janett

I arrived a few minutes before Elissa. I was met at the door by a young woman with a scarf wrapped around her neck and held up to cover the lower part of her face. She shyly introduced herself as Janett. I also met her mother, Philomena, who was even shyer than her daughter. Janett showed me to the kitchen table and proceeded to make a fried egg sandwich for my lunch, mostly using one hand while using the other to cover her face with the scarf.

Later, Elissa told me Janett was twelve years old and from Gambia. A tumor, now the size of a watermelon, had developed on one side of her face and was growing so rapidly that eating was problematic for her. She had been unable to find treatment in Gambia or in neighboring Senegal. Her mother had contacted a foundation that in turn contacted doctor Dr. David Hoffman, an oral surgeon at the Staten Island Hospital to see if he would help her daughter. Dr. Hoffman agreed. He had worked with Elissa's children before, so he asked Elissa to get the necessary visas for Janett and Philomena. But Elissa's experience told her there was much more than a visa that she would need to arrange.

Both mother and daughter would need passports, a place to stay, and someone to meet them at the airport and get them through Homeland Security. Elissa made the first point of contact communication and prepared the necessary sponsor letter and hospital letter. Then she made sure that Janett and Philomena got a whole slew of required tests, insuring they didn't have prohibitive diseases for entry into the U.S. The day before our interview, the Friday of Thanksgiving weekend, Elissa had taken Janett for her CAT scan. In the days after our interview, she would take her to five different doctors, including plastic surgeons and ear, nose, and throat specialists and bone graft doctors. Then Janett would be ready for the surgery.

I asked how many operations would be required. Elissa told me all five doctors wanted to operate at the same time because of the nature and the urgency of Janett's situation. Elissa would sit in the waiting room with Philomena while they waited for the surgery to take place, and then both mother and daughter would stay at the Dare to Dream House for the next week until the doctors felt Janett was able to travel home to Gambia. The pair would also be welcome at Dare to Dream House if Janett needed follow-up surgery in the future. All these services, including the surgery, were donated on a pro bono basis. This was a typical situation—if there was such a thing—that took place at Global Medical Relief Foundation constantly.

Ngawang and Ahmed

Elissa generously gave me not only time for the interview, but surprised me by offering me a ticket to go with her to the New York Knicks basketball game that evening where two of her GMRF boys were performing together during half-time.

One of the performers was Ngawang, a Tibetan child who had been living as a refugee in India. He had been electrocuted at age fifteen while chasing a kite, losing both arms. Because of the severity of his injuries, Ngawang and his mother, Dolma, needed to extend their stay and eventually moved to Staten Island. Ngawang had a beautiful voice.

The other performer was Ahmed, an Iraqi boy that first came to Elissa when he was six years old. He had stepped on a landmine walking home from second grade. Ahmed lost his eyesight and one arm and was badly scarred. Major General Norma Sandow of the American forces contacted Elissa to see if the damage to his body could be repaired. Elissa welcomed him at the time and for several future procedures that were required as Ahmed grew older. When Ahmed first came to her, she had a toy piano that he would constantly play. Because Elissa had always been involved in music herself, she realized early on that Ahmed was extremely talented musically.

By the time he was fifteen and had returned to GMRF for one of his many updated prosthetic fittings, Ahmed met Ngawang. The boys bonded like brothers while they were staying with Elissa. By then, Ahmed was able to play anything he heard on the keyboard. Before long he was composing songs of his own, some of which he and Elissa recorded together. At this time it was too dangerous for Ahmed to return to Iraq. As he was under age, he remained in the United States under Elissa's guardianship. Ahmed attended the Vision For The Blind program, which taught him life skills for being visually impaired. Both boys attended high school together on Staten Island. Besides singing together there, they were both on the track team, Ngawang running in front, Ahmed in back with his hand on Ngawang's shoulder.

Most of all, these two boys sang and played music together. Their talent matured until they became good enough to be invited to perform at the half-time ceremonies at the New York Knicks basketball game.

How lucky was I to witness these two young men walking onto the floor of the stadium before a massive crowd of American basketball fans? Ahmed put his hand on the shoulder of Ngawang, who walked in front, leading Ahmed to the keyboard bench, acting as Ahmed's eyes as he had become accustomed to do. Ngawang was not wearing the prostheses on his arms, but Ahmed was wearing his, even though he could not use his prosthetic hand to play. Even so, it was miraculous how much music Ahmed could bring alive from that keyboard with his one hand. Together, these two nineteen-year-old young men performed "Bridge Over Troubled Water" to an audience of twenty thousand people listening intently and then cheering mightily. Having heard the story of their lives from Elissa, I was in tears as I recorded it.

Texting with No Hands

After their performance, as Ngawang's mother, Dolma, and I were riding in the back seat of the van with Ngawang, he did something that blew my mind. Since he was not wearing his prosthetic arms, his bare arms ended at his elbows. There were small bumps of bone underneath the skin where his amputation had healed up. He wanted to text someone on his cell phone. Dolma held his phone and Ngawang texted faster with his bumps than I could ever text with my fingers.

Watching him, the word "handicapped" more or less dissolved out of my vocabulary on the spot. Elissa had said her kids could do anything. I became a believer when I saw how cleverly they adapted to doing things with and without their prosthetic arms, such as eat with utensils, or drink out of a cup, work on a computer and brush their teeth, play a guitar and turn the key in a car's ignition, ride a bicycle, and repair electronic equipment.

I had not realized how many assumptions and beliefs I held about what an amputee could and could not do, assumptions about individuals I had never even met! I learned quickly to see each one as a unique individual, and if I wanted to know what they were capable of doing with or without their prostheses, all I had to do was watch or ask, not assume.

How Would One Know Elissa?

How can I best describe to you Elissa Montanti, the woman behind this charity? Let's start with what you would see in her presence. Elissa is petite, with dark hair, and by her own description, she often touches people to show affection. Looking at pictures of her with the children she has helped, it is sometimes hard to find Elissa because she is often the shortest person in the picture. She is always holding someone's hand, hugging them or putting her hand on their shoulder while their gurney is being wheeled into an operating room. During our interview, sitting across from her at her kitchen table, I saw her face and her eyes light up like the sun as she described her work, her children, and the people she works with.

What would you hear in Elissa's presence? Primarily stories—full, detailed stories, told in her classic Staten Island accent, dropping g's at the end of some words and adding r's at the end of others. If it were stories about the children, you would hear about how they met with disaster, how their bodies and their souls paid the cost, how she found them, how many hurdles it took to get them and their parent or guardian to their first night with her in Staten Island house, the multiple appointments involved in their healing process, what other children they bonded with while spending weeks or months together at the GMRF center, the procedures they had, the doctors that did the procedures, and the tears that were shed as the newly confident child boarded a plane to go home. And such a story would be told in a matter of ten minutes, because Elissa can talk faster than you can imagine. Thank goodness I was recording our interview rather than trying to take notes! The only luxury she gives herself if she skips a few details is the phrase, "anyway, long story short," which I heard often in our interview.

Music would also be a theme of what you would hear in talking to Elissa. Twice during our interview she played recordings of music she or her GMRF kids wrote and performed. Music was a theme that stretched from the two young men who would sing "Bridge Over Troubled Water" that night all the way back to her childhood household. Elissa told me:

> *My mother loved all kinds of music, and she had a strong sweet voice. It was comforting to hear her sing along to Broadway show tunes or the smooth crooners of the day—Dean Martin, Perry Como, Connie Francis—while she vacuumed or helped Grandma Nellie with dinner. Sometimes she moved the Singer sewing machine from the basement into the dining room to listen to music while making me a new skirt and*

241

matching headband or my sister, Rita Lu, a dress ... My father preferred opera, Mario Lanza, and Ezio Pinza. Daddy was a wanderer. One time when he returned from his Merchant Marine duty in Greece, he brought home a forty-five recording of Zorba The Greek and put it on the hi-fi-console and began dancing and singing around the house.

When I asked Elissa what metaphor she thought best described her work as a Peacemaker, it was no surprise her answer was "concert master, or maybe a concert mistress." It combined her love of music and her prodigious multi-tasking skills in orchestrating everything necessary to make miracles happen for the children.

Oh, and one other thing you would hear in Elissa's presence would be her cell phone ringing. It did so eleven times during our interview. She would instantly read the text or check the caller ID. It was one of the most important tools of her trade. For example, it might be a call from the Dominican Republic about getting a visa for the child to come next week. Most of her conversations were short, as she took care of business quickly. Once I heard her "mother bear" voice come out in a call where someone was talking disparagingly about one of the GMRF children. As Elissa told me, "I don't know how to set very good boundaries for myself, but I will always protect my kids, especially if injustice is involved."

The Transparent Truth

Elissa was very transparent in our interview. The same was true of the book she wrote about herself with Jennifer Haupt entitled *I'll Stand By You*. She describes the paths she took growing up in a very close Italian family, living in an equally close Italian neighborhood on Staten Island. She describes how she inadvertently forged her way to being the founder and director of the Global Medical Relief Fund. She chronicles the mistakes she made along the way as well as the lessons she learned. She talks about her two marriages candidly as well as how driven she was in cobbling together the skills, money, and human resources to keep helping more children. She describes the overwhelming pain of nursing her mother through eleven years of cancer, and how she stuffed her feelings after losing three loved ones in a very short time during her early twenties, causing her to fall into such a "deep, dark hole" of depression and anxiety that she couldn't find her way out for four years.

However, transparency can go both ways. If she lets people see into her life, she can also see into people's lives. By my reckoning, Elissa is an empath, someone who can feel the feelings of others. The good news is this makes her the perfect person to run an organization that helps children come back from devastating situations, because she is highly tuned into their needs and the feelings. On the other hand, when combining this empathetic trait within someone as sensitive as Elissa, it means her nervous system must handle twice the load of feelings that the ordinary person deals with on a daily basis.

When her parents divorced, even though still loving each other deeply, little Elissa felt their anguish. When her mother was internally besieged by cancer but was concealing it to those around her, Elissa felt all those conflicting things even though she didn't understand them. When she saw two dogs dying of thirst by the roadside in a war zone in Iraq, she made the driver stop so she could give them the last of the water in her bottle. An empath can feel so much from those around them, they sometimes don't deal with their own feelings.

Such was the case with Elissa. She describes it as "pasting a big smile on my face all those years my mother was ill, and my boyfriend was murdered, and my beloved grandmother died."

Panic Attack

One day, while standing in line at a bank to deposit money for her employer, Elissa had her first panic attack. A panic attack is a fearsome thing. It often happens in the company of other people, but bizarrely, while the person experiencing the attack feels like they might die from everything going on inside their body and mind, the people around them often never notice. Her hands got sweaty, her throat closed up, and her knees felt like Jell-O; all she could hear was her heart beating a million miles an hour; her eyesight narrowed, and she was sure she was going to faint. The only thing that kept that from happening was her sense of embarrassment at fainting in front of strangers. Somehow, by pasting that smile on her face, she managed to endure the endless time it took for her to travel the six long feet to the teller's window.

Having a panic attack is suddenly and utterly frightening; worrying about when the next one will grab you is life altering. After the bank incident, Elissa began to lose sleep, and her heart wouldn't calm down. She couldn't be around other people without being hit by another panic attack.

243

She quit going out with friends to eat or hear music. In fact, she quit singing altogether. Somehow, she made it to work each day, but she immediately came home afterward, lit candles in her room, and crawled on the bed with her one consoling friend, Obie, her 150 pound Newfoundland. She wrote poems and journal entries and letters to God asking for help in understanding how to get back to her normal, outgoing life. She was so embarrassed she told no one what was going on, not even her sister. She began feeling physically ill, and when she saw a cardiologist, he recommended going to a counselor.

She spent two years with a psychologist who helped her see that she had compartmentalized her feelings about so many losses in so few years, that her grandmother's recent death had tipped the basket of unprocessed feelings, casting her into depression. Still, Elissa fought this information for another four years, until she ended up in a deep, dark hole from which she could not escape. The way she describes it in her book is:

> It took a miracle to help me climb out. That miracle came in the form of a fifteen-year-old boy who, at the same time that I was lost in depression, was fighting battles that made mine pale by comparison.

Kenan Malkic

The boy's name was Kenan Malkic. He lived in the town of Maglaj, Bosnia. Kenan lived with his mother, Aida, who was pregnant with a new sibling that she would eventually lose because it arrived early and the war had destroyed all the incubators for prematurely born children. His father would come home from the Front Line of battle in the horrific Bosnian War whenever he was able. At eleven, Kenan was in charge while his father was gone, doing everything to help keep his mother safe in their bombed-out community. The two of them spent a lot of time in the underground concrete shelter they shared with their neighbors.

On one of the few days when it was safe for Kenan to play outdoors with his friends that had so far survived the war, he took his prized position as goalie on the makeshift football field. As the ball whizzed past him, he chased it into the weeds, where unbeknownst to him, an undetonated landmine lay. The next thing he remembers is flying through the air with the taste of blood, dirt, and gunpowder in his mouth. The next memory after that was waking up in a hospital bed to discover he was missing both arms and a leg. The next two years were a pool of depression, pain, grit, and persistent effort for this young man and his family.

About this time on Staten Island, a friend of Elissa's had coaxed her into writing a song for a fund raiser he was throwing to gather school supplies and toys to send to Bosnian children. Reluctantly, Elissa agreed to write the song from the safety of her home, but panicked at the thought of performing it at the event. But when encouragement came as messages from her deceased mother and grandmother on the "other side," she agreed to allow a cassette tape of her singing the song she had written, "Let's Do A Miracle," to be played at the fundraiser. When she was done, she actually felt a tiny seed of finding her way out of her dark hole.

In the following weeks, she found herself wanting to do more for the Bosnians. Surprisingly, with the help of friends and her heart racing madly, she found herself going to the office of Muhamed Sacriby, Bosnia's ambassador at the United Nations. When she told him she somehow wanted to help, he pulled a letter out of his desk drawer and showed it to her. It read:

> *My name is Kenan Malkic. I am 14 years old and have stepped on a landmine. I have no arms and a leg. I am asking all good and merciful people to help me.*

And suddenly, in fact almost instantly, the seed of finding her way out of her darkness took off and bloomed. She describes it in her book:

> *'I want to help,' I said without hesitation. And for some reason I still can't explain, I knew I could do it. In hindsight it occurs to me that this boy's letter was really an answer to the letter I'd written to God, asking for help in finding my way out of the darkness that was consuming my own life. It was an answered prayer ... Once I make up my mind to do something, there's no stopping me ... I still can't believe that within just twenty-four hours, all of the roadblocks to bringing Kenan to America disappeared.*

Finding Herself At the Center of Something Bigger Than Her Fears

She went home from Muhamed's office, whom now she fondly calls Mo, and things began to happen. Kenan had been waiting for so long without hope and she knew exactly what that felt like. She wasn't going to make him wait any longer. Within a few hours, an orthopedic surgeon, who said of course he would donate his skills, called a hospital that said of course they would donate the necessary physical therapy, and all the other hospital fees would also be donated. The prosthetics company said yes. Austrian Airlines said yes to donating the airfare for Kenan and his mother. Friends and family all offered their help to cover other expenses while Kenan and his mother were in Staten Island. Elissa describes it as "finding myself at the center of something bigger than my own fears: helping another human being have a better life. It was exciting and empowering, a feeling I hadn't felt in a very long time."

She went to bed that night with one remaining question: where would Kenan and his mother stay? The anxiety started bubbling in her chest but she was determined not to let it win this time. Instead, she prayed. Elissa is thoroughly convinced that miracles exist, that nothing is a coincidence.

Elissa woke up the next morning rested and knowing clearly that Kenan and Aida would stay with her in her one bedroom apartment. She would drive them to the doctors appointments and the grocery store, even though she had a full-time job. Never mind that only yesterday driving anywhere had petrified her.

After Kenan and Aida arrived, the media wanted to come to Elissa's house. At first, there was much demand by the press to interview him. She told me, "I felt his pain, actually more fiercely than I'd ever felt my own pain. I could never stand up and say no in my own life, but I could do it for this boy I was growing to love." She minimized the number of public engagements arranged for him.

One night, prior to his surgery, a friend took Kenan to Madison Square Garden to see the New York Knicks. His name was up in lights on the stadium entrance and gifts were planned to be given to him during half-time. Aida and Elissa were surprised to see them come home soon after the start of the game.

"He seemed happy at first," the friend reported, "but about a half hour after the game began he told me he had to get out of there. The kid was freaking out. I could see it written all over his face."

When they got home, Kenan said he was going to sleep and didn't want to talk about anything.

Putting Each Other Back Together

Kenan had experienced a panic attack. A few nights later he had a full blown PTSD event, seeing flashbacks of the horrors he had seen in the war, his friend killed in front of him by a sniper's bullet, glass walls shattering, and flashes of his own landmine accident.

Aida and Elissa held him, slowing their breathing to guide his own. Elissa told Kenan she knew what he was feeling. She said:

> *You're not going to die. You're not going to die. You're here. You think you're going to die, and you think this is the end. But it's not. You are just going through a really bad time right now. And it's going to pass. I know because I had these panic attacks for four years.*

"You did?" Kenan said. He understood enough English to let her words distract his anxiety. "That night," as Elissa put it, "Kenan, Aida and I became not just close, but family. And it has been that way ever since." She was quick to add, "As I was putting him back together, he was putting me back together."

Elissa also credits Kenan with renewing her sense of humor that had gone underground during her dark days.

> *I've always had a good sense of humor, but Kenan taught me the healing power of laughter; he's one of the few people who can turn my worries into jokes and make me smile at the thing I have no control over. Kenan had always used laughter as a way to get out of trouble with his mother. Something would happen, something silly that other people don't even find funny, and Kenan and I would look at each other and bust up laughing. Then, later in bed I'd start laughing again, thinking about what happened. Before I knew it he'd text me from his bedroom downstairs to say he was laughing about the same thing.*

The details of Kenan's story are told in vivid, touching details in Elissa's book, *I'll Stand By You*. Long story short, Kenan received his prosthetics. He came back several times for new prosthetics as he grew out of them, and then finally he returned for good where he lives permanently in Elissa's basement, going to college in New York City.

He adds a dimension to GMRF that only someone who has experienced a disabling accident could add. He made videos of himself doing things with his arms that Elissa could show children overseas to give them hope. He ran alongside the bicycle of a newcomer child who was trying to learn to ride. He took them to doctors appointments and asked critical questions. He hung out with them until they were wheeled away into surgery. He became their big brother. He even walked Elissa down the aisle when she married her second husband.

Global Medical Relief Fund

Thus, the Global Medical Relief Fund was launched even before it became an official charity. Finding Kenan proved much easier than finding the second child to help. She flew to Bosnia (this woman who at one time could barely make it six feet to the teller's window), to visit hospitals in Iraq to find the next child. There were so many needy candidates, adults and children, that it proved exhausting and overwhelming. But somehow, one child's voice and smile grabbed her attention and she knew she would find a bed and a limb for that child in Staten Island.

These days, she doesn't have to go looking; the referrals come to her. They come as emails from soldiers in war zones; from reporters covering a tsunami, a typhoon, or an earthquake; from medical personnel working at disasters; from global organizations that have been contacted by a desperate parent; and from the doctors at the hospitals in the United States that provide their pro bono services.

Elissa has grown a substantial team that make miracles happen for the children. She calls them angels. The team includes not only the Shriners Hospitals for Children, but also several other hospitals and health institutions and personnel. And Elissa's team of allies has more than medical personnel on it.

Elissa's 3-P Approach

I kidded Elissa that she has a "3-P" approach to her work: Patience, Persistence, and Prayer. She told me the story of when she had flown to Haiti shortly after the epic earthquake struck in 2010. After identifying three girls who had lost limbs, she prepared about two hundred pages of the necessary paperwork. She went to the airport with the girls and their guardians, only to be turned away because she was told she needed humanitarian parole documents. Flying back to the United States, she obtained the proper paperwork and returned to Haiti a few days later having all the required documents. This time the trip to the airport, which was normally a twenty-minute ride, took two and a half hours because of the chaos created by the earthquake. Finally, as she approached the gate with her six Haitians, the immigration officer told her she had to have a letter from a doctor, verifying the children were amputees.

I said to him, "You can't see that these kids are missing arms and legs? You've got to be kidding me. This is so unfair. How can you do this! You just had this horrific earthquake. These kids can walk again with our help, and you're telling me that I need a letter from a doctor!"

Elissa returned to the United States without the Haitians for the second time in a week. People suggested she should forget the whole thing. Elissa's response was, "Forget it? You think I'm going to forget this? These poor kids I left at the airport. There's no way I'm going to forget it!"

It took about a week of going to this and that person, paying fifty dollars for each child to get the official stamp that they were, indeed, amputees. She went back the following week, picked up the children and their guardians, and finally exhaled when they closed the door on the airplane.

So here I am. We've landed at JFK airport and I go through Homeland Security. I have six Haitians with me, three kids. And the officer said, "Oh, this isn't good." I said, "What isn't good? I have all the papers, and mind you, this has been quite a journey so far." And he told me their visa had expired yesterday. I had just gotten them last week when I was there. And that was the first country that I went to that said it had expired so quick, because usually you have at least a month. This officer was not very nice. And the Haitians were looking at me, because they didn't understand hardly any English. I didn't tell him anything about why I was bringing the Haitians in. I said, 'Please, you have to understand.' He said, 'I'm sorry. Their visas expired. There's nothing we can do.'

Then this angel walks by, this tall man, and he said, "What's the problem? I asked him to please help me. I went into the

whole thing. He happened to be the head officer of Home-
land Security in charge of Customs and Borders. He talks to
the guy and they got on the phone and within forty minutes,
he said "You're OK. Don't worry about it. I said, "Oh may
God, Bless you." At this point, I told him about GMRF and
he said, 'Listen, there's no reason why you should ever have
to go through this when you come back to Homeland Secu-
rity. I would like to help you when you come into the country
with these kids.' I said, 'Really? Do you know how many
hours I have spent in Homeland Security, being up late
twenty-four hours or more and waiting.' So from that mo-
ment on he said, 'Next time you or your kids come into this
country, you call me.'

So now I call him, he assigns an officer, I meet them at the
airport, they come to me, we go to the gate, they get off the
plane, they usher them through, they don't have to wait in
line, they go right through, they fill out everything they have
to fill out, and they are finished in a half hour. And now I
know all the customs and border folks because there are dif-
ferent terminals where the kids come in. It's amazing.

Elissa doesn't consider herself a traditionally religious person, but she
prays all the time, mostly for people to be safe. Every night she prays for
all the GMRF children before going to sleep. She told me that God has a
habit of answering her prayers at five minutes to midnight, just when it
seems time has run out. She thinks it's God's way of teaching her to have
a little more patience.

And how does she finance the services she provides? All the medical
services are donated. For the other things such as food, she originally gathered money every possible way you can imagine: kindergarteners filling
a jar with pennies, her relatives and friends, local churches and service
clubs, her own paycheck, and big and little fund raisers.

She also applies for grants. She told me it is harder for her to get grants
than many charities because she is serving children both inside and outside the United States. Around 9/11, she was even receiving hate mail
about helping Iraqi children. Sometimes it is also harder for her to get
grants because the granting agencies wonder if two hundred children in

nineteen years is a meaningful enough investment of their funds. Elissa shows them the paragraph on her brochure that reads:

GMRF's scale of treatment is highly personal. We know every child and his or her mother or father or guardian by first name. GMRF and its partners welcome and care for injured children with the warmth, love, and personal attention that can only be found in a family. Every child helped by GMRF becomes an 'ambassador' who can return home not only with a healed, mended body and a new spirit of hope for life, but also an experience of 'America's best': thanks to the support of GMRF, its donors, benefactors, partners, and community volunteers.

To Expand or Not

People asked Elissa how large GMRF will get. Her thinking is:

Big is not always better. I want to keep my charity personal. I want to grow, but I never want to grow more than not know- ing who I am helping. You know I have a connection with these kids that stay here, maybe four to eight at a time. I know all of them. I know their dreams ... most of them come back. And I don't want to bring a hundred kids every year and not know each child and guardian personally.

You know, a lot of what the charity is about is the fact that we may have four different families here from four different parts of the world. It is like a mini-United Nations. Inadver- tently we are promoting healthy foreign relations, because we may have an Iraqi child here, a Haitian child, a Tibetan child all under one roof.

Elissa's Miracles

And then there was that miracle of the CBS 60 Minutes Documentary magazine on GMRF that brought her enough notoriety for donations to begin seriously rolling in. The funds received enabled her to hire two girls to help with the multiple endless tasks for operating the charity, and even enough for Elissa to start drawing her first small salary in fourteen years from the charity, instead of her supporting the charity with her paycheck as a medical assistant. She maintains her original office in the walk-in closet of her home bedroom where she continues to keep the piles of red tape documents for the children's travel and medical procedures.

Oh yes, and that other miracle in the form of Tyler Perry, the movie star, and his co-donor, MDC Partners, that purchased the building down the street from where she lives. Whereas before the children had been living in spaces donated by churches, GMRF now had The Dare to Dream House, a permanent remodeled home where the children coming to Staten Island live while Elissa's teams work to change their bodies and their lives.

I asked her what advice she might give to a young person who wanted to be a Peacemaker. Her advice was to "communicate with people so you can learn why they do what they do, what makes them tick and what they are thinking. Don't make assumptions, judge people, or draw negative conclusions."

How, you might ask, does a woman who was trained as a medical technician learn to be the CEO of a charity with a large budget and endless global challenges? Elissa is clear about this:

> There are some things that you can figure out only by taking a deep breath, jumping in, and doing; starting a charity is one of those things. For example, when the Board of Shriners Children's Hospital asked how I was going to care for the children I planned to bring here, I had some temporary options. But mostly I was making it all up as I went along. But the key was that I really did believe in myself, and I had a small but growing base of supporters who believed in me.

She learned to never take "no" for an answer and to trust that eventually she will find her way to "yes." She seeks out people who tell her what she can do rather than what she can't do. Most of all, she has learned to recognize the opportunities, the miracles, and the angels that are sent to her.

Epilogue

Six weeks after our interview, Janett underwent ten hours of surgery. A team of doctors from Staten Island Hospital, who had practiced by using 3D images from her CAT scan, removed the tumor in her jaw while keeping all of her facial nerves intact. At the same time, a second team was busy removing a bone from Janett's leg, which would be used to rebuild her jawbone. Janett is smiling again. No scarf.

Kenan has a prestigious job in New York City. He is happily married. He and his wife live in the basement of Elissa's home. Both are valuable members of the GMRF team.

Ahmed is getting a seeing-eye dog. He has received a scholarship to a college where he will major in music and fulfill his dream of becoming a music teacher. One-handed, he now plays guitar and trumpet as well as the keyboard.

Ngawang is waiting on surgery so he will be more mobile. He's working with Ahmed on songs. He's praying that he and his mom will be approved for asylum.

Ngawang and Ahmed have also performed together at Carnegie Hall before thousands of people. They received a standing ovation. Ngawang leaned over and whispered to Ahmed, "They're standing up." "How many?" asked Ahmed. "All of them."

Elissa simply doesn't have time to fall in any more dark holes. When she was recently asked to speak at a large prestigious marketing convention about how she overcame her anxiety about public speaking, she told about the time she and Kenan were addressing the U.N. when Kenan froze up, and she suddenly found her voice and has loved connecting with audiences ever since. She also told them persistence was her form of bravery.

Although there was a time when the panic attacks kept Elissa from singing, there was also a time when she sang, but not very often because she was busy with GMRF responsibilities. Today, she is singing publically every week. Boy, can she belt it out. On her website, she continues to welcome donations from large corporations and from individuals, including kindergartners.

Long story short, as of the publication of this book, this tiny dynamo of a woman, along with her allies and angels, with her prayers, patience and persistence, has served just over four hundred children from over forty-four countries. And because the children return to be re-fitted as they grow, four hundred children translate into 1400 visits for medical procedures. As the children live together at the Dare to Dream House while waiting for their procedures, they bond. And so do their guardians. They return home with increased self-esteem, increased mobility and sight, and with new friends that expand their trust in the global-ness of our world. The Global Medical Relief Fund is a stunning incubator for new Peacemakers.

Elissa's book, *I'll Stand By You*, concludes with the following words:

> *If you think about it, there are actions we can all take in our daily lives to help others in need and create a global family. I'm not talking about quitting your job, traveling across the globe, and turning your bedroom closet into an office. But sometimes we all get so busy with our lives that we place a barricade around us: a wall of I can't, I don't have time, I can't afford it. If you think about it, who really doesn't have time to give someone a smile? Listening to someone's worries for a few moments or saying a prayer doesn't cost a cent. There are dozens of little things we can do in our everyday lives that add up, make a difference, and actually put a smile on our own faces!*
>
> *Who knows where these small actions and a greater awareness will lead. You may find yourself, just like I've found myself, in exactly the right place at the right time to do something bigger than you ever could have imagined you were capable of accomplishing. And instead of quietly thinking, I can't, you'll find yourself shouting: "How could I not?"*

*We can do nothing substantial
toward changing our course on this planet,
a destructive one, without rousing ourselves,
individual by individual,
and bringing our small imperfect stones to the pile.*

—Alice Walker

CHAPTER SIXTEEN

Women Peacemakers Advice to Young Peacemakers

During my interviews with each of the Women Peacemakers I asked, "What advice would you give to another person who wanted to become a Peacemaker?" These are the answers, verbatim, they gave me.

Chido Govera

Don't give up, forgive all the hurt, believe in yourself, and have hope for the future.

Clan Mother Rachelle Figueroa

Tell them to go find an Elder.

Judith Jenya

To be a Peacemaker requires a sense of mission, purpose, and commitment to the principle and the goal. It requires a belief that is not always based on what seems possible at the moment but which one knows is possible through focused effort and adherence to the past.

More than anything it requires a belief in the value of each life and the value of making a small difference that can be multiplied. The pitfalls occur when your efforts are derailed by events and when hatred seems to have the upper hand.

They need to gain as much knowledge in as many areas as possible and have personal and professional experience in listening, taking action, developing a vision and a plan, working with volunteers, working as a volunteer, having a great vision but not expectations, learning to not take things personally, developing great flexibility, and studying aikido or other techniques of getting to your goal indirectly but surely.

Have clarity about your desired outcome but not attachment to the outcomes that happen. Be open and willing to change tactics, schedules, actions, but not stray from your basic values, principles and goals. Regard each small gain or victory as validation and encouragement, but don't dwell on the losses or discouragements as a statement about the purpose.

Be willing to walk a lonely, often solitary road and not be attached to recognition when it does or doesn't come. Treat others with respect and compassion and be willing to meet people where they are. Get angry at injustice, deceit, betrayal, and then move on. Take time for yourself and have recreation and beauty in your life.

Sister Sarah Clarke

You should try not to offend anybody, but you will always end up offending the establishment, and it's not a pleasant position to be in.

Ruchama Marton

Work at both the individual level and the system level. Both are equally important. I believe this is a feminist way of thinking.

Connie Ning

Stay under the radar of the government, who could care less about the poor as long as they are not arming themselves or getting too vocal. You have to be willing to be pretty counter-culture and be willing to get in trouble.

Stay small enough that you can make ninety-degree turns. Have a team culture with your board and staff. Every organization, nonprofit or for-profit, needs a culture. It's critical.

Admitting your mistakes is a fast track to success. And if your board can do that, you've got a great board. I couldn't do this all by myself. I would never want to run an organization by myself.

There is a spiritual component. Among other things, it carries you through the rough times, like when an employee steals from the organization. It's like having a bigger perspective. This also helps keep you from burning out. It is that spiritual component that is the grace of knowing it is not me that is making it happen.

I'd tell a Peacemaker to go for it! You can do far more than you ever dreamed you could do.

Muffy Davis

You can't be a good Peacemaker unless you take care of yourself, but at the same time you have to look outside of yourself and see what is needed that you can offer, and then learn how to serve that need.

Sister Mary Vertucci

First I would ask the young Peacemaker what path he or she was drawn to. And then I would encourage that person to move down that path that was beckoning. I would warn them they will meet obstacles, sometimes be hurt and discouraged, but whatever you are drawn to … keep seeking. And you will not only do the work, you will have much greater knowledge of who you are. If you really seek who you are in a mutually loving way, the path will open out. I would encourage you as a Peacemaker to move in that direction, and you will find happiness in what you do.

Chona Ajcot

Create opportunities for oppressed people.

Inge Sargent/Thusandi

If you can not help people up close, do it from afar.

Shahla Waliy Al Kli

Be honest.

Somboon Srikhamdokkae

You must love the people you are working for and you must have patience.

Theo Colburn

I would tell them to get a degree in endocrinology. We know more about the moon than we do what goes on in the womb. We need chemists, we need biologists, we need endocrinologists, we need people who can get into that womb environment and understand what goes on there. We need as much focus on inner-space research as we are putting into outer-space research.

Yvonne de Mello

First, you must love the people you work with. If you are motivated by interest or research or something other than love, you will never make it. If they do not see love in your eyes, they will never accept you. Second, you must understand and accept the situations of the children without pity. You have to be able to work under difficult situations, and you can't scream because you have to handle the children. Do not waste your time trying to educate the establishment, because their goal is to remain in power.

Isabel Löfgren

(Who went to work in the streets with her mother, Yvonne de Mello) If you do a kind of freelance thing like my mother does, and if you aren't well with yourself, don't depend on institutions for your well-being. You must have inner strength. Do not be attached to images or to things, and don't forget yourself. Your last resource is yourself, so take good care of yourself.

Elissa Montanti

Communicate with people so that you can learn why they do what they do, what makes them tick and what they are thinking. Don't make assumptions, judge people, or draw negative conclusions. Never take no for an answer and trust that eventually you will find your way to yes. Seek out people that tell you what you can do rather than what you can't do. Most of all, learn to recognize the opportunities, the miracles, and the angels that are sent to you.

*If you can't do great deeds,
do small deeds with great heart.
If you can't feed a hundred people
then just feed one.*

—Mother Teresa

CHAPTER SEVENTEEN

Lessons Learned from the Peacemakers

I have been gathering the stories of Peacemakers for over thirty years. Over time, I have seen similar patterns in the work of these valuable citizens of our world are doing. These are lessons about how their work comes to them, how they go about doing it, how they deal with obstacles, how they find sustenance, perseverance, and joy in the process. I share some of their patterns of wisdom below.

1. Be awake when the opportunity presents itself.

2. Develop your service in response to people's expressed sense of need. When listening for this be sure you are listening to understand their needs rather than listening to validate your preconceived ideas of what is needed.*

3. Never lose sight of your goal and never get attached to how you get there.

4. Learn who the local Peacemakers are and be respectful of their peacemaking traditions.*

5. Every day, revisit the wisdom of and your willingness to continue this work.

6. Operate from unconditional caring, not from sentimentality.

7. Making a difference in the world might be your primary form of compensation, rather than financial compensation. If you need money to do your work, be creative about sourcing it.

8. Work under the radar of oppressors when called for.

9. Work "with" not "for." Work alongside those who request your services.

10. Acknowledge, validate, and nurture the strengths of those with whom you work.

11. Work simultaneously at both the individual and the system level.

12. Pace yourself: Make a little peace, make a little dinner. Know that your work might not be completed in your lifetime.

13. Be aware peacemaking may be, but does not have to be, dangerous. Provide for your safety.

14. Be willing to hang out on the margins of society without taking it personally.

15. Practice patience and persistence; employ them both simultaneously.

16. Most of your learning will be on-the-job training or osmosis from other Peacemakers. Observe what your mentors do and don't do, and why.

17. First go small and deep with your work. Then think about the wisdom of going bigger. Many Peacemakers stay small and deep.

18. Sometimes anger works as a good motivator, but it is an unwise and dangerous plan of action.

19. Rising up out of a depression can launch amazing acts of peacemaking. Likewise, doing an act of peacemaking can, but doesn't always, dispel depression. Provide for your mental healthiness.

20. Do not use violence of any kind, including to yourself.

21. When making choices, choose what keeps you in integrity with your goals and your conscience.

22. Pray.

23. The amount of outside pressure you may feel from those that disapprove of your work may be great. Meet it with a greater amount of inner resolve, integrity, and grit.

24. When overwhelmed by what you can't do, refocus on what you can do. Then proceed with the next right thing.

● ● ●

* Items 2 and 4 come from the work of
a beloved male Peacemaker, Jon Paul Lederach.
The remaining items were gleaned
from the women in this book.

If not you, if not me, who will it be?

—Ellen Stapenhorst

CHAPTER EIGHTEEN

The Invitation

I encourage you to do more than read this book; I wholeheartedly invite you to do some conscious peacemaking of your own. Use these stories as your inspiration. Use the lessons learned from the Peacemakers as a beacon for how to identify and pursue an act of peacemaking.

Use "mutual respect" as your definition of peacemaking. By this I mean creating a situation where parties in a relationship treat each other with the same mutual respect with which they want to be treated. Acts of peacemaking are the process of creating, practicing, and supporting mutual respect.

The parties of such a situation might be neighbors on your block, a classmate in your school, two people in a marriage, a parent and a child, or citizens in a community. It might be two people dating each other, or a pet and its owner, or co-workers. On a more global scale, the relationship might be between Indigenous people and newcomers, or corporations and Mother Earth, or people of differing religious beliefs. It might even be the relationship you have with yourself, meaning are you respecting your body's physical needs, your social needs, your spiritual needs? There is no limit to the examples of relationships in our world today. Any time there is a relationship, there is an opportunity for it to be conducted with mutual respect … or not.

This is an invitation to be awake to one or two or three situations in your realm that are embroiled in a dance of domination and subordination, and to consciously choose to do something to shift it to a dance of mutual respect. Do your best, take care of yourself in the process, and consciously observe what happens as you proceed.

When you are done, write down what transpired. Describe not only what happened but how it affected you and anyone else involved. You can even record this in the empty pages at the end of this book so when your grandchildren inherit this book, they will be amazed at what you chose to contribute to the world.

Go to my website, **barbechamblissauthor.com** and click on "Submit Your Story" under the "Take Action" heading to send your peacemaking story to me. This book is not the only collection of Peacemaker stories I plan to share with the world. I am looking forward to publishing more collections of Peacemaker stories of every size, shape, origin, and corner of the earth. The more stories that are out there about conscious peacemaking, the better our world will be.

And then, please, don't go back to sleep. Be awake when the next opportunity presents itself.

In case you are still wondering—no,
it was not a wrong turn that brought you here.
You do belong here and there is
a contribution uniquely yours that is needed.
Welcome and good luck.

—Hafsat Abiola

It is said that in the Babemba tribe of South Africa, when a person acts irresponsibly or unjustly, he is placed in the centre of the village, alone and unfettered. All work ceases, and every man, woman, and child in the village gathers in a large circle around the accused individual. Then each person in the tribe speaks to the accused, one at a time, about all the good things the person in the centre of the circle has done in his lifetime. Every incident, every experience that can be recalled with any detail and accuracy is recounted. All his positive attributes, good deeds, strengths, and kindnesses are recited carefully and at length. The tribal ceremony often lasts several days. At the end, the tribal circle is broken, a joyous celebration takes a place, and the person is symbolically and literally welcomed back into the tribe.

—Alice Walker

ACKNOWLEDGEMENTS

It took one person to this write book. But it took a whole village to provide the material for this particular book. And it took another village to give this book a professional visual presence that beckons readers to it, and an audio presence that calls listeners to it.

Thank you to the nearly sixty women Peacemakers I have interviewed throughout the world, and the even greater number of people who nominated them as Peacemakers. Thank you each for giving me a window into your life, for standing up in the mantel of "Peacemaker," and for never missing a beat in your work. Thank you for being my mentors, even though neither of us were conscious of that happening.

Thank you to my dissertation committee at the Fielding Graduate Institute, men and women, for believing this was valuable research. Special thanks to the chair, Libby Douvan, who told me to ask the women their metaphors for themselves. And to Elise Boulding for cheering me on to continue the research after graduation.

Thank you to my two sons who accompanied me on some of the interviews. And thank you to my brother and two sisters who never let me give up over the thirty years of bringing this book to life. And thank you to three coaches that kept nudging me along, not letting me fall off the rails, because they believed in the Women and in me: Andrew Adleman, Nancy Murphy, Sandra Beckwith.

And to the highly skilled craftsmen and craftswomen, sometimes coming in triplets: Three editors: Adair Linn Nagata, Karen Connington, Watson Bowes. Three web designers: Christy Eller, Laurie Stone, and Lyn Howe.

Sometimes coming as individuals: Daniel Biggerstaff for offering me his studio, his voice, and his technical expertise in recording the book; David Jacobson for his videography skills and his huge heart; Deborah Payton for getting my rear in gear by sending me down a staircase in hypnosis; and Dana Bishop for translating photographs into fantastic stipple art likenesses of the women. I hope to meet you someday, Dana. Heartfelt thanks to all of you.

And to yet another triplet, the three women at Light Of The Moon, Inc.: Kaya Henley, the personalized editor; Olivia Savard, the creative marketer, and Alyssa Ohnmacht, intuitive graphic designer, layout wizard, and team leader. I thank each of you for personally accompanying me across the finish line, COVID-19 lock downs and all.

And two more thank yous: One to Providence for tossing all these helper angels in my path. Keep it up, Providence, I'm not done with this life journey, and I love having you by my side along the way.

The final thank you is to myself, for being awake when the opportunities and helpers appeared in my path, for never giving up my goals and never getting attached to how I get there, and for playing whatever part I can in waking up as many conscious Peacemakers as possible in my lifetime.

About the Author

Barbe Chambliss is a psychotherapist, professional mediator, and organic farmer dedicated to discovering and bringing forth conscious acts of peace in a progressively chaotic world. She directed the volunteer Center for Conflict Resolution in Aspen, Colorado. She has taught mediation to over 500 children and adults in rural Colorado and facilitates Restorative Justice Circles in her community.

Chambliss's PhD dissertation, entitled *Contemporary Women Peacemakers: The Hidden Side of Peacemaking*, ignited three decades of interviews with nearly sixty women across the world, exploring the nuts and bolts of how peace is actually made. Midway in this journey, she volunteered as a counselor in a Croatian camp providing safe haven for eighty children who had recently survived the Bosnian War. Shortly after the terrorist attacks in New York City, she compiled and distributed a "Working Compendium of Non-violent Responses to 9/11," and later served as a therapist on a U.S. military base to better understand the human dynamics of making war. Her work is an ongoing exploration into the practice of peacemaking, which she defines simply as people treating each other with equal respect.

Chambliss is a fourth-generation Coloradoan. She'd rather sleep under the stars than beneath a roof, and revels in being outdoors in all seasons of her beloved Rocky Mountains. She recharges her soul and does her best writing at her yurt, perched 8,000 feet high on the edge of an alpine meadow she shares with a herd of elk, a chorus of coyotes, and a family of pesky marmots. For fun she sings in a cowboy corral and plays in a marimba ensemble. Her goal is to wake up the conscious Peacemaker in as many people as possible during her life.

Made in the USA
Monee, IL
29 November 2020